Ways of Knowing Cities

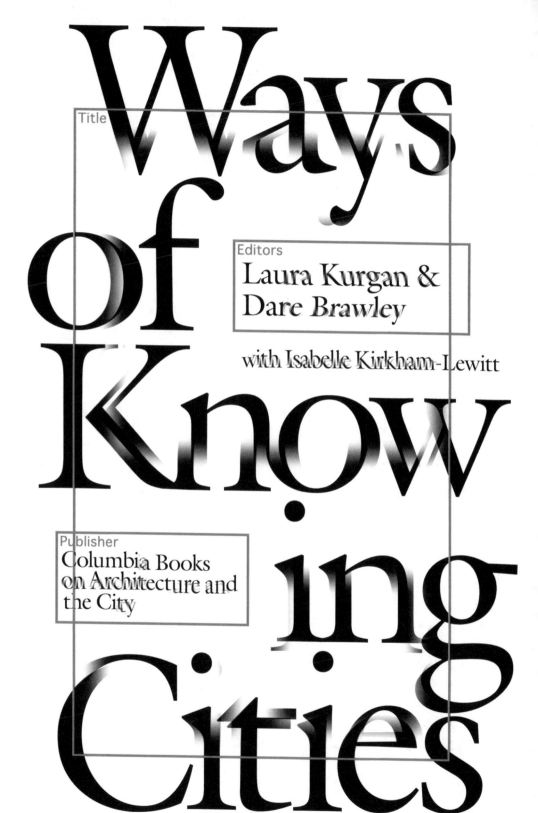

Title

Ways of Know ing Cities

Editors

Laura Kurgan & Dare Brawley

with Isabelle Kirkham-Lewitt

Publisher

Columbia Books on Architecture and the City

Infrastructures

Borders

Cities Full of Data: A Preface
Laura Kurgan

Historically, maps and data have shaped urban lives. With its capacity to represent the spatial world, data has the power to operate on, intervene in, and change the built environment around us. Cities can (and should) be investigated with data, but they are also built, renewed, and scarred by it as well. This is not simply a proposition: it is a call to action.

This book aims to address directly the modes in which cities are represented and thus inhabited. It is a book about techniques and technologies of knowledge, about the tools and practices through which cities are understood. One of those ways of knowing— and not just one among others—is mapping. This book seeks to confront the authority of maps and the data that underlies them, digital and predigital, in order to show how these representations are tools that actively redraw, rebuild, and remake cities. Going far beyond simply representing them, data has fundamentally shaped the look, layout, and lives of cities. John Snow's 1854 cholera map of London, Jacob Riis's photographic documentation of tenement life in late nineteenth-century New York City, and the Bombay Improvement Trust's response to Bombay's plague of 1896, for instance, have each demonstrated the ways in which the collection and presentation of empirical data can have radical effects on the restructuring (or the "modernization") of cities. These effects are not always progressive. Robert Moses rebuilt New York City with the help of census records and housing and transportation data, and he created a set of "slum clearance" maps that disproportionately displaced people in neighborhoods of color. In Philadelphia, and many other American cities, the federal Home Owners' Loan Corporation and the Federal Housing Administration covertly maintained a policy of racial segregation for decades by linking demographic data with mortgage-lending maps.[1]

Whereas Snow collected his information on foot and drew his map by hand, contemporary cities are prodigious generators of information: quantitative and qualitative, automated and manual. Everything—from tax and real estate information to 911 and 311 call center statistics to GPS devices in taxis and mobile phones to access card and point-of-sale swipes to health records, public opinion surveys, and social media posts and "likes"—can be acquired, analyzed, mapped, and visualized. These visualizations show us patterns, habits, clusters, secrets, flows, and stoppages. They present the city as ripe for improvement, intervention, control, regulation, and automation.

As "smart city" discourses make louder and louder claims for calculable and omniscient urban futures, the problematic histories

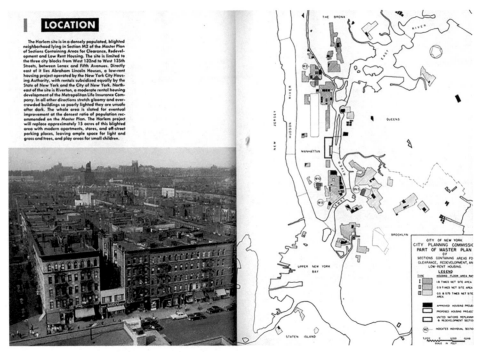

Fig 1: "Harlem: Slum Clearance Plan Under Title I of the Housing Act of 1949" (New York: Committee on Slum Clearance Plans, 1951).

of the use of data for urban "improvement" seem to fade further out of earshot. Twenty-first-century segregation and exclusion are produced and reinforced algorithmically. Redlining maps have been supplemented with predictive policing, ubiquitous dataveillance, facial recognition, and geolocation systems. The social geography of our cities is being rearranged, often automatically, with digital spatial data. It is true that data can transform our knowledge of cities in remarkable ways, sometimes in the direction of equality and justice, but we must be alert to the dangers that lurk in the smart city and in the data that shapes it.

Many of the essays that follow display a deep ambivalence about data's effects on cities—what Trevor Paglen has referred to as the "monsters in the smart city."[2] This is an apt metaphor with which to critique the ideology of data-driven cities and the explosion of machine seeing and artificial intelligence in the corporate as well as civic uses of our collectively produced data—our likes, our votes, and our movement—for profit, predictions, and policing. It is an apt metaphor, as well, for the uncertainties and biases these practices have engineered in cities. Paglen's monsters are the largely invisible mathematical and technological components busily calculating a future city, predicting the behavior of its citizens, and creating environments of fear. They are the instruments that drive the contemporary monitoring, privatizing, and policing of individuals and groups, as well as public space in cities.

Fig 2: Trevor Paglen, *Untitled* (*Reaper Drone*),
2013. C-print, 48 × 60 inches (121.9 × 152.4 cm).
Courtesy of the artist and Metro Pictures,
New York.

Caspar Vopel's 1558 map of the world represented the space
"beyond"—which is to say, the space that cartographers did not
know how to measure or represent—as inhabited by monsters,
frightening deep-sea creatures.[3] Today, there is no lack of
knowledge about how to measure and represent even the most
complex multidimensional spaces that merge the physical and
the virtual in ways unimagined only fifteen years ago. But to
most of us, the techniques generating today's monsters remain
enclosed in black boxes, opaque in their mathematical
complexity, and hidden behind daunting firewalls and terms-
and-conditions pages.

Ever since the news broke in 2015 that Cambridge Analytica
betrayed fifty million Facebook users by revealing nine hundred
points of data about each one of their profiles—their habits,
likes, and dislikes—in order to target political advertisements,
we have become painfully aware and suspicious of the algorithms
that govern our everyday lives.[4] The independent journalists
at ProPublica fought back with their own algorithm, the
"Political Ad Collector," which holds "advertisers accountable

Fig 3: A detail of the Indian Ocean from Caspar Vopel's map of the world, which includes sea monsters and deep-sea creatures, 1558. Courtesy of the Houghton Library, Harvard University.

by revealing pitches that only a targeted slice of Facebook users would otherwise see."[5] Algorithms determine (and potentially limit) what we see on social media, decide whom we are similar to and whom we might (want to) be friends with, and make suggestions about what to do, purchase, and believe. And cities are the front lines for these practices. Urban policing algorithms, which link facial recognition with rich databases, increasingly affect the movements and freedoms of millions of people around the world.

These algorithms are another way of knowing cities. There is an urgent need to represent them as such so that we can begin to unpack the black boxes that are quietly transforming urban space and its networks. Few of us are data literate enough to recognize, let alone combat, the algorithms that Virginia Eubanks has so cogently described as "automating inequality" and the ones that Safiya Noble has rightfully described as "algorithms of oppression."[6] Learning how to read data and its effects—and developing strategies and tactics for challenging its authority and its biases—is one of the most essential political tasks of our moment.

One might not have said this a few decades ago. In the mid-1990s the *Wired* generation declared the "independence of cyberspace," and an Internet service advertisement for the telecommunications company MCI described a space where there is no race, no gender, no age, no disability—"only minds."[7] A real space but one freed from physicality. "Not utopia but the Internet."[8] A decade and a half later, William Gibson, who coined the word "cyberspace," noted that in the age of Google, "cyberspace has everted. Turned itself inside out. Colonized the physical."[9] And by the time of Brexit and the 2016 US elections, data came to stand for fake news, filter bubbles, psychographic profiling, and scissor statements.[10] It seemed a rather abrupt reversal away from data optimism and toward data pessimism.

For many of those studying cities, though, this opposition was not clear-cut, and the narrative of reversal—the taming of hope by experience—seemed much too simple. Cities have never been just collections of people and buildings but rather dynamic networks of relationships that generate data, operate with data, and are transformed by data—for better and for worse. Optimism and pessimism are equally irrelevant categories here. In order to understand cities, then and now, data is unavoidable: it needs to be understood, harnessed, confronted, and critically examined. Cartographers, GIS users, and urban scholars have long researched the confusing ways in which data has shaped urban space and the ways in which those urban epistemologies have resulted in more and less spatial equality.

Understanding how data and maps shape space is urgent work, and work that cannot be done at a distance—either from data or from cities. "Spatial research" names a mode of working with spatial data to discover what can be done and undone, learned and unlearned with it.

Data is always a matter of translation. Things and people and events are observed, measured, and abstracted into numbers and pictures—static and dynamic. Not all, but much of that data has a spatial component: what was measured happened *some-where*, and that location is itself part of the data. When data is spatial and depicted on maps, the practice might as well be called data visualization.[11] Today the preeminent icon for this type of data visualization is the geographic information system (GIS) framework itself—*a way of knowing* that combines a database of information about things happening in space with a cartographic or geographic description of the physical world. Geolocation is all. Any point that has a unique address can be mapped.

Maps as images are familiar features of the media landscape. They appear each day in our newspapers and on our screens to tell us how we voted, how storms have flooded and will flood cities, what's happening on the southern border of the United States or in the Mediterranean. Maps are the background against

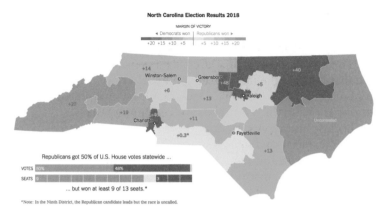

which all sorts of data have been collated to create an interpretation of a spatial condition. Urban versus rural voting patterns can be juxtaposed each election cycle; nation-states can be compared for population growth and gross domestic product; cities can be monitored for sprawl over time; neighborhoods can be differentiated according to crime statistics and high school graduation rates; social networks can be evaluated for how similar your friends are to you.

These maps show a lot.

First, they show us their own limits. Maps are, in fact, arguments about constraint. They cannot help but foreground one boundary over another: police district or school district, country or state, census tract or voting district, city block or building. Circumscribing data is never a neutral act. In terms of resolution, maps display the limits of the image-making technology they rely upon: what they can show (for example, the measurement of a pixel on a satellite image) depends on just how finely grained their sensors and representations are. Some maps let us play with these constraints—for instance, by changing the scale (or the zoom) that determines what is and is not visible at any given moment—and thus underline the irreducible nature of limitation itself.

To speak of constraint is to speak of power, and that is the second essential metadisplay made by maps. Maps, and the technologies and imaginations used to produce them, are instruments of power.[12] Not of Power but of the exercise of power in conflicts, relationships, encounters, challenges, battles, protests, and subversions. Maps are never just navigational aids or aesthetic objects; they live essentially in the force field of social, economic, and political struggle.

Unlike charts and graphs, GIS maps are spatial representations—spatial icons of statistics. The seamlessness of this type of cartographic image often allows us to overlook the fact that the map is a presentation of spatial statistics—an argument about something in the world analyzed from a dataset and projected onto a map. Therefore, we need to address data as its own entity, as a medium that informs the map. Data's limits affect not only the generation of maps but also their use. Data cannot be interpreted or read without knowing the constraints (or conditions) that govern its collection and representation. It is a part of the social, political, economic, racial, and gendered world it represents. There is no such thing as raw data. Long lists of numbers or lines of text may appear "raw," but that is merely a presentational device. Numbers and text become data only when people observe them, read them, make claims about them—and the meaning or output of this information depends on the political and social resources available to observe it. Data is always collected for a purpose and constrained by the people, institutions, or machines that collect it. Nothing about data, despite the etymology of the word, is given: not the numbers, the rules for analyzing them, or the forms in which we see them. Without observation, decision, translation, interpretation, and memory—which is to say, without intervention—there would be no data. Data is *taken*, not given.

This fact implies three provisional conclusions. First, if spatial research is about the political, aesthetic, and operational episte-mologies of cities, then data and maps must display not just their "content" but also their limits. Second, because political and ethical choices are embedded in urban data, it's essential to open up the black boxes (technical and otherwise) that generate and process it, and to exercise some agency over its meanings and uses. Third, we should acknowledge that data-driven "smart" cities have long histories (no matter how analog that "smartness" is), which often underlie the spatial conflicts that have become so visible today.

The chapters that follow propose a political orientation toward data and maps as resources for *knowing cities* differently. Some of them emphasize technical mastery, others data literacy, still others countercartographies. They all, in different terms, ask us to inter-rogate the inherited frameworks through which we think we know cities. They contest and confront the ways in which "knowledge" and "technology" are thought to be synonymous with progress in cities. Progress, after all, is just one mode of narrating historical change. Here, readers will find a multiplicity of other, more nuanced ways in which knowledge and technology can be thought together to understand the rich historicity of cities—and to rethink their futures.

LAURA KURGAN is professor of architecture at the Graduate School of Architecture, Planning, and Preservation at Columbia University, where she directs the Center for Spatial Research and the Visual Studies curriculum. She is the author of *Close Up at a Distance: Mapping, Technology, and Politics* (Zone Books, 2013). Her work explores the ethics and politics of digital mapping and its technologies; the art, science, and visualization of big and small data; and the design of environments for public engagement with maps and data. In 2009 Kurgan was awarded a United States Artists Rockefeller Fellowship.

1   For specific data on the topic, see Digital Scholarship Lab, "Renewing Inequality: Urban Renewal, Family Displacements, and Race 1955–1966," *American Panorama*, ed. Robert K. Nelson and Edward L. Ayers, http://dsl.richmond.edu/panorama/renewal/#view=0/0/1&viz=cartogram&city=newyorkNY&loc=11/40.7140/-73.8890.

2   These monsters live and work in the environment of "surveillance capitalism," a term explored by Shoshana Zuboff in her book *The Age of Surveillance Capitalism: The Fight for a Human Future at the New Frontier of Power* (New York: PublicAffairs, 2019). Trevor Paglen was a keynote speaker at the "Ways of Knowing Cities" conference at Columbia University, February 9, 2018, https://www.arch.columbia.edu/events/816-ways-of-knowing-cities; he presented recent artwork in five chapters titled *Monsters in the Smart City*, which can be viewed here: http://c4sr.columbia.edu/knowing-cities/schedule.html#tpaglen?r=sch.

3   Greg Miller, "Why Ancient Mapmakers Were Terrified of Blank Spaces: Inventing Cities, Mountains, and Monsters to Fill the Empty Spaces on Maps Is a Centuries-Old Tradition in Cartography," *National Geographic*, November 20, 2017, https://news.nationalgeographic.com/2017/11/maps-history-horror-vacui-art-cartography-blank-spaces.

4   Kevin Granville, "Facebook and Cambridge Analytica: What You Need to Know as Fallout Widens," *New York Times*, March 19, 2018, https://www.nytimes.com/2018/03/19/technology/facebook-cambridge-analytica-explained.html.

5   Jennifer Valentino-DeVries, "Outlets in Eight Countries Are Using Our Tool to Monitor Political Ads on Facebook," ProPublica, February 8, 2017, https://www.propublica.org/article/outlets-in-eight-countries-are-using-our-tool-to-monitor-political-ads-on-facebook.

6   See Virginia Eubanks, *Automating Inequality: How High-Tech Tools Profile, Police, and Punish the Poor* (New York: St. Martin's Press, 2018); and Safiya Noble, *Algorithms of Oppression: How Search Engines Reinforce Racism* (New York: New York University Press, 2018).

7   John Perry Barlow, "A Declaration of the Independence of Cyberspace," Electronic Frontier Foundation, February 8, 1996, https://www.eff.org/cyberspace-independence. This ideology was echoed in a television commercial by MCI in 1997; you can view "The Anthem" on YouTube, https://www.youtube.com/watch?v=ioVMoeCbrig.

8   MCI, "The Anthem," https://www.youtube.com/watch?v=ioVMoeCbrig.

9   William Gibson, "Google's Earth," *New York Times*, September 1, 2010, https://www.nytimes.com/2010/09/01/opinion/01gibson.html.

10   Scott Alexander, "Sort by Controversial," *Slate Star Codex*, October 30, 2018, https://slatestarcodex.com/2018/10/30/sort-by-controversial.

11   Laura Kurgan, *Close Up at a Distance: Mapping, Technology, Politics* (New York: Zone Books, 2013).

12   J. B. Harley, "Deconstructing the Map," *Cartographica* 26, no. 2 (Summer 1989): 1–20.

Ways of Knowing Cities: An Introduction
Dare Brawley

Technology is changing how we know and experience cities: sensors, satellites, machine vision, and predictive algorithms are transforming both the daily rhythms of city life and the political economic ordering of the urban world. Cities have always been instantiated through historically specific technologies, but the scale, pace, and pervasiveness of these changes are unprecedented. *Ways of Knowing Cities* addresses this accelerated condition, considering the role that technologies have played in altering how urban space and social life are structured and understood in varied locations, across different historical moments. From a broad range of disciplinary perspectives, the essays in this book investigate the relationship between "technology" and "the city" as distinct entities, and also provoke a reevaluation of these terms as analytic categories.

This reevaluation comes at a time when the very concept of the city is in flux.[1] Much of the project of urban theory has been to generalize an abstracted concept of the city by studying the spatial arrangements and social patterns of particular urban places—all too often in Europe and North America. Scholars have increasingly begun to call this parochialism into question, challenging the sites and biases upon which canonical urban theory has been based. In a call for new geographies of theory, Ananya Roy urges a closer consideration of how theory and site interact, of how cities inform "the city." She decries the "limited sites at which theoretical production is currently theorized and… the failure of imagination and epistemology that is thus engendered."[2] Roy argues for new geographies to ground theory—new forms of urban knowledge reliant upon a broader and different set of places, embodiments, and experiences. In a related critique—as a means to address the global profusion of urban forms that are arguably no longer meaningfully described by the city concept— David Wachsmuth posits that the city ought to be treated as a "category of practice, as a representation of people's relationship to urbanization processes, rather than as a category of analysis adequate to describe these processes themselves."[3] Following this, Wachsmuth diagnoses a dynamic that, together with Hillary Angelo, he describes as "methodological cityism": forms of contemporary urban analysis that are ill-equipped to describe the conditions they aim to decipher. In their view, these projects fail to fully comprehend the varied impacts of urbanization processes because they assume a particular set of scalar, social, economic, and power relationships endemic to the concept of the city that no longer hold—and take for granted certain relationships between labor and sites of production, between settlement patterns and local economic structures, between the spatial imaginaries of urban dwellers and the bounded agglomeration that is "the city."[4]

The essays contained here speak to these uncertainties within the fields of urban studies. They trace histories of urban epistemologies; untangle methodologies of theory; address sites, technologies, and discourses where the question of knowing cities is being actively worked out; and propose alternative practices for measuring and drawing urban life. Through them, a new set of concrete sites and forms of engagement comes into view, addressing topics including the proliferating apparatuses of border policing in the Mediterranean; the battles over stolen electricity in Manila; the calcification of forgotten histories of segregation within axioms of network science; the emergence of new publics through strawberry plants that monitor air quality in Amsterdam; and the evasion of police surveillance by Black queer love. Taken together, the essays in this book reveal that the ways the city, and its inhabitants, have been comprehended in moments of technological change have always been deeply political. Representations of the urban have been sites of contestation and violence, but they have also enabled spaces of resistance and delight.

Ways of Knowing Cities stages a conversation across disciplinary ways of knowing in order to interrogate how certain epistemologies are predicated on the erasure of others. To frame this conversation and future ones, the book is organized according to "Assumptions," "Infrastructures," "Softwares," "Borders," and "Maps." There are, of course, areas of overlap between these terms, as well as other meaningful commonalities across pieces not captured by these particular categories. As lenses, or as points of entry, the categories offer a guide for how the book operates together and across its individual elements—and for how the approaches in this volume play off one another. Yet, just as these organizing frames offer distinct *ways of reading* narratives, histories, technologies, sites, and urban realities, they also reveal, in the spaces between them, new urgencies and unaddressed questions.

"Assumptions" deals with *how* the city becomes legible and presents alternative modes of reading urban space and urban life. These essays provide examples of the ways in which the processes and frameworks that make sense of the city are shaped by (and in turn perpetuate) longstanding ideological positions or biases— of how colonial, racist, or neoliberal forces are masked by their presentation as "normal," commonsense, abstract, and statistically significant. The essays gathered within this frame destabilize accepted terms and question what is ordinarily considered "given" as they address the ideological and disciplinary underpinnings of how we come to know and decipher the city. In this way, they offer new histories, contextualize underlying assumptions, and propose new forms of engaging with the politics of legibility.

Orit Halpern takes up resilience, a key paradigm for contemporary urban practices, to unpack its underlying assumptions. She reminds us of the scientific origins of the term and focuses attention on how the concept has been appropriated as a logic for urban governance and intervention that naturalizes certain kinds of precarity—an epistemology of urban management that prioritizes technological fixes to the system "at the cost of the survival of any of its particular components."[5] Wendy Hui Kyong Chun traces the reflexive and historical relationship between network science and the city. Her piece unravels several studies to show how network science, which is increasingly used to describe and model the city—and which stands in for and acts as a form of urban theory (depending on whom you ask)—is rooted in a model of segregation in US cities. "Homophily"—the tendency for similar things or people to group together—is "a starting place [that] cooks the ending point it discovers… [it] imposes, naturalizes, and projects the segregation it finds," she writes.[6] Built upon midcentury urban sociology, network science eclipses its historical foundations, ignoring the ways in which urban systems are socially constructed and instead taking their forms as natural. Risk and technological innovation work together here as the inputs of and alibis for financial speculation. Simone Browne uses the film *Naz & Maalik* as an entry point to consider Sylvia Wynter's notion of "deciphering practice" as a model for crafting anticolonial futures. Browne travels to other contemporary examples of state violence perpetrated against everyday Black life, revealing how such violence is justified through statistical modes of representation and normalized through lasting forms of colonial oppression. The relationship between the film's protagonists (and the way it is interpreted by the police and FBI officers tracking and surveilling them) provides an entry point for Browne to name the ways in which Black queer love in urban spaces has radical potential to recast normalized forms of violence for what they are. The piece makes explicitly clear the political and everyday significance of deciphering— of making sense of—cities.

"Infrastructures" considers the materiality of the city, bringing together essays that examine the ways in which infrastructural systems inscribe meaning in urban environments and the ways such systems aim to both rationalize and transform the city. These essays testify to the impact of infrastructural solutions, to the ways power is materialized and contested through these systems, and to the ways cities, as purveyors of resources, are built and transformed through conflict. They name these effects as historical phenomena that also persist today despite increased deployment of smart city solutions that appear to flatten difference and inequity. Together, the essays speak to the ways that rights to the city are negotiated through infrastructure—the *technopolitics* of infrastructure.[7] At stake in each of these accounts is the ability to influence or control the conditions (and conditions of possibility) of the material city and the imaginaries, hopes, and other forms of human flourishing that this material city can enable or foreclose.

Mitch McEwen situates the crisis of water shutoffs in urban Detroit as the end point of more than half a century of design, policy, and rate-structure decisions shaping the spatial order of the city. Drawing on the work of Keller Easterling, McEwen positions these developments as a form of "extrastatecraft"—existing beyond ordinary political processes yet directly impacting the daily life, financial stability, health, and well-being of Detroit's residents. It is a story of water that reveals the way in which resource management has made, and continues to make, an unequal city. Dietmar Offenhuber interprets a program to overhaul Manila's consumer electricity grid as an example of how infrastructures usher in, and are sites of contestation over, new forms of governance in the era of the "smart city." Informality and platform urbanism are brought into direct contact and confrontation as the private utility's new program borrows the logic of improvisation from the ad hoc, fragile, contingent, and varied local electricity connections to control practices of unmetered, pilfered electrical usage. In this fraught terrain, complex responses to the smart city paradigm are possible and written into lampposts and electrical lines. Laura Kurgan, Grga Basic, and Eva Schreiner describe research and mapping work that examines the deliberate urban and infrastructural damage inflicted in Aleppo during the Syrian civil war. The power of the state to designate certain forms of infrastructure as "informal" emerges, seemingly, as a tactic of the Assad regime to control who is allowed to shape the (future) city of Aleppo.

"Softwares" tackles the "smart city," the overused moniker used to describe a wide set of practices that combine information communications technologies and contemporary urbanism. It implies, in various contexts, software, hardware, ideology, political organization, analytical regimes, or all of the above. At times "smart" urbanism is marketed as an alternative to politics. Often it is modeled on Euro-American conceptions of technology, specifically centered in a Silicon Valley ethos. Proponents of the smart city often claim that it eliminates the need for other interpretive regimes—"smart" implies an already full knowledge of the city and thus minimizes the need for other forms of knowing. The essays in this section respond to this monopoly of knowledge by proposing and recovering alternative epistemologies, (re)claiming the right to the city.

Shannon Mattern traces several histories of urban media, providing vignettes that illustrate how the city has long been transformed by communications infrastructures. Roman and Islamic epigraphy, telegraph lines that coated cities like Stockholm in dense fibrous webs, and the role of the telephone in the making of the modern skyscraper all "embody urban epistemologies and... 'program' the material city."[8] Mattern argues that the logic of "disruption," so often touted by contemporary smart city projects, is made possible by ignoring or rewriting these histories. Anita Say Chan speaks to the limits of liberalism at the heart of smart city discourse and challenges the affective politics of care—urban, social, economic—that underwrite Silicon Valley-driven urbanism. Through an ethnography of a Lima-based coding school, Chan names the ways that start-up logics are imposed along with their assumptions about the lives of tech knowledge-sector workers— even as these are deeply out of touch with their urban context— and the ways that, in their pursuit of innovation, "smart" projects often attempt to disrupt a set of imagined conditions that do not actually exist. B. Coleman summons the "escape artist" as a figure of civic engagement that provides a model for claiming rights to the city in the context of "smart" neoliberal urban governance. Whether amplifying local knowledge through a system of data collection rather than mimicking authoritative ways of measuring in Amsterdam; organizing efforts against gentrification that reinterpret official data sources in Jakarta; or physically transforming iconic symbols of modernity into layered sites with complex meanings in Mumbai, for Coleman, these discrete instances manifest the right to representation, the right to resist, and the right to disappear.

"Borders" engages in forms of practice that alter, bend, and map conditions of exclusion and violence, belonging and displacement. Each essay troubles the relationship between media, bordering practices, and urban space. They point to the complex relationships between movement, nation, and city to ask: what does citizenship mean amidst diaspora and how is it encoded in urban space? How have responses to perceived crises of migration, made in the name of defending national boundaries, altered relationships between nation, city, and territory? And what is the role of representation in these contexts?

Tinashe Mushakavanhu and Nontsikelelo Mutiti, a graphic designer and journalist pair, discuss an ongoing project to construct an archive of Zimbabwean literature: Reading Zimbabwe. Moving between the archive as a whole and the work of author Dambudzo Marechera within it, the essay traces how literature demarcates and is demarcated by expectations of emplacement and othering— how it creates and sustains often vexed ideas of home and belonging. Reading Zimbabwe aims to map national identity and diaspora through taking up "issues of memory, the afterlives of colonialism, and the forms of narrative that are commensurate to telling a nation's stories."[9] In a second piece, Mutiti describes a series of recent design projects that engage African diasporic urban experiences, mapping a countercity through hair braiding salons and other spaces and practices of Black hair aesthetics. Maribel Casas-Cortés and Sebastian Cobarrubias address the constellation of mechanisms that have been used to alter the ways that migration is policed in the European Union. New technologies have allowed for practices of border externalization by which migrants are tracked and stopped far before the geographic borders of the countries they are attempting to reach. This creates new kinds of interstitial spaces, new conceptions of nation and city. Lorenzo

Pezzani and Charles Heller recount migration in the Mediterranean. They argue that the policing of migrants in this landscape is a form of media practice where the sea itself is "mobilized in the context of border control to constitute a perilous liquid mass."[10] Their work reveals the ways in which these media practices, ways of knowing, have created "hostile environments." Their project, Forensic Oceanography, uses the same techniques of detection and image-making that are used to render migration illegal but shifts the object of focus to the violence of the border itself.

The final lens explicitly examines "Maps" as a key technology of urban research—of knowing the city—and offers possibilities for alternative cartographies. The essays here provide examples of critical practices that bring multiple disciplinary apparatuses to bear on making and interpreting representations of the city in maps and archival material. Each piece addresses fundamental tensions inherent in flattened representations of the city and its social processes—the tensions between lived experience and geographic measures, between fixing time and examining space, between authoritative explication and interpreted narrative. They each offer suggestions for how the "worlding" ability of maps might be enacted, as well as new, more pluralistic approaches to reading and making the city through its representation.

Eve Blau describes a collaborative project from the Harvard Mellon Urban Initiative, which experiments with techniques for studying, accumulating, and reading urban archival materials. Through investigations in Berlin, Boston, Istanbul, and Mumbai, *Urban Intermedia: City, Archive, Narrative* explicitly attempts to develop a method for urban research across and between disciplinary perspectives "through a shared media language," enacted through the literal assembly of archival materials in animated narrative collages.[11] Matthew W. Wilson provides a history of animated maps in order to communicate how they push the boundaries of cartographic interpretation. Drawing on cinema theory to reinterpret these representational forms, he argues that "'maps that move' might mobilize design to think about the intervention in cartography differently, as shifting the ways the world is experienced and represented, to be *for space* in all its liveliness, surprise, and disruption."[12] In the context of the recent surge of interest in, and accessibility of, geographic information systems softwares, Leah Meisterlin revisits the key building blocks of all geographic analysis: measures of location, area, and distance. In particular, she describes recent work on reformulating understandings of distance and charts, with remarkable clarity, the way that the "analytical assumptions and geographic preconceptions" built into tools of geographic analysis have created and "reinforced a totalizing map logic that (literally, figuratively, and representationally) bounds the types of knowledge produced via cartographic reasoning."[13] The impact of this work is profound, as it suggests nothing less than a reformulation of the very ground on which cartography sits.

Addressing themselves to the contentious and varied relationships between technology and the urban, the essays gathered in this book offer diverse geographies, prose, objects of analysis, and modes of interpretation. Each piece operates at a different register, whether transforming current theoretical approaches, reading cultural forms, or offering concrete tactics. Across and between these varied approaches, they problematize the city "container," in some cases explicitly constructing analytic geographies based on experience, in others defining place relationally and sketching out meaningful codependences that cross sites and scales. In response to present uncertainties within the fields of urban studies and to the far too limited locations through which the city is currently theorized, these essays extend many points of entry, signposts, and models for thinking and making cities anew. Premised on the urban as a process rather than as a discrete site, the essays that follow catalyze more robust, more creative, and more far-reaching ways to think about the relationship between the city and the information systems that enable, engage, and express it at a critical juncture in our collective urban life.

DARE BRAWLEY is a researcher
and designer. She is assistant
director of the Center for Spatial
Research at the Graduate School
of Architecture, Planning,
and Preservation at Columbia
University. Her work focuses on
the interactions of technology,
urban governance, and spatial
politics using methods from critical
urban studies and geographic
information systems. Her work has
been exhibited at and published
by the Venice Architecture
Biennial, Storefront for Art and
Architecture, the Architectural
League, the Lincoln Institute of
Land Policy, and the Chicago
Architecture Biennial.

1   See, for example, the work
of the Urban Theory Lab. Neil
Brenner, "Theses on Urbanization,"
Public Culture 25, no. 1 (January
2013): 85–114, https://doi.org/
10.1215/08992363-1890477; Neil
Brenner, *Implosions/Explosions:
Towards a Study of Planetary
Urbanization* (Berlin: JOVIS, 2014),
http://public.eblib.com/choice/
publicfullrecord.aspx?p=4566677;
Neil Brenner and Christian Schmid,
"Towards a New Epistemology of
the Urban?," *City* 19, no. 2–3 (May
4, 2015): 151–182, https://doi.org/
10.1080/13604813.2015.1014712;
Neil Brenner, "Debating Planetary
Urbanization: For an Engaged
Pluralism," *Environment and
Planning D: Society and Space* 36,
no. 3 (June 1, 2018): 570–590,
https://doi.org/10.1177/
0263775818757510.

2   Ananya Roy, "The 21st-
Century Metropolis: New
Geographies of Theory," *Regional
Studies* 43, no. 6 (July 2009):
819–830, https://doi.org/
10.1080/00343400701809665.

3   David Wachsmuth, "City
as Ideology: Reconciling the
Explosion of the City Form with
the Tenacity of the City Concept,"
*Environment and Planning D:
Society and Space* 32, no. 1 (February
1, 2014): 87, https://doi.org/
10.1068/d21911.

4   Hillary Angelo and David
Wachsmuth, "Urbanizing Urban
Political Ecology: A Critique
of Methodological Cityism,"
*International Journal of Urban and
Regional Research* 39, no. 1 (January
2015): 16–27, https://doi.org/
10.1111/%28ISSN%291468-2427/
issues.

5   See Orit Halpern, "Hopeful
Resilience," in this volume.

6   See Wendy Hui Kyong
Chun, "Ways of Knowing ~~Cities~~
Networks," in this volume.

7   Brian Larkin, "The Politics
and Poetics of Infrastructure,"
Annual Review of Anthropology
42, no. 1 (October 21, 2013):
327–343, https://doi.org/10.1146/
annurev-anthro-092412-155522.

8   See Shannon Mattern, "Ether
and Ore: An Archaeology of Urban
Intelligences," in this volume.

9   See Tinashe Mushakavanhu
and Nontsikelelo Mutiti, "Minding
the Gaps: Navigating Absences in
the Zimbabwean Imaginaries,"
in this volume.

10   See Lorenzo Pezzani
and Charles Heller, "'Hostile
Environment'(s): Sensing Migration
across Weaponized Terrains," in
this volume.

11   See Eve Blau, "Urban
Intermedia: City, Archive,
Narrative," in this volume.

12   See Matthew W. Wilson,
"Maps that Move," in this volume.

13   See Leah Meisterlin,
"Cartographies of Distance,"
in this volume.

Hopeful Resilience

Orit Halpern

22

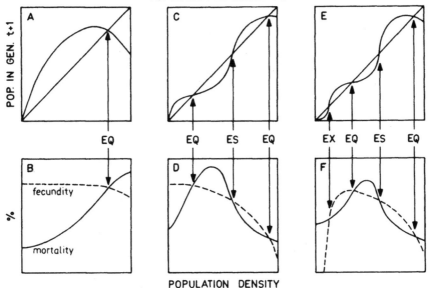

Fig 1: Diagram, "Resilience and Stability of Ecological Systems," demonstrating theoretical examples of various reproduction curves (a, c, and e) and their derivation from the contributions of fecundity and mortality (b, d, and f). From C. S. Holling, "Resilience and Stability of Ecological Systems," *Annual Review of Ecological Systems* 4, no. 1 (November 1973).

From the tailings of large open-pit mines and omnipresent data centers with seemingly infinite data to the overconcentration of capital in the hands of the few, we appear to be in an age of dense accumulation, feeling the weight of what once seemed so light.[1] The Internet and information have become concrete, utilizing the earth's sand and metals to transmit its data in a manner not so different from the construction of roads and buildings.

So much weight makes us dream of being plastic and light, mobile, modulatory, capable of bearing all these materialities while sustaining the technical and economic fantasies of eternal growth and novel change. It is perhaps of little surprise, then, that since the 1970s, the word "resilience" has become a figure of hope for planners, entrepreneurs, policy makers, and environmentalists alike. Resilience is a system's ability to absorb shock and continue functioning. The best system is one that can bear the weight, so to speak, of dynamic change and flexibly respond to the accumulations of population, matter, contaminants, and money. The best ecology is one that can keep operating under pressure.

The 1970s marked the rise of another myth-reality: finance capital and derivatives. Finance is often presumed to be featherlight and mobile, unattached to earthly matters. It is often argued that financial instruments, too, are to be detached from the social and material processes that make commodities— to be understood instead as money making more money. However, as the recent 2008 "crisis" demonstrated, nothing could be further from the truth. Derivatives are financial instruments that allow a certain amount of something (mortgages, minerals, oil, gold, tables, anything) to be traded at some point in the future at an agreed-upon price. One can also, for example, bet on the cancellation of an order or on some other event that might change the future price of an underlying commodity or security. The result is that the size of derivatives markets far exceeds the world's actual gross domestic product by twenty times and has grown exponentially, by 25 percent per year over the last twenty-five years.[2]

Despite being seemingly abstract and delinked from the present, derivatives also drive human actions. People build homes, take out mortgages, and subsequently suffer when these markets fluctuate. As cultural theorist Randy Martin has argued, the derivative—rather than separating itself from social processes of production and reproduction—actually demonstrates the increased interrelatedness, globalization, and socialization of debt.[3] By tying disparate actions and objects together into a single assembled bundle of reallocated risks to trade, derivatives make us more indebted both to each other and to the earth itself, which is often the literal matter of these exchanges. The political and ethical question thus becomes how we might activate this increased indebtedness in new ways, ways that are less amenable to the strict market logics of neoliberal, and perhaps now neo-extractionary, economics.

What then is the relationship between speculation and resilience? The materialities of geology, ecology, and algorithms are not necessarily new, but they are the substrates of a new epistemology, mode of governmentality, and form of territory. How is this new relationship between time, ecology, and economy then related to human habitation and, even more importantly, how is it controlling the future of human life? To elucidate this relationship means asking how economy and ecology were rescripted in the 1970s and what effect this rescripting had on human habitation and life. To this end, it may be helpful to consider the term "planetary urbanization" as defined by Neil Brenner and Christian Schmid.[4] In this concept, the older categories of nature and polis cease to be. In a world where nature no longer exists and where automation, technology, and the political economic functions once assigned to the urban are dispersed into every space on the planet, we are faced with new conceptions of territory and *oikos*.

Such forms of planetary urbanization, perhaps also labeled by nonurbanists "the era of the Anthropocene," have unveiled the geological materiality of things otherwise considered social and technical—financial instruments, digital media, and information economies—and have forced us to question the tactics and strategies, or the affective techniques, we continue to use to speculate upon earthly destruction. How can we make sense of two simultaneous but seemingly incommensurable conditions: the material weight and geological timeliness of our earthly actions and the speed and mobility of globalized, computational, and machine-traded capital?

These questions emerged for me, quite viscerally, while doing fieldwork on logistics and "smart" cities. I became concerned with the forms of speculation and hope that continue to facilitate the ongoing penetration of computation—in terms of "smart" cities, grids, logistical systems, and finance—into the earth. For architecture, the question becomes one of thinking about how time and space are organized to allow for the continuous operation of development and design when there is widespread recognition that current forms of urban planning, growth, and development are injurious to humans and to other forms of life. In order to begin confronting the logics of derivation, extraction, and speculation in negative futures that justify the sacrifice of certain lives as necessary to survival and even growth—what I am calling "resilient hope"—I want to discuss two scenes from my research: one in West Bengal, in India, and the other in New York City, in the United States. While seemingly disparate, these sites and their relation to financialization and extraction better elucidate the forms of hope and speculation currently allowing us to continue myths of economic and technical growth while also embracing a future understood as finite and catastrophic.

Fig 2: Bouldering in Siliguri, India, 2016.
Photograph courtesy of the author.

DISASTER SPECULATION

In March 2016 I went to West Bengal to investigate urban development in Kolkata and to see how Chinese capital was reformulating territory.[5] I visited the city of Siliguri, located near India's border with China, Nepal, and Bangladesh, on a floodplain of the Himalayas. As an essential site in the vast river systems central to life throughout the region, the city is also a major site of extraction. Boulders and sand mined from the riverbeds are used for road and building construction, which there is currently a great deal of in the region. The Asian Development Bank has been investing large sums of money to develop a new "silk road" as part of a broader Asian Highway plan to increase and improve infrastructure throughout South and Southeast Asia. Accompanying this speculative infrastructure is a real estate development boom largely catering to foreign investment. Both the roads and the condos demand massive financing and, of course, concrete. Concrete, in turn, demands waterworn sand particles that are clean, smooth, hard, without clay or chemical coatings or other contaminants, and usually dredged from a river or a seabed. The material demands of development at this scale require a multitude of often disposable laborers mining endlessly under deplorable conditions—and contribute to sinking water levels around Siliguri and drying up (thereby threatening) a major source of water for India and Bangladesh.

Some six hundred kilometers south of Siliguri lies Kolkata. One of the largest and densest settlements on the planet, the city was central to the development of capitalism and has long been at the heart of global trade and commerce.

Situated between Kolkata's IT park and the airport lies Rajarhat New Town. Rajarhat was developed as a space for high-tech corporations—one that could accommodate the luxury housing speculatively desired by their workers—but high-tech industry did not shift its central operations from other cities such as Bangalore, nor did many foreign corporations open their offices there. With foreign corporations being slow or reluctant to relocate to this zone, what exists in Rajarhat today are secondary service providers to central operations located elsewhere. Not only has Rajarhat failed to achieve its intended designation of "smart city," but some of its developments are not even hooked into the information and bandwidth infrastructures that are their purported raison d'être. While much of the new housing in Rajarhat, not to mention across India, has never been (and might never be) occupied, having been bought solely for speculation by domestic and foreign investors, construction continues full-speed ahead on luxury condos and office parks. One of the more violent demonstrations of this disjointed development occurred on March 31, 2016, when a recently built overpass collapsed, killing many. This collapse was the result of overly rapid construction (which, in this case, meant poor-quality concrete), corruption, and the velocity of speculation and derivation in the real estate sector.

This rapid speculation emanates from the fact that most of these developments, both the office parks and the residential towers, are heavily leveraged. In a manner consistent throughout the subcontinent, both the cost and the debt of the state and the developers were likely credit-swapped long before ground ever broke—and profits likely were reaped by large investment banks located in the global financial hubs of Mumbai, New York, Frankfurt, and London. While the function of zones like Rajarhat beyond financialization is unclear, their development has, as a result of the complex and entangled histories of caste, colonialism, and capitalism, already cost some thirty thousand people their homes. Since most of these people are from lower castes and never owned the land they lived on, they have been easily dispossessed by eminent domain, often with little remuneration. As a result, tens of thousands of people have been forced to relocate and occupy the ubiquitous shantytowns of Kolkata—which lack any public health or sanitation infrastructure, as well as electrical grids—and seek transitory work in locations like the port, where they often supply, under enormous duress, the kind of labor that in other contexts would be automated. No longer capable of unloading and loading ships with the efficiency and productivity required of them, dockworkers are forced to retire by their late thirties. Individuals are literally being worked to death.

RISING CURRENTS

Mirroring these scenes of graphic, territorial-scale violence are a set of marketing, technological, and logistical endeavors that participate in a positive speculation on precarity and environmental destruction. One of the more astounding recent demonstrations of this hopeful speculation—the 2010 exhibition *Rising Currents: Projects for the New York Waterfront* at New York's Museum of Modern Art—focused on the future devastation of New York City (a harbinger, perhaps, of the real devastation of Hurricane Sandy two years later). The exhibition invited the city's premier architecture and urban design firms to design for a city ravaged by sea-level rise as a result of global warming. One of the most popular projects exhibited was Oyster-tecture, by Kate Orff/SCAPE, a project that by 2017 had

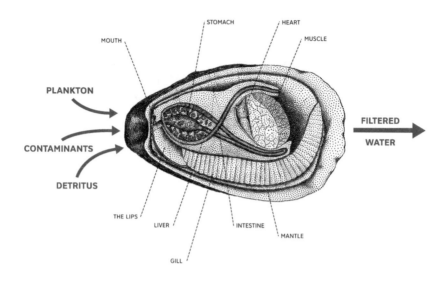

Fig 3: SCAPE, bio-filter diagram from Oyster-tecture, as exhibited in *Rising Currents: Projects for New York's Waterfront*, 2010. Courtesy of SCAPE.

generated around $60 million in funding.[6] The project, sited on Staten Island, proposes to grow oyster reefs as ecological barriers. The very recruitment of another organism's body for and as infrastructure poses historically situated questions about what makes this new mode of managing speculation, populations, and futurity novel. How are these forms of speculation related to the discourse of "resilience"? The irony is that in serving as infrastructure, the oysters would slowly die off as a result of their dirty and inhospitable environment marked by rising water acidity and temperature. This state of being used to death perhaps even goes beyond the terms often invoked to critique neoliberalism, such as extraction and subsumption. This death, beautifully rendered by the architects, embraces terminal destruction as aesthetically pleasing—the inevitable devastation not just of oysters but also of much of New York City by tidal waters.

Another project in the same exhibition, New Aqueous City, by nARCHITECTS, also aestheticizes this destruction with a proposal for new zoning measures and "bottom up" design strategies, which include inflatable barriers, flotation devices for buildings, and new seawalls.[7] A video that accompanies the proposal depicts a storm surge and narrated, by way of the architectural intervention, its survival.

In the video, we see rising waters offer new real estate and agricultural opportunities: islands and barriers, public waterfronts, and aqueous neighborhoods. When the big storm finally hits one of these aqueous neighborhoods (we are given the subtitle "Storm Surge"), individuals calmly gather on the roof of what appears to be a fancy condominium, prepared for evacuation. A helicopter swoops into the frame; all is beautiful, the light is gentle, and there is no wind or rain. It looks rather pleasant. These images resemble nothing of the devastated environment that Hurricane Katrina wrought on New Orleans, which, unlike

Fig 4: nARCHITECTS, New Aqueous City, stills from an animation for *Rising Currents: Projects for New York's Waterfront*, https://www.youtube.com/watch?v=O7folAgxX-. Courtesy of nARCHITECTS.

Sandy, had people actually evacuated by helicopter. In light of these recent historical referents, one cannot help but wonder who is being left behind.

The question here is not the quality or conception of these projects—both have great merit—but rather the aesthetics. How knowledge and power are being made visible and how violence is being affectively rendered are pressing concerns for designers.

RESILIENT LOGICS

From the recent fetish for making architectural renderings look used, dilapidated, or degraded in quality to reports by entities such as Deutsche Bank on the potential risks and rewards for investors created by climate change, a new sentiment of positive affect for negative futures is emerging. It is crucial to think about automated algorithms (the software but also the concrete infrastructure of global finance) alongside their material and physical impact on the earth and on human life. These images are indoctrinated by what I call "resilient hope," an emergent paradigm that links the high-tech computational infrastructures of ubiquitous computing and "smartness," data centers and finance, to the more concrete extractive or exploitative economies of bodies, such as those in West Bengal or New York City. Combined, resilience and technology create a form of preemptive infrastructural governance that naturalizes precarity, sacrifice, and violence as a necessary economic value rather than a politically derived option.

Resilience has a peculiar logic. It is not about a future that is better but rather about an ecology that can absorb constant shocks while maintaining its functionality and organization. Following the work of Bruce Braun and Stephanie Wakefield, one can call it a state of permanent management without ideas of progress, change, or improvement.[8] The irony is that this hopeless situation is actually met with hopeful speculation, usually through new forms of temporal management in finance and technology. Thus, real estate speculation can continue to occur on new silk roads and never-occupied "smart" developments, even as the Himalayan floodplains are destroyed, because the end never arrives but is simply delayed or, to put it more appropriately, derived.

Resilience plays an important role in many different fields, from economics to engineering to forestry.[9] The understanding of resilience most crucial to this discussion was first forged in ecology discourse during the 1970s and in the work of C. S. Holling, who established a key distinction between "stability" and "resilience."[10] Working from a systems perspective and interested in the question of how humans might best manage elements of ecosystems that were of commercial interest (salmon, wood, etc.), Holling developed the concept of resilience to contest the premise that ecosystems were most healthy when they quickly returned to an equilibrium state after being disturbed. Holling called the return to a state of equilibrium "stability," but argued that stable systems were often unable to compensate for significant and swift environmental changes. As Holling put it, the "stability view [of ecosystem management] emphasizes the equilibrium, the maintenance of a predictable world, and the harvesting of nature's excess production with as little fluctuation as possible." Yet this very approach assures that "a chance and rare event that previously could be absorbed can trigger a sudden dramatic change and loss of structural integrity of the system."

Resilience, by contrast, denoted for Holling the capacity of a system *itself* to change in periods of intense external perturbation as a mode of persistence. The concept of resilience enabled a management approach to ecosystems that "would emphasize the need to keep options open, the need to view events in a regional rather than a local context, and the need to emphasize heterogeneity." Resilience is, in this sense, defined in relationship to crisis and states of exception; that is, it is a virtue when such states are assumed to be either quasi-constant or the most relevant for managerial actions. Holling also underscored that the movement from valuing stability to valuing resilience depended upon an epistemological shift: "Flowing from this would be not the presumption of sufficient knowledge, but the recognition of our ignorance: not the assumption that future events are expected, but that they will be unexpected."[11]

Contemporary planning, finance, and design practice abstract the concept of resilience from an ecological systems approach and transform it into an all-purpose epistemology and value. These fields posit resilience as a general strategy for managing uncertainty without an endpoint while also presuming that our world is so complex that unexpected events are, indeed, the norm. Resilience also functions in the landscape of planning and management to collapse the distinction between *emergence* (which would simply denote something new) and *emergency* (which denotes something new that threatens). In this sense, the term operates in the interest of producing a world where any change can be technically managed and assimilated while maintaining the ongoing survival of the system even at the cost of the survival of any of its particular components, be they individuals, ecosystems, or species.

Nowhere is this better exemplified than in the aforementioned examples of New York City, where the slogan after the devastation of Hurricane Sandy in 2012 is "Fix and Fortify." There might not be a clearer statement about the stance of urban planners toward geo-ecological trauma. Planning, it is posed, must assume and assimilate future, unknowable shocks—ones that may come in any form, including threats to security, economies, or environments. In the cases discussed, the real destruction of New York City was initially taken as an opportunity for innovation, design thinking, and real estate speculation. MoMA's discourse was abundantly positive:

MoMA and P.S.1 Contemporary Art Center joined forces to address one of the most *urgent challenges* facing the nation's largest city: sea-level rise resulting from global climate change. Though the national debate on infrastructure is currently focused on "shovel-ready" projects that will *stimulate the economy*, we now have an important *opportunity to foster new research* and *fresh thinking* about the use of New York City's harbor and coastline. As in past economic recessions, *construction has slowed* dramatically in New York, and much of the city's *remarkable pool of architectural talent is available* to focus on innovation.[12]

This rather stunning statement turns economic tragedy—the labor crisis in architecture after 2007—and the imagined coming environmental apocalypse into an opportunity for technical, aesthetic, and economic speculation. A literal transformation of emergency into emergence; a model for managing perceived and real risks, not through solving the problem but through absorbing shocks and modulating the way environment is managed.

These logics pervade the landscape of large logistical and computational environments. Returning to the initial example of the imagined but never realized high-bandwidth smart city of Rajarhat, the development of so-called smart cities follows a logic of software development. That is, every present state of the smart city is understood as a demo or prototype of a future smart city; every operation is understood in terms of testing and updating. As a consequence, there is never a finished product but rather infinitely replicable yet always preliminary versions of these cities around the globe. Engineers openly speak of these cities as experiments and tests—admitting the system did not work but could be improved in the next instantiation elsewhere in the world. This idea of infrastructure as demo avoids any actual questions of whether its construction impacts the planet, labor, or its inhabitants, and it assimilates, by way of deferral, any difficulty or challenge into the next version. This design logic allows the management and negotiation of risks through derivation (from an imagined origin) in a manner that avoids ever having to encounter or take responsibility for the impact of respective events—whether related to weather, the economy, or security—on the world. This evasion of encounter with the world happens because the credit has already been swapped, or the version has already been rendered obsolete, before anyone took the time to evaluate the implications of the original bet or question the actual process being deployed. If a prototype "fails," which is to say it is found ecologically or economically suboptimal or unresilient, then this failure does not provoke a wide-scale structural change in approach (the next development has already been planned) but rather a modulation of the current strategy—an assimilation of the adverse event, or any form of resistance, into the next model that maintains the basic operations of the ecology or system. Derivation and resilience are thus married. The subprime mortgage "crisis" of 2008 might exemplify this, for from the logic of the derivative, there was no crisis and nothing changed; what is true of finance also often holds true today for urban planning and development.

RESILIENCE AND DERIVATION

Resilience is tied to a concept of the future that is always a version, perhaps a derivative replica, of another moment. It is a concept of time in which difference is not historical or progressive but repetitive in practice—constantly producing different territories. It is a self-referential difference, only measured or understood in relation to the many other versions of smart cities, all built by the same corporate and national assemblages. This kind of self-reference—in which evaluation is linked to the management and curtailment of temporality into very short intervals—mitigates the need to actually find out the "true" value or the actual impacts of a project, an investment, or a bet on the world. As Melinda Cooper has noted in discussing weather futures, contemporary markets have now produced derivatives that are literally producing value from betting on adverse and unpredictable events in *relation to one another*, rather than as discrete occurrences with lived impacts. She notes:

> As a futures methodology, scenario planning is designed to foster decision-making under conditions of uncertainty. Its focus is not risk as such, but rather the radical uncertainty of unknowable contingencies—events for which it is impossible to assign a probability distribution on the basis of past frequencies… In the process, it is the very relationship between the measurable "substance" of the commodity—its stored value—and the event-related nature of price that is reworked: where traditional derivatives contracts traded in the future prices of commodities, financial derivatives trade in futures of futures, turning promise itself into the means and ends of accumulation.[13]

Fig 5: Rajarhat, India, 2016. Photograph courtesy of the author.

Time here is not a relationship to the spatial circulation of goods, labor, and commodities but a thing-in-itself, a nonhistorical but also nongeological or nonenvironmental time; it is time as a pure ecology of self-reference. The equation Cooper implies is somewhat new. She argues that if before, at least since the nineteenth century, the futures markets bet on the change in price of commodity over time (time = money), now we bet on time = time. This future is not one that can be predicted as it does not rely on past data. Financial markets therefore "hedge" bets. Derivatives can be traded and make profits long before the results of the investments are known, and, in fact, those who repackage and circulate risks (in mortgage markets but now also in insurance and weather futures markets) are betting on agglomerations of dispersed risks and futures, not on the relationship between the "measurable substance" or "stored value" of a commodity and its future price. This provokes new practices, most significantly around measurement, since time no longer equals money; rather, money derives from time itself. The form of time here is speculative, not predictive. This logic is materialized through engineering and design, through the production of test beds, demos, or prototypes: speculation on a future that is always multiple and elastic. Perhaps that explains why architectural projects, like the ones mentioned above, have a certain love for the animation and renarration of disaster. They are a constant reminder that change itself is a medium for speculation. If the Cold War was about testing and simulation as a means to avoid the unthinkable yet nonetheless predictable (nuclear war), the formula has now changed.[14] This distinction is best summarized in the line between risk and uncertainty first articulated in the 1920s by economist Frank Knight. According to Knight, uncertainty, unlike risk, has no clearly defined endpoints or values; it offers no clear-cut terminal events.[15] What follows is that the test no longer serves as a simulation of life but rather makes human life itself an experiment for technological futures. This "uncertainty" embeds itself in our technologies, both architectural and financial. Thus, in financial markets we continually swap, derive, and leverage never fully accounted for risks in the hope that circulation will defer any need to actually represent or confront it. In infrastructure, engineering, and computing, we do the same. We prototype, develop, and demo building management systems or "smart" infrastructure. We optimize and produce resilient environments through self-referential calculus that compares performance only to the previous version of a building, electrical grid, and so forth. The entire discourse of "smart" cities is invested in evading top-down planning in the interest of offering data-driven systems that literally use population as a resource, a medium, and a test bed for new forms of development, extraction, speculation, and life.

As future risk transforms into uncertainty, high technology (particularly "smart" and "ubiquitous" computing infrastructures) becomes both the language *and* the practice to imagine our future. Instead of looking for utopian answers to questions regarding the future, we should focus on quantitative and algorithmic methods, on logistics, on how to move things—not on where things end up or on measuring the impacts of these actions. Resilience, now coupled with infrastructures of ubiquitous computing and logistics, becomes the dominant method for engaging with possible urban collapse (and also the collapse of more sui generis infrastructures of transport, energy grids, financial systems, etc.). At the same time, a term like "smartness" becomes a new catchphrase for an emerging form of technical rationality that, by continuously collecting data in a self-referential manner, is able to constantly defer future results or evaluation and assume the responsibility of managing this structurally uncertain future. What results is the development of forms of financial instrumentation and accounting that no longer (need to) engage with, alienate, or translate extraction from a historical, geological, or biological framework of value.

One of the key (and troubling) consequences of these two operations that shape and form many logistical territories—the practice of demoing, prototyping, and versioning the imaginary and a discourse of resilience—is that they obscure the differences between catastrophes. While every crisis event—for example, the 2008 subprime mortgage collapse or the Tohoku earthquake of 2011—is different, within the demo logic that underwrites the production of smart and resilient cities, supply chains, and infrastructures, all catastrophes appear the same. Differences are subsumed under the general concept of an ongoing crisis without a clear event structure. It is precisely this evacuation of differences, in temporalities and societal structures, that is most concerning in the extraordinary rise of ubiquitous computing and high-tech infrastructures— either as solutions to political, social, environmental, and historical problems in urban design and planning, or as engines for producing new forms of territory and governance. This logic also prompts us to consider possible alternatives: Can we narrate alternative histories? Can we produce environments and designs that encounter the loss and ruin of our planet differently and that imagine actions *other* than the continued and resilient circulation of capital? We must fundamentally transform the current practice of deferring negative futures by demoing another mode. This requires examining the social movements, construction projects, and many efforts in the arts, humanities, sciences, and politics that have challenged the positive embrace of end times and fought to reintroduce other forms of time and life into space.

With these questions, I return to the opening scenes of this essay, which make visible the ethical and political implications of a world where derivation, extraction, and resilience are married in such a way that the planet (as well as all its forms of life) is a massive medium for the development of "smart" technologies. When concrete first emerged as an ideal material in modern architecture and in art, it was in the interest of producing another world that was not yet here: utopia. Today, we face a different challenge: imagining another world that also recognizes the tragedy that has occurred and still is occurring in most life on the planet. This demands a change of tense for design and politics. A new imaginary and new tactics for rethinking the forms of futurity we wish to inhabit also demand that we understand the relationship between financialization, ecology, habitat, and environment differently. Finance does not replace the social or our connection to the world but could, as many suggest, actually serve as a site to recognize how seriously internetworked and codependent we are—how thoroughly socially produced and contested our debt to each other and to the planet is.[16] Making ourselves indebted in new ways to the many Others that occupy the earth might spark not merely a negative speculation on catastrophic futures but also new forms of care, which are increasingly imperative. A close examination of finance, environment, and habitat could become the bedrock from which new futures emerge. We cannot dream of creative destruction, since we have indeed already destroyed the world, nor can we continue to embrace a world without futures.

Special thanks to Brett Neilson and Ned Rossiter for their support of this research through their ARC grant Logistical Worlds, for their excellent feedback, and for their discussion of the piece. Also thanks to Robert Mitchell, who contributed greatly to developing these ideas.

ORIT HALPERN is associate professor at Concordia University in Montréal. Her work bridges the histories of science, computing, and cybernetics with design and art practice—with a focus on histories and practices of big data, interactivity, and ubiquitous computing.

1   A version of this essay was originally published in *e-flux*, April 17, 2017, https://www.e-flux.com/architecture/accumulation/96421/hopeful-resilience.

2   Randy Martin, "What Difference Do Derivatives Make? From the Technical to the Political Conjuncture," *Culture Unbound: Journal of Current Cultural Research* 6, no. 1 (2014): 193.

3   Martin, "What Difference Do Derivatives Make?," 189–210.

4   Neil Brenner and Christian Schmid, "Planetary Urbanization," in *Urban Constellations*, ed. Matthew Gandy (Berlin: Jovis, 2011), 10–13.

5   This research trip was conducted as part of the Logistical Worlds research project, http://logisticalworlds.org.

6   "Oyster-tecture," October 31, 2017, *99% Invisible* podcast, produced by Emmett Fitzgerald, episode 282, https://99percentinvisible.org/episode/oyster-tecture.

7   For more information on this project, see "MoMA Rising Currents," NARCHITECTS, http://narchitects.com/work/moma-rising-currents.

8   Bruce Braun and Stephanie Wakefield, "Living Infrastructure, Government, and Destituent Power" (paper presented at "Infrastructure, Environment, and Life in the Anthropocene" conference, Concordia University, October 19–20, 2015), 1–16.

9   Since the nineteenth century, the "modulus of resilience" has served in material sciences as a measure of the capacity of materials such as woods and metals to return to their original shapes after an impact. In other fields, resilience tends to name ways in which ecosystems, individuals, communities, corporations, states, and the like respond to stress, adversity, and rapid change.

10   C. S. Holling, "Resilience and Stability of Ecological Systems," *Annual Review of Ecological Systems* 4, no. 1 (November 1973): 1–23.

11   For all quotes by Holling, see Holling, "Resilience and Stability of Ecological Systems," 21.

12   See the curatorial statement on MoMA's website, "Rising Currents: Projects for New York's Waterfront," Museum of Modern Art, https://www.moma.org/calendar/exhibitions/1028?locale=en (emphasis mine).

13   Melinda Cooper, "Turbulent Worlds: Financial Markets and Environmental Crisis," *Theory, Culture, & Society* 27, no. 2–3 (May 2010): 173–178.

14   It is important to recognize that there are also alternative histories of temporality and control within computing coming from cybernetics. In the work on organizations and economics from figures such as Herbert Simon, and in the work on neural nets coming from the heritage of Warren McCulloch and Walter Pitts, ideas of "fuzzy" problems and logic were prevalent, and preemption, not prediction, was a dominant theme. These influences went on to be very important and influential in engineering and financial culture, particularly through the figure of Nicholas Negroponte and through architectural collectives such as Archigram and the Metabolists. For more information, see Orit Halpern, "Cybernetic Rationality," *Distinktion: Journal of Social Theory* 15, no. 2 (2014): 223–238; Judy L. Klein, Paul Erickson, Lorraine Daston, Rebecca Lemov, Thomas Sturm, and Michael D. Gordin, *How Reason Almost Lost Its Mind: The Strange Career of Cold War Rationality* (Chicago: University of Chicago Press, 2013).

15   Frank H. Knight, *Risk, Uncertainty, and Profit* (Boston: Houghton Mifflin, 1921), http://www.econlib.org/library/Knight/knRUP.html.

16   Similar arguments in relation to derivatives and credit swapping have been made by David Graeber in *Debt: The First 5000 Years* (New York: Melville Press, 2011); see also Martin, "What Difference Do Derivatives Make?," 193.

Ways of Knowing ~~Cities~~ Networks

Wendy Hui Kyong Chun

36

I would like to wager the following: to understand how networking technologies define cities, urban life, and politics, we need to understand how cities define networks. Discussions of smart cities—of how information systems enable, engage, and express the city—must be supplemented with considerations of how the city enables, engages, and expresses information systems. Why? Because at the core of networks lies a "practice," to use David Wachsmuth's term, of the segregated and segregating city.[1]

PART 1: CITY-NETWORK AS VIRTUAL PROXY

There is a growing consensus—across many disciplines and sectors—that cities can be analyzed through the networks that traverse and constitute them. This consensus is remarkable because it is arguably the only one that exists across the divided fields of urban studies and urban science. For instance, Christian Schmid, a critical urban studies scholar and professor of sociology, argues that "urban space… is permeated by all kinds of networks that connect it to the inside and outside, and whose extension is either local or global depending on its function: networks of trade, production, capital, daily routine communication and migration… urban space thus can be understood by means of the networks that run through it and determine it."[2] The MIT Media Lab's City Science Initiative— whose methodology is antithetical and even hostile to Schmid's—similarly contends that "understanding the mechanisms of tie formation in cities is the key to the development of a general theory for a city's growth."[3] Although there are important differences between these two formulations, they both emphasize the importance of networks in understanding urban space. Why? And what emerges from this confluence?

To link cities and networks, networks and geography, is hardly profound or new. One of the first maps of the early Internet, when it was Arpanet, represented server clients geographically, recalling earlier transportation network maps (figures 1 and 2).

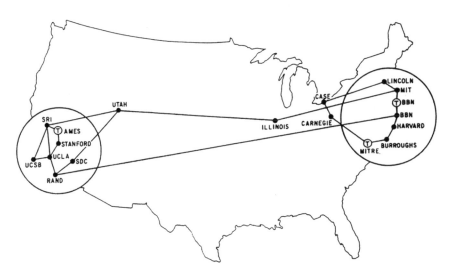

Fig 1: Arpanet, early map, September 1971,
http://www.policy.hu/inetclass/arpaNet.html.

Fig 2: A detail from Alexander Williams's
*Telegraph and Railroad Map of the New England
States*, 1854, https://www.loc.gov/item/
98688383. Courtesy of Library of Congress,
Geography and Map Division.

The term "network" originally meant "work in which threads, wires, etc., are crossed or interlaced in the fashion of a net"—basically anything fashioned to *look* like a net. The modern definition of "network"—a collection of inter-related things represented by lines and nodes—is linked to movement and circulation; in particular, transportation and telephone lines.[4] Modern networks are profoundly metaphorical: they are metaphors of metaphors and metaphors of cities. They encapsulate transport and transfer, vehicles and tenors. They both map and abstract movement and space. They are haunted by cities, itineraries, and dreams of navigating urban spaces.

Neuromancer and *Snow Crash*, the science fiction bibles of the dot-com era and "precursors" to the modern Internet, make the metaphorical relationship between cities and networks clear. William Gibson coined the term "cyberspace" in 1983 but developed it most fully in his 1984 novel *Neuromancer*. Cyberspace was "a consensual hallucination… like city lights, receding… the color of Chiba Sky."[5] The term "cyberspace," of course, combines cybernetics and space; but cybernetics itself implies navigation and space, stemming from the Greek word *kybernetes*, meaning steersman or governor.[6] Neal Stephenson coined the term "metaverse" in 1992 to describe a street-based, virtual-reality online universe. Both cyberspace and the metaverse evoke control, albeit in very different ways: cyberspace conjures outer space, expansive frontiers, and bodiless exultation. The metaverse, which allegedly inspired Second Life and avatars, was developed in Stephenson's *Snow Crash* as a built environment, with divided neighborhoods along the "Street." The metaverse mimicked the deeply divided and ethnically segregated physical world outside it.[7] It emphasized walls, gated communities, and ethnic enclaves: the disintegration of the United States into franchised enclaves, "Mr. Lee's Greater Hong Kong" or "Picket Plantations," run by corporations. *Snow Crash* offered a vision of out-of-control segregation that seems more prescient today than ever before. The imaginary of networks has moved from cyberspace, with its embrace of so-called bodiless anonymity, to the metaverse and its vision of deeply segregated and fragmented city-states. At the core of social networks and their modes of agency are theories of divided yet connected cities: of small worlds, neighbors, and friends. The metaphor of the neighborhood dominates navigational methods: "k-nearest neighbor methods," which classify nodes based on the identities of their nearest neighbors, "k means testing," which partitions nodes into clusters or neighborhoods based on propinquity, and "homophily," which assumes that similarity breeds connection. Embedded within all of these are practices of the city: experiences and representations of a segregated place in which space, geography, and physical distance magically come to define and encapsulate urban centers.

"Urban Characteristics Attributable to Density-Driven Tie Formation," by Wei Pan et al., which was published in *Nature Communications* in 2013, reveals how the move toward universal equations for cities assumes and blindly perpetuates the history of US segregation by transforming historical and institutional racism into so-called "random defaults."[8] Given the history of US residential segregation, these "data-driven" models can be verified as true only if they reproduce segregation. In these models, truth is repetition: the likely future equals the abstracted past. However, rather than simply dismiss this work as racist, we need to redeploy this kind of work as proof of segregation.

PART 2: NAVIGATING MAGIC NUMBERS AND LINES

Urban studies has been recently sideswiped by physicists, such as Geoffrey West, who have been celebrated as "solving the city." West, in an interview with the *New York Times*, explains that he invented urban science because he "didn't want to be constrained by the old methods of social science, and he had little patience for the unconstrained speculations of architects." According to West, urban theory is "a field without principles [like] physics before Kepler pioneered the laws of planetary motion in the seventeenth century."[9] In his most well-known and controversial intervention—the article "Growth, Innovation, Scaling, and the Pace of Life in Cities," coauthored with Luis Bettencourt and others—West contends that urban development is superlinear, that the growth of material resources or social activities follows the following equation: $Y(t) = Y_0 N(t)^\beta$. Y here denotes "material resources (such as energy or infrastructure) or measures of social activity (such as wealth, patents, and pollution); Y_0 is a normalization constant. The exponent β reflects general dynamic rules at play across the urban system."[10] The article argues that quantities that reflect wealth creation innovation have an exponential growth β of 1.12 percent, while those tied to material infrastructure have a β of less than 1 percent (0.8 percent), which means they decay over time. Comparing the similarities and differences between cities and organisms, it maintains that as populations grow, "major innovation cycles must be generated at a continually accelerating rate to sustain growth and avoid stagnation or collapse."[11] Although the article and formula received a lot of attention from the mainstream press and politicians, it has understandably been dismissed within urban studies. Ignoring it has not, however, made it go away. In fact, as Brendan Gleeson has written, it has become "emblematic of a contemporary decline in the influence and reach of urban social science."[12] This decline is because of a fundamental difference between urban social science and "urban revolutionaries" who eschew the premise of urban studies: that cities are social, rather than natural, artifacts.

To combat this decline, Gleeson calls on "the social sciences to offer the conceptual—that is *theoretical*—means for human urban aspiration."[13] Absolutely, but to do so, urban studies must engage, not ignore, urban science because it is not as simple as natural versus social. Consider, in this vein, "Urban Characteristics Attributable to Density-Driven Tie Formation."[14] The article seeks to one-up formulations by physicists, such as West, by revealing that superlinear growth is actually a special case of another relation: $\rho \ln \rho$, where ρ equals the number of nodes per unit area. That is, growth is determined by the number of social ties formed between individuals. This relation thus describes the "efficient creation of ideas and increased productivity in cities." The authors claim that this simple bottom-up model "provides a robust and accurate fit for the dependency of city characteristics with city-size, ranging from individual-level dyadic interactions (number of acquaintances, volume of communication) to population-level interactions (contagious disease rates, patenting activity, economic productivity and crime)"; and that it links micro ties to macro trends "without the need to appeal to heterogeneity, modularity, specialization or hierarchy."[15]

Pan's model relies on the creation of a simple, analytical equation for the number of social ties formed between individuals, with population density as its only single parameter: $T(\rho) = \rho \ln \rho + C' \rho$. Where $T(\rho)$ is the social tie density, ρ, again, is the number of ties per node, and $C' = 2 \ln r_{max} + \ln \pi$ (r_{max} is a urban mobility "boundary"). To test the accuracy of theoretical $T(\rho)$, they simulate tie formation for various settings and show that their model produces diffusion rates remarkably similar to those of superlinear growth (where β = 1.16). The generated diffusion rate, they argue, is a proxy for the amount and speed of information flow and data adaptation. Because this proxy accurately reproduces empirically measured factors, such as the spread of HIV/ AIDS infections and the correlation between GDP and population in European cities, "the surprisingly similar scaling exponent across many different urban indicators suggests a common mechanism behind them. Social tie density and information flow, therefore, offer a parsimonious, generative link between human communication patterns, human mobility patterns and the characteristics of urban economies, without the need to appeal to hierarchy, specialization or social constructs."[16]

This model, like all network science models, assumes and entails abstraction. Network science reduces real-world phenomena to a series of nodes and edges, points and lines, which are in turn modeled to expose the patterns governing seemingly disparate behaviors, from friendship to financial crises. Network science depends on drastic simplifications; however, it is alleged:

> By stripping away the confounding details of a complicated world, by searching for the core of a problem, we can often learn things about connected systems that we would never guess from studying them directly. The cost is that the methods we use are often abstract, and the results are hard to apply directly to real applications.[17]

The findings of network science are "hard to apply directly to real applications" because they are vast simplifications of vast simplifications. Each of the two phases of network theory—initial abstraction/representation followed by mathematical modeling—produces its own type of abstraction. The first phase is "applied" and "epistemological": it suggests and explicates "for given research domains, how to abstract phenomena into networks." In terms of Pan's article, real-world interactions are abstracted into social ties, diffusion rates, and graphs. One decides what is a node and what is an edge. The second phase is "pure" network theory: it deals "with formalized aspects of network representations such as degree distributions, closure, communities, etc., and how they relate to each other. In such pure network science, the corresponding theories are mathematical—theories of networks."[18] The goal in this stage is to build a model that reproduces the abstraction produced in the prior stage. Whatever does so is then considered true or causal. This two-step process highlights the tightrope that network science walks between empiricism and modeling: network science models not the real world but the initial representation and truth that repeats this abstraction. That Pan's model reproduces the abstraction of Bettencourt's is taken as evidence that it is correct. Further, Pan's model is better than other models because it is parsimonious. According to Occam's rule, simpler solutions are always better.

Pan's model is deemed true because it reproduces the past, or because it reproduces past abstractions such as superlinear growth. This mode of verification assumes that things that repeat are identical—repetition is identity: the likely future equals abstractions of the past. The reproduction of the abstract superlinear relationship, which again is another theory, and empirical data are both taken as proof. In order to show that $\rho \ln \rho$ is true, they show that this relationship produces a curve that matches the simulation of tie formation (figure 3).

To understand why this relation explains urban communication patterns, they then hypothesize that a "city's productivity is related to how far information travels and how fast its citizens gain access to innovations and information."[19] To test this hypothesis, they examine how information flow scales with population density—quantifying the functional relationship between typology and the speed of information spread. They do so by simulating two different models of contagion for information spread, and by comparing these simulations to their theoretical predictions (figure 4).

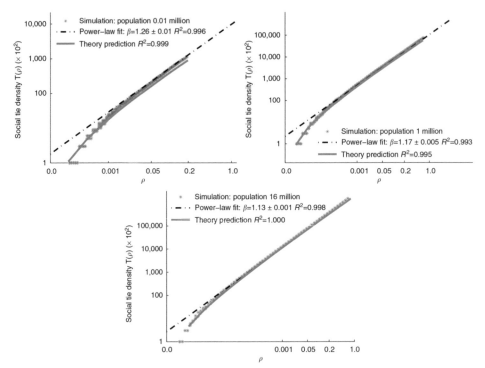

Fig 3: "The number of social ties as function of grid sizes and urban mobility limits. The number of ties $T(\rho)$ plotted as a function of ρ for various grid sizes N. The data points represent the average over $n = 30$ realizations of the simulation described in the text, while the solid green line is the theoretical expression equation (5). The dashed line is a fit to the form $T(\rho) \sim \rho^\beta$. As can be seen in each case, the agreement between theory and simulation is excellent. The best fit to the scaling exponent yields a value of $\beta \approx 1.15$ independent of N. Note that the measured value of the exponent in empirical data is $1.1 \leq \beta \leq 1.3$." Figures 3–5 from Wei Pan, Gourab Ghoshal, Coco Krumme, Manuel Cebrian, and Alex Pentland, "Urban Characteristics Attributable to Density-Driven Tie Formation," *Nature Communications* 4, no. 1 (2013): 3–5. © Wei Pan et al.

Lastly, to prove their hypothesis is true, they study the prevalence of HIV/AIDS infections in cities in the United States and plot the prevalence of HIV in ninety metropolitan areas in 2008 as a function of population density. They also plot the overall GDP per square kilometer in NUST-2 (Nomenclature of Territorial Units for Statistics level 2) regions in the European Union as a function of population density and size (figure 5).

All of the above rely on proxies: on the diffusion rate along ties as a proxy for the quantity and speed of information flow and idea adaptation; on AIDS as a proxy for all infection and contagion. Proxies, however, as Boaz Levin and Vera Tollman have argued, are fundamentally ambivalent. They are "a pharmakon—cure and poison woven into the fabric of networks—where action and stance seem to be masked, calculated, and remote-controlled."[20] They both elucidate and obscure the relationship between action and cause, correlation and causality. Proxies are spaces for approximation and speculation. They are empirically known variables used to infer the value of otherwise unobservable or immeasurable others. As such, they are "a kind of concession to imprecision, and an incomplete foray into an unknown terrain."[21] As Cathy O'Neil has argued, proxies are used when modelers don't have access to the thing they want to measure, and because of this, they open up the possibility of duplicity and discrimination.

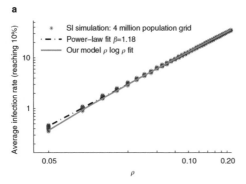
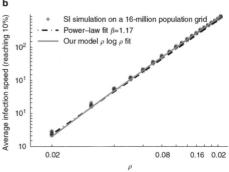

Fig 4: "The spreading rate as a function of density for two different contagion models. (a) The mean spreading rate as a function of density ρ. The points correspond to $n=30$ realizations of simulations of the SI model on a 200 × 200 grid. The dashed line corresponds to a fit of the form $R(\rho)\sim\rho^{1+\alpha}$ with $\alpha=0.18$. The solid line is a fit to the social-tie density model. (b) The mean spreading rate as a function of ρ under the complex contagion diffusion model based on $n=30$ realizations of simulations. The dashed line corresponds to the power–law fit of the form $R(\rho)\sim\rho^{1+\alpha}$ with $\alpha=0.17$. Once again the solid line is the fit to the model described in the paper. In both cases, the social-tie density model provides a better fit than a simple power–law with much lower mean-square errors (29% and 41% lower respectively)."

"Folks building WMDs," she writes, "routinely lack data for the behaviors they're most interested in. So they substitute stand-in data, or proxies. They draw statistical correlations between a person's zip code or language patterns and her potential to pay back a loan or handle a job. These correlations are discriminatory, and some of them illegal."[22] Proxies, in other words, are not just stand-ins, they are also agents. They can take a cut.

Proxies, though, are not categorically bad. Global climate change models rely on proxies. Proxies are necessary, and we cannot attack a model simply for using them. Pan's article, however, uses simulated diffusion rates as a proxy for the amount and speed of information flow, without examining the relationship between geography, population density, and societal interactions. As noted earlier, the authors' move toward spatial distance and population enables them to create models for social diffusion without considering hierarchy, heterogeneity, and the like. Why does this elegant mathematical equation obviate the need for hierarchy? Or, to put it bluntly: why are spatial distance and geography such a good proxy for hierarchy?

This model takes as its ground truth the following equation for rank friendship:

$$P_{ij} \propto \frac{1}{rank_i(j)}$$

Crucially, the equation is taken from an analysis of LiveJournal users in "Geographic Routing in Social Networks," by David Liben-Nowell et al., in order to relate geography to social networking friendships.[23]

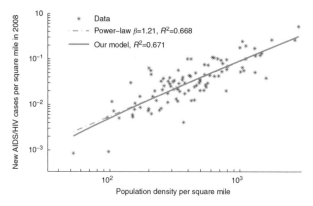

Fig 5a: "Spreading rate of HIV as a function of density in US Metropolitan Statistical Areas. The relationship between density and HIV/AIDS spreading rate of the 90 metropolitan statistical areas from recent Centers for Disease Control and Prevention and US Census surveys. As is visible, the model captures the qualitative trends in the data."

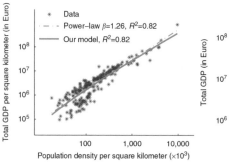
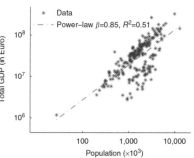

Fig 5b: "Correlation between GDP and population, as well as correlation between GDP and population density for all 247 NUST-2 regions in the European Union. Left panel: correlation between density and GDP, suggesting a strong correlation with a super-linear functional form as predicted by the model. A pure power–law fit to the data is also shown for illustrative purposes. Right panel: the correlation between population and GDP this time showing a sublinear functional form. However, the poor R^2-value suggests that raw population does not correlate, as well as density with GDP growth in cities."

PART 3: WHO IS YOUR NEIGHBOR?

Liben-Nowell et al. seek to understand how to navigate small worlds. In network science, small worlds and the Milgram mail experiment, which sought to calculate the degree of distance between people, are foundational. The Milgram mail experiment measured how many "hops" it took for a letter, sent by a randomly chosen person in Omaha or Wichita, to be received by another randomly chosen person in Boston. The trick was that the sender could send the package only to someone they knew on a first-name basis. The experiment allegedly showed that most packages reached the addressee in Boston within six hops. Hence, we live in a small world where we are, at most, six degrees apart from everyone. Jon Kleinberg, who has done some of the best work on small worlds, has used Saul Steinberg's "View from Ninth Avenue" cover for *The New Yorker* to describe a navigable small world (figure 6).

In Kleinberg's model of a navigable small world, every person has random connections beyond their immediate neighborhood, but these connections reflect geographical distance. People have immediate neighbors and then longer-distance friendships, where distance is either geographical or organizational. As Steinberg's drawing shows, the important thing is that each "block," from the perspective of the person looking out, comprises more physical distance: the distance from Ninth to Tenth Avenue, for instance, equals the distance from the Hudson River to the Pacific Ocean. That is, these blocks, like the Richter scale, transform exponential relations into linear ones. The question then becomes, how are these small worlds constructed and navigated? What enables one to move from block to block?

Fig 6: Saul Steinberg, *View of the World from 9th Avenue*, cover of *The New Yorker*, March 29, 1976. © The Saul Steinberg Foundation/Artists Rights Society (ARS), New York. Cover reprinted with permission of *The New Yorker* magazine. All rights reserved.

Liben-Nowell modeled the probability of these longer-distance friendships as rank friendships, based solely on distance. To do so, he first engaged in a thought experiment to prove that the LiveJournal network was indeed a navigable small world. He simulated a version of the message-forwarding experiment using only geographic information to choose the next person who would get the message. LiveJournal is a small world because most messages reach their target within four hops (figure 7).

He then produced a distance-based equation to explain how this navigability works. Crucially, unlike others (Duncan Watts, for example) who build models based on organization and hierarchy, Liben-Nowell's model used only population density and geography. Liben-Nowell and his coauthors chose geography because they argued that although interests and occupations might be naturally hierarchical, "geography is far more naturally expressed in 2D Euclidian space" and "embedding geographic proximity within a tree heart hierarchy is not possible without significant distortion."[24]

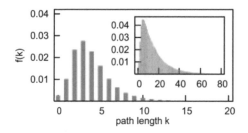

Fig 7: "Results of GEOGREEDY on LiveJournal. In each of 500,000 trials, a source s and target t are chosen randomly; at each step, the message is forwarded from the current message-holder u to the friend v of u geographically closest to t. If $d(v,t) > d(u,t)$, then the chain is considered to have failed. The fraction $f(k)$ of pairs in which the chain reaches t's city in exactly k steps is shown (12.78% chains completed; median 4, $\mu = 4.12$, $\sigma = 2.54$ for completed chains). (*Inset*) For 80.16% completed, median 12, $\mu = 16.74$, $\sigma = 17.84$; if $d(v,t) > d(u,t)$ then u picks a random person in the same city as u to pass the message to, and the chain fails only if there is no such person available." From David Liben-Nowell et al., "Geographic Routing in Social Networks," *Proceedings of the National Academy of Sciences, USA* 102, no. 33 (2005): 11624. © 2019 National Academy of Sciences, USA.

In this model, geography, against all experience to the contrary, enables the imagining of a flat system—there is no 3D architecture. It is basically like Gibson's cyberspace. It divides the earth's surface into "small squares... each person u in the network has an arbitrarily chosen neighbor in each of the four adjacent grid points: north, east, south, and west. In addition to these four neighbors, person u has a long-range link to a fifth person chosen according to rank-based friendship, that is to the probability that u chooses v as her long-range link is inversely proportional to $rank_u(v)$."[25] The model never questions why these neighbors exist—why neighbors are likely to be friends and why the probability of connection is linked to geography.

At the heart of network science is the principle of *homophily*: the axiom that "similarity breeds connection," that birds of a feather flock together. Homophily structures networks by creating clusters; and in doing so, it also makes networks searchable.[26] It grounds network growth and dynamics by fostering and predicting the likelihood of ties. Homophily—now a "common sense" concept that slips between effect and cause—assumes and creates segregation; it presumes consensus and similarity within local clusters, making segregation a default characteristic of network neighborhoods. That network analytics produces real-life echo chambers should surprise no one because a retrograde identity politics drives homophily. As Jon Kleinberg and David Easley explain: "one of the most basic notions governing the structure of social networks is homophily—the principle that we tend to be similar to our friends."[27] To make this point, they point to the distribution of "our" friends. They write:

Typically, your friends don't look like a random sample of the underlying population. Viewed collectively, your friends are generally similar to you along racial and ethnic dimensions: they are similar in age; and they are also similar in characteristics that are more or less mutable, including the places they live, their occupations, their interests, beliefs, and opinions. Clearly most of us have specific friendships that cross all these boundaries; but in aggregate, the pervasive fact is that links in a social network tend to connect people who are similar to one another.[28]

This description naturalizes discrimination. Homophily is no longer something to be accounted for but rather something that "naturally" accounts for and justifies persistence of inequality within facially equal systems. Homophily as a starting place cooks the ending point it discovers. Segregation is what's recovered if homophily is assumed. Homophily as a grounding principle imposes, naturalizes, and projects the segregation it finds.

Kleinberg and Easley turn to US residential segregation to prove the naturalness of homophily. They write that "one of the most readily perceived effects of homophily is the formation of ethnically and racially homogeneous neighborhoods in cities."[29] To prove this theoretically, they move from "representation" to "model"—turning to the "Schelling model" of segregation, a simulation that maps the movement of "two distinct types of agents" in a grid. The grounding constraint is the desire of each agent "to have at least some other agents of its own as type of neighbors."[30] Showing results for this simulation, they note that spatial segregation happens even when no individual agent seeks it: the example for $t=4$ (therefore, each agent would be happy in an equal setting, since they have four neighbors who are different and four who are the same) yields overwhelmingly segregated results (figure 8).

In response, they write:

> Segregation does *not* happen because it has been subtly built into the model: agents are willing to be in the minority, and they could all be satisfied if only we were able to carefully arrange them in an integrated pattern. The problem is that, from a random start, it is very hard for the collection of agents to find such integrated patterns... In the long run, the process tends to cause segregated regions to grow at the expense of more integrated ones. The overall effect is one in which the local preferences of individual agents have produced a global pattern that none of them necessarily intended.
>
> This point is ultimately at the heart of the model: although segregation in real life is amplified by a genuine desire within some fraction of the population to belong to large clusters of similar people—either to avoid people who belong to other groups, or to acquire a critical mass of members from one's own group—such factors are not necessary for segregation to occur. The underpinnings of segregation are already present in a system where individuals simply want to avoid being in too extreme a minority in their own local area.[31]

I cite this interpretation at length because it reveals the dangers of homophily. The long history and legacy of race-based slavery within the US is completely erased, as well as the importance of desegregation to the civil rights movement. There are no random initial conditions. The "initial conditions" found within the United States and the very grounding presumption that agents have a preference regarding the number of "alike" neighbors are problematic. This desire not to be a minority—and to move if one is—maps most accurately the situation of white flight, a response to desegregation. Further, taken as an explanation for gentrification, it portrays the movement of minorities to more affordable and less desirable areas as voluntary, rather than as the result of rising rents and taxes.

Most importantly, if it finds that institutions are to blame for segregation, it is because institutional actions are rendered invisible in these models.

Thomas C. Schelling's now classic "Dynamic Models of Segregation"—published in 1971 during the heart of the civil rights movement and at the beginning of forced school desegregation—makes this deliberate erasure of institutions and economics, as well as its engagement with white flight (or "neighborhood tipping"), clear.[32] In the paper, Schelling acknowledges deliberately excluding two main processes of segregation: organized action (he does not even mention the history of slavery and legally enforced segregation) and economic segregation, even though "economic segregation might statistically explain some initial degree of segregation."[33] Economic assumptions, however, are embedded at all levels of his model. Deliberate analogies to both economics and evolution ground his analysis of the "surprising results" of unorganized individual behavior. He uses economic language to explain what he openly terms "discriminatory behavior."[34] At the heart of his model lies immutable difference: "I assume," he asserts:

> a population exhaustively divided into two groups; everyone's membership is permanent and recognizable. Everybody is assumed to care about the color of the people he lives among and able to observe the number of blacks and whites that occupy a piece of territory. Everybody has a particular location at any moment; and everybody is capable of moving if he is dissatisfied with the color mixture where he is. The numbers of blacks and whites, their color preferences, and the sizes of "neighborhoods" will be manipulated.[35]

These assumptions are troubling and loaded, for they erase the fluidity of racial identity within the United States, in particular the "one-drop rule," which grounded segregation and effectively made black and white identity not about visible differences. As well, homophily maps hate as love. How do you show you love the same? By running away when others show up.[36]

The links between homophily and US segregation are deep and profound. The term "homophily" was actually first coined in 1954 by sociologists Paul Lazarsfeld and Robert Merton in a text that analyzed the friendship patterns within two towns. Yet absent from every single reference to this work is the fact that this text studied segregation within the United States. The piece—which coined the terms "homophily" and "heterophily" together (inspired by friendship categorizations of the "savage Trobrianders whose native idiom at least distinguishes friendships within one's in-group from friendships outside this social circle")—looked at "Craftown, a project of some seven hundred families in New Jersey, and Hilltown, a bi-racial, low-rent project of about eight hundred families in western Pennsylvania."[37] Lazarsfeld and Merton did not assume homophily as a grounding principle, nor did they find homophily to be "naturally" present. Rather, documenting both homophily and heterophily, they asked: "what are the dynamic processes through which the similarity or opposition of values shape the formation, maintenance, and disruption of close friendships?"[38] According to the study, homophily is one instance of friendship formation—and one that emerges by studying the interactions between "liberal" and "illiberal" white residents of Hilltown. The responses of the black residents

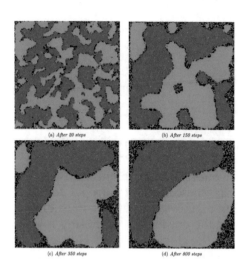

Fig 8: "Four intermediate points in a simulation of the Schelling model with a threshold t of 4, on a 150-by-150 grid with 10,000 agents of each type. As the rounds of movement progress, large homogeneous regions on the grid grow at the expense of smaller, narrower regions." From David Easley and Jon Kleinberg, *Networks, Crowds, and Markets: Reasoning about a Highly Connected World* (New York: Cambridge University Press, 2010), 114. © David Easley and Jon Kleinberg, 2010. Courtesy of Cambridge University Press through PLSclear.

were ignored, since all these residents were classified as "liberal." The very concept of homophily thus presumes segregation.

What to do with this? How can we learn from history so we don't reproduce it? We need to repeat, but in a very different way and in a very different register, the question "Who is your neighbor?"

PART 4: WHO IS YOUR NEIGHBOR?

To conclude, let me offer some suggestions. We need to engage mathematical models of cities and not simply ignore them, for it is through engaging them that a different dialogue might emerge. Let's ask: what does $\rho\ln\rho$ actually prove? What does its insight—which is both acutely obvious and blind—that geography encapsulates hierarchy (and that it makes it linear) do? Where do we go from here?

Intriguingly, Pan's article talks about the difference human experience makes—in particular, how human experience blinds us to overall structures: "[M]ost great cities are exceptions in their own right: a New Yorker feels out of place in Los Angeles, Paris or Shanghai. However, this exceptionalism may be more due to our attention to human-scale details than to the underlying structures."[39] This insistence on underlying structures is important and actually resonates strongly with Carl H. Nightingale's sweeping examination of the history of segregation across global cities in *Segregation: A Global History of Divided Cities*.[40] Nightingale argues that three factors—governments, networks of intellectual exchange, and the institutions associated with the modern real-estate industry—have consistently fostered segregation. Richard Rothstein's *The Color of Law* similarly uses the US legal system as the most parsimonious description, indicator, and reason behind geographical segregation.[41]

The question "Who is your neighbor?" has driven Judeo-Christian ethics as well as political theory. Homophily seeks to cut through this Gordian knot. It seeks to make this ethical dilemma trivial by making your neighbor yourself. To express it very simply in an algorithm:

```
if homophily = true
    neighbor := self
    neighbor.love := self.love
    ethics := narcissism
    society := segregated.hopelessly
end if
```

What if, instead, we took up Freud's challenge that the neighbor also invokes hostility?[42]

And what if we once more looked at the question of experience? David Wachsmuth argues in "City as Ideology" that "these ideological tropes do not endure simply because elite actors want them to; they continue to correspond to a common experience of urban society, and thereby influence scholarly as well as everyday understandings of urbanization in the global North."[43] How can we understand and engage everyday understandings—our habits—of the city? These experiences and habits are ties that bind: they are what underlie what is represented as information diffusion and as links more generally. As I've argued extensively elsewhere, links are habitual actions. Information is habit. So the questions before us are these: What new worlds could we create if we started by interrogating the institutions and other embedded actors within the human and habitual actions? What if we viewed these seemingly isolated habits, these connections, as shards of others embedded within ourselves that we constantly reproduce so they appear like simple lines? This would mean engaging, rather than erasing, questions of hierarchy, difference, and institutional infrastructure. It would mean revisiting Pan's conclusion that the "city's productivity is related to how far information travels and how fast its citizens gain access to innovations and information" through questions of capital investment, communications infrastructure, and factors that foster residential segregation such as zoning laws, property taxes, mortgage loan programs, low-income housing projects, and the like. Pan's article and argument could be used to show the effects of discriminatory urban policies and practices, as well as the importance of "indifferent" infrastructures as the basis for any network connection.

Further, what if we produced models based on heterophily, rather than homophily? What if we saw these lines not simply in terms of similarity but also in terms of opposition and indifference? Vi Hart and Nicky Case, in their remarkable remodeling of Schelling, the "Parable of the Polygons," make the relationship between initial conditions and history explicit.[44] Playing on the "shapes" of society, their interactive online model takes the desire for desegregation, not segregation, as the default. Each agent (triangles and squares) moves in order to increase diversity, not reduce it, based on baseline heterophily. The lessons learned, thanks to Hart and Case, are as follows:

1   Small individual bias → Large collective bias.
     When someone says a culture is shapist, they're not saying the
     individuals in it are shapist. They're not attacking you personally.
2   The past haunts the present.
     Your bedroom floor doesn't stop being dirty just coz you stopped
     dropping food all over the carpet. Creating equality is like staying
     clean: it takes work. And it's always a work in progress.

3   Demand diversity near you.
    If small biases created the mess we're in, small anti-biases might fix it. Look around you. Your friends, your colleagues, that conference you're attending. If you're all triangles, you're missing out on some amazing squares in your life—that's unfair to everyone. Reach out, beyond your immediate neighbors.[45]

Hostility, antagonism, mutual indifference and difference. These are all concepts that we need to engage in order to displace and open the future that our networked cities and models increasingly close through their predictions and visions.

This research was undertaken, in part, thanks to funding from the Canada 150 Research Chairs Program.

WENDY HUI KYONG CHUN is Simon Fraser University's Canada 150 Research Chair in New Media in the School of Communication. She is the author of *Control and Freedom: Power and Paranoia in the Age of Fiber Optics* (MIT Press, 2006), *Programmed Visions: Software and Memory* (MIT Press, 2011), *Updating to Remain the Same: Habitual New Media* (MIT Press, 2016), and co-author of *Pattern Discrimination* (University of Minnesota and Meson Press, 2019). She was previously professor and chair of the Department of Modern Culture and Media at Brown University.

1   David Wachsmuth, "City as Ideology: Reconciling the Explosion of the City Form with the Tenacity of the City Concept," *Environment and Planning D: Society and Space* 32, no. 1 (2014): 75–90.

2   Christian Schmid, "Theory," in *Switzerland: An Urban Portrait*, ed. Roger Diener, Jacques Bernard Herzog, Marcel Meili, Pierre de Meuron, and Christian Schmid (Basel: Birkhäuser, 2006), 163–224.

3   Wei Pan, Gourab Ghoshal, Coco Krumme, Manuel Cebrian, and Alex Pentland, "Urban Characteristics Attributable to Density-Driven Tie Formation," *Nature Communications* 4, no. 1 (2013): 2.

4   *Oxford English Dictionary*, third edition, s.v. "network," https://www.oed.com/view/Entry/126342.

5   William Gibson, *Neuromancer* (New York: Ace Books, 1984), 51–52.

6   *Oxford English Dictionary*, third edition, s.v. "cybernetics," https://www.oed.com/view/Entry/46486.

7   Stephenson writes, "[A]s Hiro approaches the Street, he sees two young couples… climbing down out of Port Zero, which is the local port of entry and monorail stop… They could strike up a conversation: Hiro in the U-Stor-It in L.A. and the four teenagers probably on a couch in a suburb of Chicago, each with their own laptop. But they probably won't talk to each other, any more than they would in Reality." Neal Stephenson, *Snow Crash* (New York: Bantam Books, 1992), 36.

8   Pan et al., "Urban Characteristics," 1–7.

9   It is not just urban theory and architecture that are in West's quantifying crosshairs: he has also, just as controversially, taken on organismic biology. Biologists, especially organismic biologists who believe that the structure of the organism is important, that biology is somehow profoundly biological, have pushed back against West. See Jonah Lehrer, "A Physicist Solves the City," *New York Times*, December 17, 2010, https://www.nytimes.com/2010/12/19/magazine/19Urban_West-t.html.

10   Luis Bettencourt, Jose Lobo, Dirk Helbing, Christian Kuehnert, and Geoffrey West, "Growth, Innovation, Scaling, and the Pace of Life in Cities," *Proceedings of the National Academy of Sciences, USA* 104, no. 17 (2007): 7301–7306.

11   Bettencourt et al., "Growth, Innovation, Scaling, and the Pace of Life in Cities," 7302.

12   Brendan Gleeson, "What Role for Social Science in the 'Urban Age'?," *International Journal of Urban and Regional Research* 37, no. 5 (2013): 1839–1851.

13   Gleeson, "What Role for Social Science?," 1848.

14   Pan et al., "Urban Characteristics," 1–7.

15   Pan et al., "Urban Characteristics," 1.

16   Pan et al., "Urban Characteristics," 2.

17   Duncan J. Watts, *6 Degrees: The Science of a Connected Age* (New York: W. W. Norton, 2004), 24.

18   Ulrik Brandes et al., "What Is Network Science?," *Network Science* 1, no. 1 (2013): 5.

19   Pan et al., "Urban Characteristics," 4.

20   Boaz Levin and Vera Tollman, "Introduction: Proxy Politics," in *Proxy Politics: Power and Subversion in a Networked Age*, ed. Research Center for Proxy Politics (Berlin: Archive Books, 2018), 10.

21   Levin and Tollman, "Introduction: Proxy Politics," 10.

22   Cathy O'Neil, *Weapons of Math Destruction: How Big Data Increases Inequality and Threatens Democracy* (New York: Crown, 2016), 17–18.

23   David Liben-Nowell, Jasmine Novak, Ravi Kumar, Prabhakar Raghavan, and Andrew Tomkins, "Geographic Routing in Social Networks," *Proceedings of the National Academy of Sciences, USA* 102, no. 33 (2005): 11623–11628.

24   Liben-Nowell et al., "Geographic Routing in Social Networks," 11625.

25   Liben-Nowell et al., "Geographic Routing in Social Networks," 11626.

26   See P. V. Marsden, "Homogeneity in Confiding Relations," *Social Networks* 10, no. 1 (1988): 57–76.

27   David Easley and Jon Kleinberg, *Networks, Crowds, and Markets: Reasoning about a Highly Connected World* (New York: Cambridge University Press, 2010), 77.

28   Easley and Kleinberg, *Networks, Crowds, and Markets*, 77–78.

29   Easley and Kleinberg, *Networks, Crowds, and Markets*, 96.

30   Easley and Kleinberg, *Networks, Crowds, and Markets*, 97.

31   Easley and Kleinberg, *Networks, Crowds, and Markets*, 101.

32   In 1972 the NAACP filed a class-action lawsuit, Morgan v. Hennigan, against the Boston School Committee for allowing segregation to exist in public schools in Cambridge, MA, where Harvard University is located. See Thomas C. Schelling, "Dynamic Models of Segregation," *Journal of Mathematical Sociology* 1, no. 2 (1971): 143–186.

33   Schelling writes: "[E]conomists are familiar with systems that lead to aggregate results that the individual neither intends nor needs to be aware of, results that sometimes have no recognizable counterpart at the level of the individual. The creation of money by a commercial banking system is one; the way savings decisions cause depressions or inflations is another. Similarly, biological evolution is responsible for a lot of sorting and separating, but the little creatures that mate and reproduce and forage for food would be amazed to know that they were bringing about separation of species, territorial sorting, or the extinction of species." Schelling also uses the term "incentives" to explain segregation: from preferences to avoidance to economic constraints. Schelling, "Dynamic Models of Segregation," 145–148.

34   At the start of this article, Schelling explains: "This article is about the kinds of segregation—or separation, or sorting—that can result from discriminatory individual behavior. By 'discriminatory,' I mean reflecting an awareness, conscious or unconscious, of sex or age or religion or color or whatever the basis of segregation is, an awareness that influences decisions on where to live, whom to sit by, what occupation to join or avoid, whom to play with or whom to talk to." Schelling, "Dynamic Models of Segregation," 144.

35   Schelling, "Dynamic Models of Segregation," 149.

36   Pan similarly misunderstands white flight and racism. In fact, he describes the white flight as "a search for an idealized, small, low-density, locally oriented community," and he hypothesizes moves between urban and suburban centers as "back and forth shifts… facilitated by incomplete understanding of the benefits afforded by urban density." Pan et al., "Urban Characteristics," 6.

37   Paul Lazarsfeld and Robert Merton, "Friendship as Social Process: A Substantive and Methodological Analysis," in *Freedom and Control in Modern Society*, ed. Morroe Berger, Theodore Abel, and Charles Page (New York: Van Nostrand, 1954), 18–66.

38   Lazarsfeld and Merton, "Friendship as Social Process," 27–28.

39   Pan et al., "Urban Characteristics," 6.

40   Carl Husemoller Nightingale, *Segregation: A Global History of Divided Cities* (Chicago: University of Chicago Press, 2012).

41   Richard Rothstein, *The Color of Law: A Forgotten History of How Our Government Segregated America* (New York: Liveright Publishing Corporation, 2017).

42   For more on this, see Kenneth Reinhard, "Freud, My Neighbor," *American Imago* 54, no. 2 (Summer 1997): 165–195.

43   Wachsmuth, "City as Ideology."

44   Vi Hart and Nicky Case, "Parable of the Polygons: A Playable Post on the Shape of Society," http://ncase. me/polygons.

45   Hart and Case, "Parable of the Polygons."

For Maalik, Naz, Brittany & Alexis: Or, Deliberate Acts of Disruption in City Space

Simone Browne

54

"If you're here with the NYPD or you're with the FBI, welcome, sincerely. We expect you here." This is the brief greeting spoken by an imam at the beginning of a prayer gathering depicted in the 2015 film *Naz & Maalik* (directed by Jay Dockendorf).[1] This welcoming to the mosque is a recognition of and, perhaps, a reckoning with the seeming inevitability of police surveillance and monitoring of Muslim communities, by, for example, the (now disbanded) Demographic Unit of the New York Police Department (NYPD). Of course, the surveillance of Muslims in the United States is not a recent phenomenon; mosques and Muslim student groups were being infiltrated by plainclothes cops or through the work of FBI informants and by way of "create and capture" long before the current president (then candidate) proclaimed: "I want surveillance of certain mosques, okay... and you know what? We've had it before and we'll have it again."[2] One need only look to the thousands of pages of declassified FBI files on Muhammad Ali, Malcolm X, Elijah Muhammad, and the Nation of Islam that reveal, through redaction and nondisclosure, the extent of the state's targeted actions.

Naz & Maalik follows the title characters, two Black, queer, Muslim teenagers, as they move in and around Brooklyn by foot, bike, and train in the course of one day. Their conversations range widely, skimming topics from the gentrification of Brooklyn to the Qur'an, bystander intervention, prisons, and profiling at airports. At one point, they are approached by a white, greasy-haired undercover NYPD cop who attempts to entrap the two into buying a gun. Unsuccessful, the cop reports the teenagers to an FBI agent sitting in a black sedan. These scenes depict "create and capture": the making of informants whereby the FBI (allegedly) outfits its targets with terrorist starter kits in order to manufacture and then seemingly foil terrorist plots.[3] Maalik and Naz sell various things (Catholic saint cards, lottery tickets, perfumed oils) along Fulton Street to raise some cash, but it is their loving on each other in public that makes them illegible to the FBI. Their acts of loving on each other while moving through the city—while riding the L train, for instance—are cautious because of the homo-antagonistic surveillance of family, school, and the public. This illegibility renders them all the more suspicious to the FBI agent in the black sedan.

I want to hold on to the Maaliks and the Nazes, but not *Naz & Maalik*, for how they allow me to think with what Sylvia Wynter calls the "practice of decipherment" in her essay "Rethinking 'Aesthetics': Notes towards a Deciphering Practice." In it, she writes about a mode of critique that "seeks to identify not what texts and their signifying practice can be interpreted to mean but what they can be deciphered to *do*," and how.[4] It is a way of getting at, as Rinaldo Walcott puts it in his discussion of that same essay, "a reconstituted universalism proffered from the vantage point of the subaltern and the dispossessed."[5] Therefore it moves toward altering our current epistemological order rather than merely being a form of criticism that is enfolded into, as Wynter puts it, "the instituting of the 'figure of man' and its related middle-class subject (and the latter's self-representation as a genetically determined rather than discursively instituted mode of being)."[6] Black queer love in public makes possible an anticolonial reading of the Maaliks and the Nazes in the time of (for example) stop and frisk, the police torture that is Chicago's Homan Square, the FBI's proposed Shared Responsibility Committees, its "Don't Be a Puppet" website, and the Department of Homeland Security's monitoring of Black Lives Matter movements.

With this frame, I turn to, first, the leaked Unclassified/For Official Use Only FBI intelligence assessment "Black Identity Extremists Likely Motivated to Target Law Enforcement Officers" (2016) and then briefly to the recent documentary *Whose Streets?* (directed by Sabaah Folayan, 2017), which offers guideposts for anticolonial action. In this way, what follows is not an essay strictly on US surveillance policies with regard to the war on terror, or on state and state-sanctioned violence against everyday Black life. Instead, by foregrounding *Naz & Maalik* (again, for the sake of the Maaliks and the Nazes rather than the film itself) and asking what this text "can be deciphered to do," I am suggesting that Black queer love of Black people is a liberatory practice and strategy for confronting the gendered violences of anti-Black police terror. This claim is obvious and not revelatory; see, for example, Black Lives Matter—Toronto's list of demands and their queer-positive Freedom School for children, or the Movement for Black Lives' platform statement: "We are intentional about amplifying the particular experience of state and gendered violence that Black queer, trans, gender nonconforming, women and intersex people face."[7] But calling attention to Black queer love of Black people as a liberatory practice suggests that it is a deliberate enactment of anticolonial politics against a colonial system and all of its makings: white supremacy, capitalist exploitation, the white settler state's logic of indigenous dispossession and bureaucratic disavowal, anti-Black terrorism, and heteropatriarchal violence. I use the term "anticolonial" intentionally, as decolonial transformations can be fleeting. They morph and mutate. They can be reincorporated, or structurally adjusted, so to speak, into new systems of violence. "Anticolonial" calls attention to the continuous groundwork and deliberate acts of disruption that are necessary to hold the world that we want to get to someday—a world that is something other than this colonial one—to its promise of liberation.

Prepared by the FBI's Domestic Terrorism Analysis Unit, the August 2016 intelligence assessment marks the creation of a new classification: the Black Identity Extremist (BIE). The FBI defines this identity, in a rather incomplete, confounding, and probably deliberate fashion, as "individuals who seek, wholly or in part, through unlawful acts of force or violence, in response to perceived racism and injustice in American society and some [*sic*] do so in

furtherance of establishing a separate black homeland or autonomous black social institutions, communities, or governing
organizations within the United States."[8] The document cites the
killing of Michael Brown in Ferguson, Missouri, in August 2014
and the grand jury's decision not to indict the cop who killed him
as the "very likely" impetus for the rise of this new classification—
one that is now part of the FBI's catalogue on the surveillance
of Black life and the criminalization of Black political struggle.
According to the leaked document:

> The FBI assesses it is very likely that BIEs' perceptions of unjust
> treatment of African Americans and the perceived unchallenged
> illegitimate actions of law enforcement will inspire premeditated
> attacks against law enforcement over the next year. This may
> also lead to an increase in BIE group memberships, collaboration
> among BIE groups, or the appearance of additional violent lone
> offenders motivated by BIE rhetoric. The FBI further assesses it
> is very likely additional controversial police shootings of African
> Americans and the associated legal proceedings will continue to
> serve as drivers for violence against law enforcement.[9]

I quote from the leaked document at length here because it
is an instrument of the FBI's power to index certain Black political
struggles as internal threats to US national security. This indexing
functions as the state's alibi and its justification for the repression
of any critique or response from Black people when it comes to
state violence against Black people and their communities. This
leaked twelve-page threat assessment is documentary evidence
of the sources and methods of the state's anti-Black surveillance
rationales. The document states that "The FBI only uses likelihood expressions" and "does not derive judgments via statistical
analysis"; instead it claims to present "analytic judgments."[10]
However, these analytic judgments ("The FBI assesses" and "it is
very likely" when it comes to "*perceptions* of unjust treatment")
work to produce that very statistical analysis, where "very likely"
is equated with "highly probable" and a rate of "80–95%."[11] It
is a spurious correlation indeed. However, if we are to take such
certainty at face value, then we must read the use of future tense in
"will continue to serve" as an unintentional admission that police
shootings of Black people will continue along with decisions not
to indict, acquittals, or, as in the case of the now former cop who
killed Terence Crutcher in Tulsa, Oklahoma, in 2016, all charges
being removed from record.[12] The rhetoric of statistics as objective, empirical truth—when they are in fact not—is part and parcel
of the FBI's intelligence sources and methods that work to name
Black political struggle as an ideological and statistically verifiable
threat to police power. The threat assessment does not include
any credible specifics about future violent acts targeted at police;
instead it only offers the BIE as a category manufactured to trigger,

For Maalik, Naz, Brittany & Alexis: Or, Deliberate Acts of Disruption in City Space

one could guess, the bureau's counterintelligence tools, which include the recruiting of informants and other methods of discrediting and disruption.

In *Whose Streets?*, Brittany Ferrell, cofounder of the St. Louis-based organization Millennial Activists United, calls for a different future tense, one that centers a Black queer critique of our current governing order. The documentary follows Ferrell and her partner, Alexis Templeton, throughout their activist work, or caretaking, during the Ferguson uprising and beyond: recording a highway shutdown, their wedding, movement work, community meetings with elected officials, Ferguson October, protests, disruptive acts, and loving acts. Millennial Activists United is a grassroots organization created by Black queer women.[13] Their ways of caring demonstrate what Black queer revolutionary love makes possible and what it looks like to love Black people in public space, like their shutdown of Interstate 70 (where a motorist violently drove through the protestors' human barricade). Their love is strategic, and it is dutiful—they echo Assata Shakur's words throughout the documentary: "It is our duty to fight for our freedom. It is our duty to win. We must love each other and support each other. We have nothing to lose but our chains"—and it can be summed up in three words: Black Lives Matter.[14]

At one point in the documentary, Ferrell outlines a method for a deciphering practice: "I just challenge these ideas of normality… if your normal is limited opportunities for people of color, why aren't you questioning that normal? If that normal is an eighteen-year-old teenager laying in the street for four hours, but that's your normal, right? Everybody wants things to be normal. I feel like if you are not questioning 'normal,' you are not paying attention." If you are not questioning colonial forms of domination, then you are willfully not paying attention. Although Wynter's deciphering practice is focused on the texts, like film, that shape the imaginaries of our current governing order, we can still look to it as a means of reading our present to make anticolonial futures. Or, as Ferrell aptly puts it, "it's that feeling that keeps me going." If not, we remain, as Wynter warns, "accomplices in an 'epistemic contract,'" which functions not in the name of liberation but to replicate our current governing order.[15]

SIMONE BROWNE is associate
professor in the Department of
African and African Diaspora
Studies at the University of Texas
at Austin. Her book *Dark Matters:
On the Surveillance of Blackness*
(Duke University Press, 2015) was
awarded the 2016 Lora Romero
First Book Publication Prize by
the American Studies Association,
the 2016 Surveillance Studies
Book Prize by the Surveillance
Studies Network, and the 2015
Donald McGannon Award for
Social and Ethical Relevance in
Communications Technology
Research. She is also a member of
Deep Lab, a feminist collaborative
composed of artists, engineers,
hackers, writers, and theorists.

1   A version of this essay was
originally published in *Cinema
Journal* 57, no. 4 (Summer
2018): 138–142.

2   "Trump: I Want Surveillance
of Certain Mosques," Associated
Press, November 21, 2015,
https://www.youtube.com/
watch?v=RQUwtYWLR3E.

3   For examples of this
build-a-terrorist practice, see Glenn
Greenwald, "Why Does the FBI
Have to Manufacture Its Own
Plots If Terrorism and Isis Are Such
Grave Threats?," *The Intercept*,
February 26, 2015, https://
theintercept.com/2015/02/26/
fbi-manufacture-plots-
terrorism-isis-grave-threats.

4   Sylvia Wynter, "Rethinking
'Aesthetics': Notes towards a
Deciphering Practice," in *Ex-Iles:
Essays on Caribbean Cinema*, ed.
Mbye B. Cham (Trenton, NJ: Africa
World Press, 1992), 266.

5   Rinaldo Walcott,
"Reconstructing Manhood; or, The
Drag of Black Masculinity," *Small
Axe* 13, no. 1 (2009): 83.

6   Wynter, "Rethinking
'Aesthetics,'" 265.

7   The Movement for Black
Lives, "Platform," https://
policy.m4bl.org/platform. For
more information on Black Lives
Matter–Toronto's Freedom
School, visit their website: http://
freedomschool.ca. See also Cathy
J. Cohen, "Punks, Bulldaggers,
and Welfare Queens: The Radical
Potential of Queer Politics?,"
GLQ 3, no. 4 (1997): 437–465.

8   The leaked document
continues by noting that "This
desire for physical or psychological
separation is typically based on
either a religious or political belief
system, which is sometimes formed
around or includes a belief in racial
superiority or supremacy." The
leaked document makes no reference
to the "alt-right" movement or
any other nomenclature that
names white supremacist and white
nationalist groups, organizations,
ideology, and their calls for the
establishment of a white ethnostate.
FBI Counterterrorism Division,
"Federal Bureau of Investigation
Intelligence Assessment: Black
Identity Extremists Likely Motivated
to Target Law Enforcement
Officers" (August 3, 2017), 2,
https://www.documentcloud.org/
documents/4067711-BIE-
Redacted.html.

9   FBI Counterterrorism
Division, "Federal Bureau
of Investigation Intelligence
Assessment," 8.

10   FBI Counterterrorism
Division, "Federal Bureau
of Investigation Intelligence
Assessment," 8.

11   FBI Counterterrorism
Division, "Federal Bureau
of Investigation Intelligence
Assessment," 8.

12   David Moye, "Police Officer
Who Killed Terence Crutcher Has
Manslaughter Charge Expunged
from Record," Black Voices,
Huffington Post, October 27, 2017,
http://www.huffingtonpost.ca/
entry/terence-crutcher-betty-
shelby-record_us_
59f376e0e4b077d8dfc97210.

13   See http://fundersforjustice.
org/millennial-activists-united.

14   Assata Shakur, *Assata: An
Autobiography* (Chicago: Lawrence
Hill Books, 1987), 52.

15   Wynter, "Rethinking
'Aesthetics,'" 258.

Watercraft: Water Infrastructure and Its Protocols of Sprawl and Displacement

Infrastructures

Mitch McEwen

60

Recently I found myself on a bus in New Orleans on a resilience tour.[1] Structured like a tourist experience, a resilience tour replaces history with disaster and culture with climate change. The primary audience for such a tour is funders and bureaucrats (by invitation only). The leaders of this tour were also funders and bureaucrats. Much of the resilience narrative focused on water: floodwater, canal outfalls, water retention, aquifer subsidence, sewage water. At one point, the tour guide offhandedly mentioned a boil-water advisory. "That boil-water alert," I said. "Can you connect the dots between these water quality issues and recovery infrastructures? You've talked a lot about drainage and flooding, but what about the water supply?" The tour proceeded with more discussion of water retention, flooding, sewage, and groundwater. "Yes, yes," I said. "But what about the drinking water supply?"

"That's different water," the bureaucrat-guide answered.

WATER HAS NEVER BEEN MODERN

In my fifteen years of work and study in the field of architecture, water has become only more important. In the early 2000s, water played a significant supporting role in the pragmatic critique of topological formalism. Roofs leaked, and famous architecture offices were sued for the leaky buildings they completed around the turn of the millennium. Soon after, the realities of climate change hit coastal cities throughout the world. In New York City, the notion of rising currents started as a museum-led provocation at the Museum of Modern Art in 2010.[2] Just a few years later, Hurricane Sandy made this notion real and urgent enough—shutting down downtown Manhattan and initiating a planning process that continues to this day. Residents of the Rockaways are now well versed in the idea of the five-hundred-year storm.

However, whether in terms of rain or storm surge, architectural concerns for water still sit rather comfortably in the architectural canon's Renaissance imagination. Those Vitruvian virtues of architecture—*utilitas, firmitas, venustas*—demand some dryness. For architecture to be strong, stable, and durable, a Vitruvian architecture must manage water like it manages snow, or thresholds, or gravity. Water is considered yet another

1   A version of this essay was originally published in *Perspecta 50: Urban Divides*, ed. Meghan McAllister and Mahdi Sabbagh (September 2017); reprinted with permission from the Yale School of Architecture.

2   See *Rising Currents: Projects for New York's Waterfront*, Museum of Modern Art, New York, March 24–October 11, 2010, https://www.moma.org/calendar/exhibitions/1028.

force against which architecture defines its endurance and stability.

My own work is intersected by water in more destabilizing ways. When water and sewage are considered as moments or phases in a process, the relationship of water to the ground and to houses reveals architecture and infrastructure as machines—machines for living and machines for making people human. Water not only makes people human, but the architecture of water and its processes makes some people more human than others. This aspect, which I call "watercraft," demands a political role for architecture that breaks from the Renaissance and the modern—and might even demand a significant shift in what it means to be an architect.

WATERCRAFT

As a new infrastructure logic, watercraft builds off of Keller Easterling's notion of "extrastatecraft."[3] Like extrastatecraft, watercraft is beyond the governance of statecraft; it is the management of privatizing and respatializing resources. It is fluid, yet it is capable of evicting residents, criminalizing households, and rendering faucets, fixtures, and toilets useless—all through the manipulation of a spreadsheet. Detroit presents a site for thinking through repair and reparations, subsidies and sewage—through the infrastructures of water processing. This includes, significantly, the watercraft of shutoffs. The important thing here is the understanding that water shutoffs are not a bug but a feature. Shutoffs are a feature of water networks, where treatment and maintenance processes are centralized and water delivery is widely distributed to subsidize sprawl. The watercraft of shutoffs is as much defined by austerity politics and *Homo economicus* as sewer lines and interceptors.

3   Keller Easterling, *Extrastatecraft: The Power of Infrastructure Space* (London: Verso, 2014).

WATER SPACE

In Detroit we see the emergence of infrastructure and resource management accompany a new spatial order within the city. Mapping water and sewage in Detroit reveals that water infrastructure works very efficiently to subsidize sprawl and exploit city centers. This may be similar to the dynamics of transportation or the processes of urban renewal and demolition, but cannot be reduced to the power of privileged location or direct displacement. Water space demands thinking differently about the power dynamics of space—beyond connection and displacement.

When we think of the urban center and suburban periphery in power dynamics, we often consider transportation and displacement as the key spatial patterns. Transportation infrastructure, for instance, focuses primarily on moving the suburban resident to and from employment in the city. Displacement occurs when enterprises that employ or entertain these suburban residents accrue the capacity to demolish former residential neighborhoods, or when those suburban residents relocate.

The subsidy of sprawl through water networks can operate very similarly to that of transit networks, but often far less visibly. Likewise, the suburban exploitation of the city center through water space does not necessarily demand the displacement of residents. The features of water infrastructure produce mechanisms of displacement. These mechanisms may be decentralized and direct, as in the case of the water shutoffs in Detroit, or centralized and indirect, as in the case of neighborhood impact around wastewater treatment plants.

To imagine that this infrastructure study might be relevant in architecture—and vice versa—is to take seriously Henri Lefebvre's argument that space is actually space: consistent from the abstract space of mathematics to the lived space of the city and its streets. The infrastructure of water and sewage reveals one mechanism by which the space of the spreadsheet performs in the space of the house.

DETROIT WATERCRAFT

Detroit, then, serves as an important site to consider this hypothesis. After Chicago and Toronto, Detroit is the third largest metropolitan area on the Great Lakes. While Chicago has engineered large-scale systems of water and sewage management since the 1840s, Detroit developed a single large-scale system over a rather short period of time—largely through the career of a single engineer named Charles Hubbard.[4]

Over the course of the twentieth century, the relationship between Detroit's water and its houses staged the extreme terms for an austerity policy that has yet to be undone. Once Detroit's central water and sewage infrastructures were built (1940), and as the network of suburban water delivery expanded (1950s and 1960s), the concentration of

4   Whet Moser, "Chicago: 100 Years of Flooding and Excrement," *Chicago Magazine*, April 18, 2013, https://www.chicagomag.com/Chicago-Magazine/The-312/April-2013/Chicago-150-Years-of-Flooding-and-Excrement.

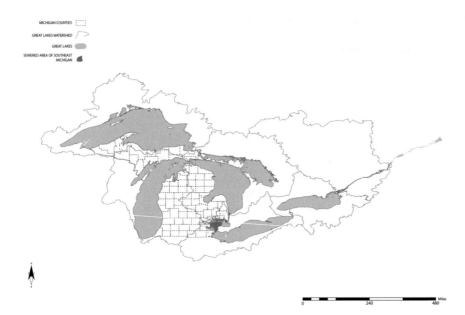

MICHIGAN COUNTIES
GREAT LAKES WATERSHED
GREAT LAKES
SEWERED AREA OF SOUTHEAST
MICHIGAN

Miles
0   240   480

Fig 1: The Great Lakes region, Michigan counties, and surrounding landmasses. Courtesy of the author.

sewage overflows and processing remained in central Detroit. The cost of maintaining these infrastructures also remained centralized in Detroit and, increasingly, were transferred to the Detroit resident as "water bills." This arrangement of infrastructure and its costs, even more than civil service pensions, created the urgency for Detroit's famed Emergency Management in 2012. And in this arrangement of planned austerity, the abstract tools of spreadsheets, GIS, and real-time data intersected the very mid-twentieth century mechanisms of pumps, sewer interceptors, asphalt, and wastewater treatment plants.

WATER MACHINES (TESTING PUMPS, FILTERS, AND CONCRETE)

In 1912, following a typhoid epidemic, Detroit's Board of Water Commissioners organized a water taste test for the residents of Detroit.[5] The taste test took place at Chauncey Hurlbut Memorial Gate, the entrance to a fifty-six-acre farm that had been purchased by the Board of Water Commissioners and opened as Water Works Park, a public park, in 1893.[6] The point of the taste test was to audition public-filtered freshwater pumped from the intake pipe in Lake St. Clair—a filtration system engineered by Charles Hubbell to take advantage of recent innovations in concrete and calcium hypochlorite.[7]

5   On December 2, 1923, DWSD formally opened the largest filtration plant in the world; see Michael Daisy and Richard Hughes, *The Detroit Water and Sewerage Department: The First 300 Years* (Detroit: Detroit Water and Sewerage Department, 2002).

6   City of Detroit, *Journal of the Common Council of the City of Detroit: From the Time of Its First Organization* (1895), 590, https://catalog.hathitrust.org/Record/008607297.

7   "History of the Detroit Water and Sewage Department (DWSD) 1900 to present," *Glow Bass*, February 5, 2011, http://glowbass.com/history-of-the-detroit-water-and-sewage-department-dwsd-1900-to-present; see also Daisy and Hughes, *First 300 Years*.

8   The plant is located at 9300 West Jefferson Avenue in Detroit.

Fig 2: Chauncey Hurlbut Memorial Gate at the entrance to Water Works Park when it was publicly accessible at the end of the nineteenth century. Courtesy of the Detroit Publishing Company collection at the Library of Congress.

Soon after the 1912 taste test, the city commissioned Hubbell to undertake a research project on sewage measurement and processing. The mega-infrastructure project that became the Detroit Wastewater Treatment Plant (WWTP) started with Hubbell's measurement of feces solids, population, and intake, culminating decades later in the design of the WWTP collection structure.[8] Construction of the Detroit WWTP was finalized on New Year's Day in 1940, financed largely by a complex loan from the federal government.[9] Eventually, over seven thousand miles of sewage and stormwater pipe, both combined and separated, would fork from this plant to the suburbs like data trees.[10]

A century after the 1912 taste test, a network of eight-inch concrete mains for filtered water has rooted itself in the ground and extended across thousands of pipe miles to serve water and waste processing for roughly three million people—constituting one of the most extensive water and sewage systems in the United States and collected into one of the largest wastewater treatment plants in the world.[11] Located in southwest Detroit near the confluence of the Rouge River and Detroit River, this wastewater plant was built and paid for by the City of Detroit. Yet Detroit residents today have a precarious relationship to the plant and its integrated water service network. Residents who live next to the Detroit WWTP find their

9   Hubbell, Roth & Clark, Inc., *The First 30 Years: 1915–1945*, 2015, accessed October 15, 2016, http://www.hrc-engr.com/pubs/hrc_first_30.pdf.

10   As of 2015, the Wastewater Treatment Plant serviced the needs of 35 percent of the state's population contained within Detroit and seventy-six other communities in a service area of more than 946 square miles. See "Wastewater Treatment Plant," Detroit Water and Sewerage Department, accessed December 4, 2016, http://archive.dwsd.org/pages_n/facilities_wastewater.html. Based on the mapping analysis included here by the author, sewered roads that are directly served by the WWTP add up to approximately 7,125 linear miles.

11   "Detroit Wastewater Treatment Plant Fact Sheet," Detroit Water and Sewerage Department, 2013, http://www.michigan.gov/documents/deq/deq-wrd-npdes-DetroitWWTP_FS_415425_7.pdf.

Fig 3: Gate and sign at Water Works Park fence, Detroit, 2016. Photograph courtesy of the author.

water bills routinely higher than the value of their homes.[12]

WATER BUREAUCRACY: TOO BIG TO FAIL

Today the Detroit Water and Sewerage Department (DWSD) network, leased to the Great Lakes Water Authority, serves 3.2 million residents. Less than 700,000 of those serviced residents live in the city of Detroit, but the sewage processing occurs entirely within the city.[13] There is no one definitive way to calculate the cost of serving each node (read "taxable property") in the system. The farther away a node is from the source of intake or processing, the more line it takes to connect that freshwater to faucet or toilet, and the more maintenance along the length of the line. Conversely, the side effects of sewage processing—smells and potential overflows, including the bacterial risk of exposure during overflows—are borne most heavily by those who are closest to the processing facilities.

Both these direct relationships—the increased cost of service based on distance from the water source and the side effects of proximity to sewage— reveal the way suburban points of access cost more to maintain and incur less of the direct detriments.

Despite this, the DWSD funding model was developed based on revenue from individual consumption, even though the consumption data for intake and

12   Minimum bid on a Wayne County tax foreclosure auction is $500. As of 2015, the average debt of Detroit water customers is $663; see Ryan Felton, "Detroit Water Shut-offs Resume—and Residents Continue to Struggle with Bills," *Metro Times*, July 6, 2016, http://www.metrotimes.com/ Blogs/archives/2016/07/06/ detroit-water-shut-offs-resume- and-residents-continue-to-struggle- with-bills.

13   Sewage processing is located at the Jefferson Wastewater Treatment Plant; see V. Farr, "Sewer Map," Detroit Water and Sewerage Department IT-GIS, September 6, 2014, http://www.detroitmi.gov/ Portals/0/docs/GLWA/Water_ Sewer_Maps_Guide_1.pdf.

sewage resist consistent measurement. To fulfill this consumer model of pricing, usage is monitored and drainage is estimated at each point of use—creating an expense itself, a kind of built-in maintenance of information. As the system expanded into the suburbs from the 1940s through the 1970s, the management of the water and sewage infrastructure shifted from an engineering model to a revenue model—aping the management of private business—despite there being no market established for determining water prices.

To analyze the spatial assets and risks managed by Detroit's watercraft, the coupling of water filtration and sewage under a joint authority is key. This dual authority was formalized at the height of the Department of Water Service's suburban expansion in 1966, but its potential can be traced back to the nineteenth century in relation to Detroit's position on an international border.[14] While the processes of water intake have remained unencumbered since the late nineteenth century, the processing of sewage has consistently failed to maintain clean waterways, from the city's first sewer in 1836 to the present day. While this failure is largely because of Detroit's combined sewer system, it cannot be disassociated from the suburban service expansion.[15]

The consolidation of sewer management with water management in 1966 coincided with the implementation of telemetered sensing devices for monitoring water levels in sewers and the centralization of stormwater treatment. Thus, a large part of the runoff from storms—including the entire runoff from small storms and the highly contaminated first flush of very large storms—would be retained in the system for complete treatment at the regional wastewater plant. An additional benefit of this stormwater monitoring and remote control system would be the potential reduction of basement flooding, thereby preserving the value of single-family homes that found themselves connected to an overflowing sewer line during heavy rain events.[16] This consolidation centralized the effects of flooding—shifting the risk impacts of heavy rain events from the metro-area single family house to the City of Detroit.

With the emergence of the Environmental Protection Agency and the Clean Water Act of 1972, the federal government sued the state of Michigan for its combined sewer overflow (CSO) into the freshwater of the Detroit River.[17] This lawsuit continued for decades, giving the state's judicial courts—

14   Gerald Remus, DWSD director, led the expansion into the suburbs in Robert Moses fashion. Remus wrote on September 8, 1966: "The program calls for the development of an area-wide waste collection system, tighter stormwater control and beautification of our lakes and rivers. It also eliminates the need for small, ineffective and costly waste treatment plants which have sprung up in the area." City of Detroit, Department of Water Service, Agency Report (archival material), 1966.

15   A combined sewer system collects rainwater runoff, domestic sewage, and industrial wastewater into one pipe that, in normal conditions, is all delivered to a wastewater treatment plant. Combined sewers can cause serious water pollution problems during combined sewer overflow events when wet weather flows exceed the sewage treatment plant capacity and untreated stormwater and wastewater discharges directly to nearby bodies of water. See EPA, "Combined Sewer Overflows (CSOs)," October 16, 2016, https://www.epa.gov/npdes/combined-sewer-overflows-csos.

16   Pollution Control Program for the Detroit Regional Watershed 1966, Section VIII, Stormwater Overflow Control, 21.

17   "In 1977, the Environmental Protection Agency (EPA) sued the City of Detroit, DWSD, and the State of Michigan, alleging that Detroit's sewage system did not satisfy the requirements of the FWPCA. Following negotiations between the parties, a consent judgment was entered by this court, requiring the City to adopt a user charge system and have it fully implemented and effective on all bills after January 1, 1980." CITY OF DETROIT, BY DETROIT WATER V. STATE. 594 F. Supp. 574 (E.D. Michigan. September 28, 1984), http://law.justia.com/cases/federal/district-courts/FSupp/594/574/1900910.

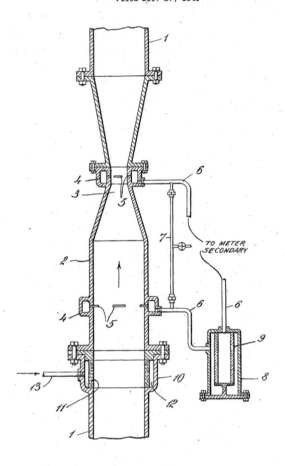

INVENTOR
GREGORY A. PETROE

BY
Pennie, Davis, Marvin, Edmonds
ATTORNEYS

Fig 4: Meter invention used for measuring sewage flows, by Gregory A. Petroe, 1943. US Patent Publication Number US2337921 A.

CITY OF DETROIT
DEPARTMENT OF WATER SUPPLY

POLLUTION CONTROL PROGRAM
for the
DETROIT REGIONAL WATERSHED
July 1966

— Detroit Wastewater Treatment Plant (WWTP)

Fig 5: Map of pollution control program for the Detroit regional watershed, by the Detroit Department of Water Service, 1966. Courtesy of the Detroit Water and Sewerage Department.

not engineers, planners, or democratically elected officials—a leading role in the management of Detroit's urban and suburban watercraft.

Despite the long-standing coupling of sewage processing and water delivery, the constellation of watercraft infrastructure owned by the City of Detroit remains legally blocked from charging suburban customers for the cost of centralized infrastructure.[18] Judicial rulings in the 1980s found that stormwater could not be considered a cost allocated to the owners of asphalt that generated runoff because stormwater itself could not be traced back to an individual user or customer.[19] The repeated spatial patterns of the suburb—highways and strip malls, parking lots and grass lawns—tend toward the spread of impermeable surfaces. The infrastructural cost of the stormwater running off these surfaces, however, remains centralized in the City of Detroit.

SCALE PROBLEM

Imagine if the highway system of a metropolitan region had been owned and maintained by the city at the height of suburban expansion. Similar to the management style of Robert Moses in mid-twentieth-century New York City, the central city could craft tolls to cover operating costs and even generate a surplus. Imagine if the ownership was so robust that it included the streets to each individual suburban house, right up to its garage door. Now, imagine that as suburban wealth climbed and city investment fell, the city failed to wield its power to demand any tolls and instead was left to pay for every pothole along thousands of miles of roads, pushing these costs to its own residents. That is, effectively, the Detroit water situation—where the costly traffic is sewage, not automobiles. The result is decades of a reverse subsidy, from the city to the suburbs, culminating recently in the cutting off of urban residents from what should be an abundant—even free—water supply.

Sociologists have begun tracing the racial dimensions of power and political influence that engendered this paradox of a monopoly with no accrued benefit.[20] The decades of Detroit's demographic shift into a black majority correspond to the same decades of "Rate Settlement Agreements," which involved federal court intervention and consistently beneficial rate terms for suburban water service. For decades, beginning in the 1970s, a

18   "30 percent of the sewer systems (26 of 77 communities) that send flows to the Detroit WWTP are combined sewers... Many of the conventional sanitary sewers in the remaining 70 percent of the service area take on storm water flow from footing drains that are connected to the sanitary sewer rather than to a sump in the basement. Like combined sewers, sanitary sewers with storm water flows can become overloaded and cause sanitary sewer overflows, or SSOs, to the Rouge and Detroit rivers." City of Detroit, "Overview of Storm Water," http://www.detroitmi.gov/ How-Do-I/Find/Storm-Water.

19   "Stormwater, unlike sewage or other industrial waste, is obviously a result of weather conditions and the amount of rainfall treated and therefore is not a waste created by any particular user or recipient of services." CITY OF DETROIT, BY DETROIT WATER, § 2(A) (1984).

20   Dana Kornberg, "The Structural Origins of Territorial Stigma: Water and Racial Politics in Metropolitan Detroit, 1950s to 2010s," *International Journal of Urban and Regional Research* 40, no. 2 (2016): 263–284, https:// deepblue.lib.umich.edu/bitstream/ handle/2027.42/134438/ ijur12343_am.pdf?sequence=2 &isAllowed=y.

single judge oversaw a judicial process that set water rates for each suburban county served by Detroit's water infrastructure.[21] These rates were reached through structured negotiation, rather than through Detroit's utility charging rates as a monopoly or pricing through market-based competition.

As alluded to already, the suburb-city divide is usually narrated through a history of transportation infrastructure. As any comprehensive primer on the history of American sprawl notes, following World War II, government subsidies supported the marketplace for suburban housing with the passage of the Federal-Aid Highway Act of 1956, partially due to intense lobbying by the National Association of Realtors. "Further enabling homeownership through the expansion of roadways into, out of, and between cities, the law's unprecedented level of funding for highway construction resulted in an otherwise impossible level of suburban development."[22] As accustomed as we are to the narrative of transportation and mortgages being the primary means of subsidizing and enabling racialized suburban expansion, the infrastructure of sewer lines and water lines subsidizes the same patterns of development.

Studying water in Detroit and its intersection with racialized geographies of inner-city and suburban sprawl uncovers the ways in which water infrastructure and transportation planning act as expensive enablers of white flight to the American suburb. As we face an era in which access to water will be increasingly important—because of rising flood levels, increased storm events, and the aging of early industrial infrastructure, among other issues—analyzing the infrastructure of urban water becomes critical for locating the spatial protocols of urban divides today.

EMERGENCY WATER

Despite the City of Detroit's coordinated planning and urban design efforts to support neighborhoods outside of its privately capitalized downtown, water shutoffs continue to act as a more direct lever to displace residents. At the peak of shutoffs in fall 2015, the city averaged two thousand residential shutoffs per week.[23] Indeed, the focus of Detroit's watercraft has been on displacing nonpaying residents more than businesses—the number of residential shutoffs is more than four times that of businesses. While 2015 saw Detroit water service shut off to approximately

21   Judge John Feikens of the United States District Court, Eastern District of Michigan, Southern Division, United States of America. See CITY OF DETROIT, 1984.

22   Vishaan Chakrabarti, *A Country of Cities: A Manifesto for an Urban America* (New York: Metropolis Books, 2013), 31.

23   Joel Kurth, "Detroit Hits Residents on Water Shut-offs as Businesses Slide," *Detroit News*, March 31, 2016, https://www. detroitnews.com/story/news/ local/detroit-city/2016/03/31/ detroit-water-shutoffs/82497496.

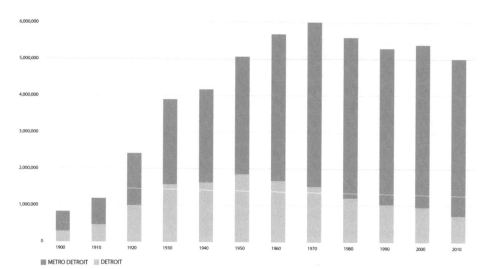

7,000,000
6,000,000
5,000,000
4,000,000
3,000,000
2,000,000
1,000,000
0

1900 1910 1920 1930 1940 1950 1960 1970 1980 1990 2000 2010

■ METRO DETROIT ■ DETROIT

23,300 homes, water service continued for thousands of businesses that owed millions of dollars to DWSD.[24]

The Nation magazine, prior to the atrocity of poisoned water in Flint, Michigan, called Detroit "ground zero" in the new fight for water rights.[25] The state of Michigan appointed an emergency manager in Detroit in 2013 to oversee financial operations, effectively seizing legal authority from the mayor and the city council for two years. Water shutoffs in Detroit started getting local media attention in 2014, and Detroit activists even managed to successfully involve the United Nations in the human rights aspects of the water shutoffs.[26] More than half of Detroit's 200,000 households with water accounts had bills at least sixty days past due, and the DWSD announced water service shutoffs for those who were sixty days delinquent and owed more than $150.[27] Within a year, national public health officials and international human rights organizations decried the situation, calling it a "possible public health catastrophe."[28]

Yet the DWSD continued to shut off water to thousands of residents. Detroit residents and activists have compared DWSD's accounting-based service stoppages to previous modes of displacement and urban land clearing, including blight removal and eminent domain. One Highland Park resident organizing protests in the municipality called water shutoffs "the newest form of

Fig 6: As the city's population continues to decline, the suburban population stays relatively stable. Chart by the author, based on US Census data. See *US Bureau of the Census*, "Census of Population and Housing: Decennial Census," https://www.census.gov/prod/www/decennial.html.

24   Kurth, "Detroit Hits Residents on Water Shut-offs."

25   Laura Gottesdiener, "Detroit Is Ground Zero in the New Fight for Water Rights," *The Nation*, July 15, 2015, http://www.thenation.com/article/detroit-is-ground-zero-in-the-new-fight-for-water-rights.

26   "Detroit's Water Shut-Offs Target the Poor, Vulnerable and African Americans," United Nations Human Rights Office of the High Commissioner, October 20, 2014, http://www.ohchr.org/EN/NewsEvents/Pages/DisplayNews.aspx?NewsID=15190&LangID=E.

27   Joel Kurth, "Detroiters Struggle to Survive without City Water," *Detroit News*, December 14, 2015, http://www.detroitnews.com/story/news/local/detroit-city/2015/12/14/detroiters-struggle-survive-without-city-water/77263784.

urban renewal."[29] Since Emergency Management, water bills in the inner city have become data in a point-based algorithm of urban desertification. Based on real-time monitoring of outstanding water bills, the DWSD disperses a fleet of contractors to shut off water service, point by point.

When residents' water is shut off, they are not only rendered bereft of flushing toilets and bathing water but also risk child protective services' taking their children away due to reduced sanitation. A precarious situation becomes more precarious, placing more pressure on the city's health, foster care, and social work services. The ease of turning water back on masks the real issue: the relationship between service disruption and the implicit criminalization of those who disrupt the disruption (by, for instance, blocking contractor trucks from accessing a street or directly manipulating the shutoff valve with a wrench).[30]

Despite the fact that the majority of households served by DWSD infrastructure are in the suburbs, the water shutoffs have occurred almost exclusively within city limits.[31] After the city declared bankruptcy, Emergency Management rule in Detroit extended to the governance of the DWSD. In this way, Emergency Management operated similarly to the "zone" in Easterling's analysis: "[T]he zone embodies bifurcated or multiple forms of sovereignty that leverage the state to relinquish its resources in exchange for forms of global competition… It is not a means by which nations attack each other, but a means by which both state and non-state actors cooperate at someone else's expense—usually the expense of labor."[32] Under Emergency Management, the entire city became a zone-like territory for two years.

Since the return to democratic control, DWSD infrastructure has been leased to a new entity: the Great Lakes Water Authority. The emergency manager negotiated DWSD, an almost two-hundred-year-old not-for-profit water department, into a forty-year lease agreement with suburban counties. This authority now leases the suburban water and sewerage infrastructure from DWSD for $50 million annually, or approximately $21 per year per suburban resident—a paltry sum considering the capitalization of this investment.

The watercraft of Detroit's suburban sprawl enables the same "fantasy town" that early

28   Full quote from Dr. Wendy Johnson, the former medical director of the Cleveland Department of Public Health: "I was shocked by the draconian measures employed by the Detroit Water Department… Water shutoffs set-up the possibility of public health catastrophe—that's what we see in poor African and Central American countries." In Martina Guzmán, "Exploring the Public Health Consequences of Detroit's Water Shutoffs," *Model D*, October 6, 2015, http://www.modeldmedia.com/features/water-shut-offs-100615.aspx.

29   *The Water Front*, directed by Liz Miller (Reading, PA: Bullfrog Films, 2007), DVD.

30   Clinton Kirby, "Detroit: Got a Wrench? Turn Your Water Back On," *Liberty Road Media*, July 1, 2014, https://libertyroadmedia.wordpress.com/2014/07/01/detroit-got-a-wrench-turn-your-water-back-on.

31   Lindsey Wahowiak, "Access to Water Surfaces as Human Rights Issue as Poor in Detroit Lose Services: Sanitation at Risk," *Nation's Health*, October 14, 2014, http://thenationshealth.aphapublications.org/content/44/8/1.3.full.

32   Easterling, *Extrastatecraft*, 148.

twentieth-century company towns imagined as bourgeois utopias, according to historian Robert Fishman.[33] Fishman argues that these suburban bourgeois utopias hid the industrial production that enabled their standard of living. In the case of Detroit's watercraft, the apparatuses that are obfuscated by distance are not the industrial source of labor but the central urban infrastructure necessary for collective basic services. Rather than registering the sensibility of the immense subsidy, the protocols of switches and shutoffs instead highlight the income and wealth disparity between residents of Detroit and residents of the suburbs. Through the distribution of combined sewer overflow, the centralization of wastewater treatment, and the income sifting associated with shutoffs, the watercraft of blackwater processing perpetuates a racialized order of the city and the suburbs.

Analyzing the regional and central aspects of water infrastructure in Detroit reveals a disturbing long-term tendency of reverse subsidy (from the city to the suburb), irrespective of the proliferation of data points and real-time information built into the system. Through Detroit's watercraft, the allocation of water becomes not a resource but a service— something more akin to wireless telephones. This field of resource allocation evolves the urban divide from a geometry of lines (redlining) to one of points (on/off). These are points of service blockage and desertification. The emergence of a new urban divide that registers as a scattering of control points reveals a matrix of resources and crises managed in service of suburban sprawl and white middle-class settlement and to the detriment of a largely black city.[34]

As a city of single-family homes—surrounded by suburbs of sprawling single-family homes— Detroit presents a false image of individualization, a spatial pretense for the customer-service paradigm of infrastructure access. In actuality, the pollutants (and related costs) that flow through water and sewage infrastructure result from complex overlaps between territories, large surfaces of streets and driveways, combined stormwater collection, central water-intake systems, and freshwater and sewage distribution and collection through thousands of miles of pipes. The pollutants and waste processing that generate costs are an effect of the surface matter that water flows over and the branching vectors that sewage travels along, not the point of the house.

33   Robert Fishman, *Bourgeois Utopias: The Rise and Fall of Suburbia* (New York: Basic Books, 1987).

34   The term "settlement" is used here with all the associations of Eyal Weizman's work in Palestine, purposefully distinct from "gentrification." See Eyal Weizman, *Hollow Land: Israel's Architecture of Occupation* (London: Verso, 2007).

With extensive asphalt and impermeable surfaces shedding water into sewers and storm drains, the low-density sprawl of the Detroit suburbs produces literally toxic effects.

These effects are not distributed evenly—not as a cloud, or even a patchwork. Rather, they are centralized. During heavy rain events, the material sludge of combined sewer overflow gets released at points within the oldest central areas of Detroit, points plotting a line at the Detroit River, as well as the border between Detroit and its western suburbs. It is important to understand that these points have environmental qualities and risks that cannot be separated from the suburban geography that the watercraft infrastructure serves.

EMERGENCY MANAGEMENT AND THE "BLUE ECONOMY"

Today metropolitan Detroit's management of water operates as a showcase of new modes of infrastructure, a just-in-time deployment of switches through wrenches and spreadsheets. A choreography of spatial controls has evolved quickly in Detroit through innovations in management, governance, and resource control, as the city has shifted from democracy to Emergency Management and back. Throughout these shifts, water has been a medium for an intense and radical set of protocols—whether related to data gathering through pumps and monitors, price setting through closed-door agreements, or shutting off service to residents.

Since the mid-twentieth century, water infrastructure has evolved from a centralized resource for an industrializing city into a sprawling regional network. In studying this territory of water management around Detroit and its suburbs, one finds ongoing protocols of suburban expansion and environmental ghettoization of the urban black poor. From Detroit to the suburbs, water access and sewage processing are subsidized by the poor in majority black American and Latino neighborhoods to enhance capacity for the wealthy in majority white enclaves.

The most nationally recognized tragedy around water allocation from the Great Lakes has been the state-managed poisoning of Flint. While that instance involved a poisonous, temporary allocation of water from the Flint River, the circumstances are not unrelated. The impetus to craft a temporary

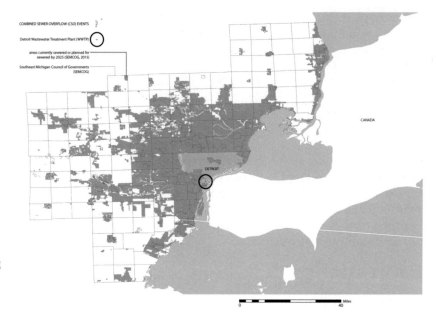

Fig 7: Sewered area around Detroit and combined sewer overflow locations. Courtesy of the author, based on data from Southeast Michigan Council of Governments (SEMCOG) GIS.

water source arose from the transition of the Detroit-based DWSD water system to a new pipeline: the Karegnondi Water Authority (KWA). After having been served by DWSD water since 1967, Flint's Emergency Management signed on to receive untreated water from KWA in 2013.[35] This new KWA pipeline was not planned by Flint to serve Flint residents. It was planned by Genesee County to open that suburban county to the "Blue Economy"—namely, development sites for industrial use of untreated water, primarily for water bottling plants and fracking.[36]

WATERCRAFT AS EXTRASTATECRAFT

Keller Easterling's notion of "extrastatecraft" becomes especially useful in understanding the regional water system as "infrastructure space"—as something shaped by geology, urban form, socioeconomics, and policy. In the crafting of water resources and policy, there is no neutral ground. As Easterling notes, "The aggressions within infrastructure space often occur with no defining moments and no satisfying declaration of an enemy. The consequential evidence may be found in the innocuous details—an invisible buildup of neglect or a silent form of attrition."[37]

Key to the contemporary effects of this infrastructure space is the network of resources, protocols, and switches (what Easterling terms "active forms")

35   Diane Bukowski, "Bi-Partisan Deal Led to Flint Water Poisoning for Profit: The Karegnondi Water Authority (KWA)," *Voice of Detroit*, February 15, 2016, http://voiceofdetroit.net/2016/02/15/bi-partisan-deal-led-to-flint-water-poisoning-for-profit-the-karegnondi-water-authority-kwa.

36   Allie Gross, "Emails Reveal Flint EM and State Advised Not to Join the KWA—It Was Never about Saving Money," *Detroit Metro Times*, February 13, 2016, http://www.metrotimes.com/Blogs/archives/2016/02/13/emails-reveal-flint-should-never-have-joined-kwa-andnbspit-was-never-about-saving-money#.

37   Easterling, *Extrastatecraft*, 149.

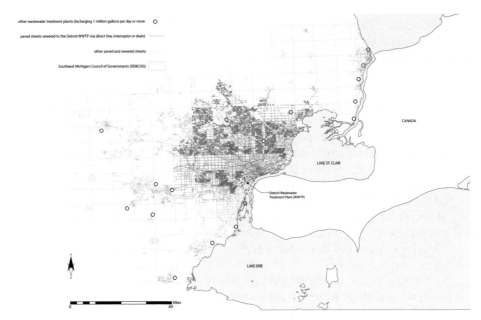

CANADA

LAKE ST. CLAIR

Detroit Wastewater
Treatment Plant (WWTP)

LAKE ERIE

Miles
0   40

deployed in the DWSD's self-proclaimed "shut-off procedures."[38] Rather than considering the shutoffs as a rupture in infrastructure, this analysis considers the termination of running water to selected nodes in the city as a performance itself of a mode of urban infrastructure. In tracing such banalities as stormwater runoff and sewage handling, the resource protocols at work in the dialectic between Detroit and its suburbs become legible as processes for transferring risk and even displacing residents.

It is within the terrain of this water network that splays out across more than a thousand square miles—the urban and the formerly urban, the suburban, the formerly agricultural turned urban sprawl, and the new pastoral of Detroit—that a new form of urban renewal emerges. Like previous forms of urban renewal, these processes require pushing certain residents out of neighborhoods to make way for new development. Unlike the last century's forms, which produced a tabula rasa defined by a closed polygon, these operations proceed from point to point, parcel to parcel, household to household. The geometry is more dot matrix or cellular automata than bounded Euclidian form. A line is formed from interceptor to suburban house, and the risks associated with that line are transferred to the single point of wastewater processing, the centralized points of CSO, and the dispersed points of houses belonging to individual customers who face water shutoffs.

Fig 8: Paved streets serviced directly by the Detroit Wastewater Treatment Plant on Jefferson (denoted by dashed circle). Facilities that support gray streets are noted with a black circle. Many of these facilities also discharge sediment-dewatering wastewater. The dark gray streets are the minimum currently serviced. Many facilities that support streets coded as light gray also discharge sediment-dewatering wastewater. Courtesy of the author, based on Detroit Water and Sewerage Department GIS, SEMCOG GIS, and Wastewater Master Plan, Executive Summary, October 2003.

38 "Shut-off procedures begin if payment has not been received by the due date stated in the Final Notice. If service is terminated, full payment of the past due balance is required and a deposit may also be required." "Customer Service: Past Due Accounts and Shutoffs," Detroit Water and Sewerage Department, February 14, 2017, http://archive.dwsd.org/pages_n/customer_service.html.

The cellular point of the inner-city house denied water services is linked to the infrastructural space of watercraft via remote control. As Easterling explains in *Extrastatecraft*:

> A remote control effects change indirectly or from some distance away, often without being detected... [A] nation indirectly floods a city when it builds a dam downstream... A mass-produced suburb, remote from the center, drains the city of its population. Any switch in any of the networks of infrastructure space can act like a remote—as a valve that may control flows of cars, electricity, microwaves, or broadband capacity somewhere down the line.[39]

39   Easterling, *Extrastatecraft*, 227.

In the case of the desertification of points via Detroit's watercraft, it is important to note that the remote control in effect here does not begin with water. The data that feeds into the algorithm of shutoffs becomes binary in relation to a temporality—currently payment that is forty-five days late—and a monetary figure: the amount owed.[40] This numerical figure is based on a calculated cost for water and sewage service. The monetary cost bundles together water and sewage as dual services of an authority that itself is subject to negotiations and rate controls by the judiciary. In other words, at no point is a market involved, despite the monetization and bundling of the resources. At no point does demand exceed supply. The customer-service mode of infrastructure management and the remote control switch of shutoffs have been layered over a delivery of resources that is highly centralized and controlled.

40   "Customer Service: Past Due Accounts and Shutoffs."

In an ominous way, Detroit's watercraft could be considered a pioneer in the US evolution of smart infrastructure. DWSD's systems were partially computerized to monitor CSO failure as early as 1980, as part of a restitution for a 1966 EPA finding.[41] Point-by-point water shutoffs might be considered the culmination of decades of sensor-based monitoring and data collection, which could not have existed in the era of paper files and printed Sanborn maps. Only the instant transfer of data between agencies, searchable databases, and information-based systems mapping (such as GIS) could make this house-by-house switch infrastructure possible.

41   Michigan Department of Natural Resources, *Detroit River Remedial Action Plan, Stage I* (1991), 3–7, https://www.epa.gov/sites/production/files/2013–12/documents/1991_detroitriverrapstg1.pdf.

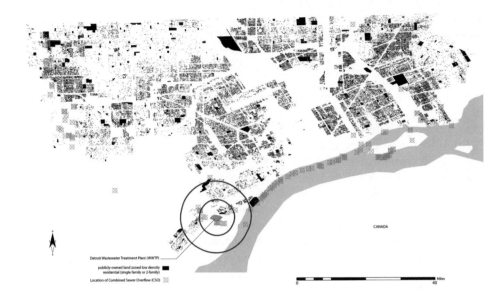

Detroit Wastewater Treatment Plant (WWTP)
publicly-owned land zoned low density
residential (single family or 2-family)
Location of Combined Sewer Overflow (CSO)

CANADA

Miles
0   40

The water shutoffs in Detroit complete a
computerization of the city that dates back to the
1980s but can be compared to Reyner Banham's
reading of Archigram decades prior. As architectural
theorist Anthony Vidler provides in a metareading
of Archigram, their "'Zoom City,' 'Computer City,'
'Off-the-Peg City,' 'Completely Expendable City,'
and 'Plug-in City'—were important as much for the
technology on which they were predicated as for
their aesthetic qualities."[42]

The watercraft of Detroit is, likewise, able
to render the city "completely expendable,"
perhaps because there is no image of what its mach-
inations look like. In this operation, the "computer
city" becomes aformal. Its illegibility makes it
politically inaccessible. Philosopher Slavoj Žižek
asserts that hegemony directs us toward false points
of binary decisions that render the operations of
ideology illegible. The inner-city house is this
false point in space, rendering the ideology of watercraft illegible. The focus on the individual switch
obscures the larger public investment and ownership
of thousands of miles of sewer and water lines—
more than a thousand square miles of territory
that feed stormwater into the network—and the
ongoing centralized points of sewage impact
(whether CSO or the stench of almost a billion
gallons per day of wastewater treatment at one
centralized facility).

Fig 9: Residential land
becomes publicly owned for
many reasons, including tax
liens, vacancy, and water-bill
foreclosures. This map shows
the extent of publicly owned
low-density residential land
in Detroit (zoned for one- or
two-family houses, shown
in gray) and its relationship
to combined sewer overflow
locations (shown in black).
Courtesy of the author.

42   Anthony Vidler, "Cities of
Tomorrow: Technology, Ecology,
and Architecture," *Artforum* 51, no.
1 (September 2012): 134.

FIELD OF SWITCHES

The water shutoffs and the watercraft that enables them draws separation not between city and suburb but within the line that connects the two, creating an autonomous authority of customer service that can be deployed to transfer risk from one point on the line toward another. This might even, tragically, be considered an antidemocratic enactment of interdependent active forms. As Easterling notes, "[B]roadband urbanists might offer an alternative organ of design—not an object form like a master plan, but an active form or an interplay of spatial variables... Broadband space can similarly be redesigned as a kind of software or a machine of interdependencies."[43] With Detroit's watercraft, the open public resource of the Great Lakes becomes a service, turned off as easily as a Netflix account. The water authority operates like a communications provider. Over time, the house without water access can be rendered unlivable, deemed unsanitary and unfit for families. The house becomes a dumb vessel, similar to a "bricked" cellphone—an inert object.

The spatial variables at play in Detroit's watercraft include the allocation of large landscape projects for water catchment and the accounting of those costs, the calculation of flow for ever-escalating peak rain events, and the distribution of excess capacity across thousands of miles of pipe and sewer lines. Across all of that, the single detached house becomes a node and a symbol for the distribution of resources across a territory. Broadband urbanism here appears as a tool of neoliberalism and even as a means of criminalizing the black urban poor.

The logic and language of customer service is itself a form of extrastatecraft that shapes infrastructural space.[44] Through Detroit's watercraft, the entire nonhomeless population of the city can be recast as customers. The water-delivery network is wielded as an instrument of debt collection. Watercraft participates in the shift from a political paradigm of citizens with access to public resources to a paradigm of customers being served.

THE COMING STATE OF ECOLOGICAL EMERGENCY

This essay aims to participate in the dissensus of the demands for water access in Detroit, not by staking claims of rights or speech but through making visible that which was not visible, namely the territories

43   Easterling, *Extrastatecraft*, 133.

44   Easterling, *Extrastatecraft*, 177.

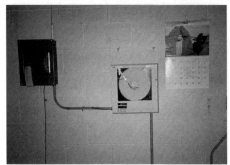

and spatial economies of watercraft. As Jacques Rancière states, "Dissensus is not the confrontation between interests or opinions. It is the manifestation of a distance of the sensible from itself."[45] Here, the sensible includes the asphalt of suburban sprawl, the topography of stormwater runoff, the vectors of processing sewage and stormwater, the thousands of miles of sewer and water lines sprawling into the suburbs. There is a distance between these spatial facts and the houses shut off from the water network due to the private matter of bill collections. Visualizing the spatial effects produced by these resource allocations—via remote controls and switches—becomes both a design problem and a politics.

The water shutoffs in Detroit, ongoing since Emergency Management, reveal a mode of

Fig 10: Meter pits, data loggers, Venturi meters, and other devices for measuring the flow of water and sewage between counties, primarily for the purposes of rate setting. Courtesy of the Detroit Water and Sewerage Department.

45   Jacques Rancière and Steve Corcoran, *Dissensus: On Politics and Aesthetics* (London: Continuum, 2010), 7.

infrastructure that channels resource protection toward the protection of a status quo of suburban sprawl. Building off fifty years of metered suburban expansion, the shutoffs arrive as a deployment of technologies of switches, real-time data management, and customer-service protocols. This analysis of watercraft cannot be reduced to a nostalgia for the "natural," an awareness of ecology, or a bemoaning of the politicization of water. As international activists and critics of globalization have noted, ecological emergency can be wielded as both cause and effect of austerity policy.

The collective authors of *The Coming Insurrection* state, "Tracking, transparency, certification, eco-taxes, environmental excellence, and the policing of water, all give us an idea of the coming state of ecological emergency."[46]

Even the most cogent theories of our current era of (fossil fuel-based) crisis tend to rely much more on land and landscape as a means of locating interrelated processes. The very term "Anthropocene" derives from work in geology. When Bruno Latour describes the involution of nature and society evident in the contemporary era, he speaks of landscape: "What happened to the landscape, for earlier generations, is now happening to the whole Earth: its gradual artificialization is making the nation of 'nature'; as obsolete as that of 'wilderness.'"[47] Perhaps the involution of nature and society in water, urban water, is even more difficult to make sensible. Water is not only threatened by artifice, it is complicated still by our own feces and—even more distancing—by the feces of others.

If we, as practitioners of the built environment, seek to engage modes of infrastructure in our spatial practices, we must develop new methods to reveal and counter the fluid forms of reverse subsidy, displacement, and privatization of resources. This may be more important and more urgent than designing ways of keeping our coasts above water.

46   The Invisible Committee, *The Coming Insurrection* (Los Angeles: Semiotext(e), 2009), 78.

47   Bruno Latour, *Facing Gaia: Eight Lectures on the New Climatic Regime* (Cambridge, UK: Polity Press, 2017), 121.

MITCH MCEWEN is assistant professor of architecture at Princeton University School of Architecture. She is principal of McEwen Studio and co-founder of A(n) Office, an architecture collaborative of studios in Detroit, Los Angeles, and Brooklyn.

Destabilizing the Platform: Improvisation on the Electric Grid

Dietmar Offenhuber

84

Fig 1: A panorama of Paco, Manila, highlighting the tamperproof wire for supplying electricity to households. Photograph by Antonella Amesberger.

The discursive space of urban technology is filled with platforms: open data platforms, "smart city" and "Internet of things" platforms, crowdsourcing platforms, platform companies, and platform economies.[1] As the central metaphor of urban tech, the meaning of "platform" is taken for granted yet surprisingly hard to pin down. It oscillates between technical infrastructure, social arrangement, and organizational principle. In technical terms, the platform is an environment governed by a set of predefined rules: standards, protocols, and interfaces that define the conditions under which software runs, data is stored, and devices connect. The platform is an enabling infrastructure for higher-level applications, a space of possibilities that prescribes not the "what" but the "how." The platform is meant to disappear behind the applications it facilitates, but it often ends up producing friction through incompatibilities, unmet dependencies, or version requirements. In the domain of urban technologies, platforms are ubiquitous; they offer access to data, mediate citizen complaints, allow apps and websites to make queries about the state of urban infrastructure, and provide a space for interaction among various groups. At what point did the idea of individual applications interacting under the governance of the platform become an appropriate framework for thinking about the city?

A decade ago, the urbanist Dan Hill reflected on the increasing presence of data infrastructures in everyday urban space and proposed that we consider the street itself as a platform. In his call for urban data governance, Hill focused not on futuristic technologies but on the mundane assemblage of sensors, networks, and commercial consumer services that already in 2008 occupied a substantial footprint in the city: "Without this infrastructure, the street only half-exists."[2] The techno-heterotopia of countless digital services he described that turn a casual stroll down a street into an online experience, however, was messy and prone to miscommunication—reflecting common difficulties with computing platforms, like getting software to run or a printer to connect. Thus, the diversity of data flows extracted from and projected into urban space demanded a framework of governance to make these data flows accessible and to regulate the conditions under which this provision takes place.

The subtle irony of embracing a slightly dysfunctional digital future, however, was lost on the many city evangelists inspired by Hill's text. Today, the idea of the city as an operating system is commonplace—used to describe civic technologies, smart city solutions, commercial companies such as Uber or Airbnb,[3] and economic and political theory.[4] Defining and implementing the rules and protocols of a citywide "urban operating system" is a considerable planning challenge that requires substantial time and resources. Once the platform is finished, we are told, magical things will happen. This view, however, creates a chicken-and-egg problem: if the platform is the prerequisite for collective engagement, how do platforms themselves take shape?

The world of open-source development, where every tool depends on countless other tools, offers a model for the art of building a plane while flying it. Its platforms are discursive and introspective—focused not only on their final use but also on their process of development. Anthropologist Chris Kelty describes the process in his concept of recursive publics: a public that is concerned with building and maintaining the infrastructure that is at the same time the basis of its discourse.[5] This perspective renders the system as a bricolage, a permanently unfinished beta version, whose components are always in flux.[6] Many established platform services have their origins in improvisation. Airbnb famously emerged from a quick hack to organize sleeping places for the attendees of a design conference in San Francisco. Unlike computing platforms, urban data platforms, however, are rarely fully defined in advance and then used precisely as anticipated. They are instead a product of improvisation, ad hoc decisions, and renegotiations. In the dynamics of improvisational governance, platforms are continuously dismantled and rebuilt.

In 2015 a new digital infrastructure landed in the city of Manila with a series of advertisements heralding a new product by Meralco, the private distribution utility company serving electricity to the metropolitan area. The product was Kuryente Load: a prepaid electricity scheme with a smart meter that promises to help customers better monitor and plan their electricity consumption. The electricity budget controlled by the smart meter is rechargeable via prepaid cards sold in convenience stores—which, similar to prepaid mobile phone schemes, have higher rates than a regular subscription and are mostly targeted at low-income communities whose members often struggle to afford their electric bills. As of late 2017, Meralco had already installed eighty thousand smart meters, and it plans to roll out more than three million devices throughout the country by 2024.[7]

The advertisements and press releases provided by the company offer no hints about its underlying motivations. The company's rhetoric around smart grid technology appears indistinguishable from other smart city initiatives around the world. However, while the exchangeability of smart city arguments illustrates Adam Greenfield and Nurri Kim's critique of the smart city as generic, timeless, and placeless—and while, especially in the case of smart city projects in the global South, it is often suspected that corporate salespeople sell boiler-plate technology to cities desperate for modernization without considering local needs—this does not seem to be the case here.[8] Meralco's smart meter rollout is deeply connected to the local context and comes with specific expectations, but neither of these circumstances is obvious.

Electricity costs are a grave concern for many of Manila's residents. The Philippines has, in absolute terms, one of the highest electricity rates in the world, despite being plagued by regular brownouts and system outages.[9] High costs and low service quality can largely be attributed to the hands-off approach of full privatization pursued by the Philippine government. Rapid urbanization has left much of the country struggling with the inadequate provision of essential infrastructure services. With the sweeping Electricity Power Industry

Fig 2: Improvised repair of a streetlight in Paco,
Manila. Photograph by Konstantin Jagsch.

Destabilizing the Platform: Improvisation on the Electric Grid

Reform Act of 2001, the public hand withdrew from service provision, and the country's grid was fully privatized, leaving the provider landscape fragmented.[10] At the present moment, electricity generation cannot keep up with demand and is additionally hampered by an inefficient distribution network. The smart meter rollout by Meralco, which does not generate but instead distributes electricity, is concerned with system loss, which may not be surprising to anyone contemplating the streetscape of Manila, with its electric poles overburdened with a massive clutter of cables.

Manila's electric infrastructure blends with the surroundings; electricity poles are used to support simple structures, cables to affix fiesta decorations or to dry laundry. Examples of appropriation and repair are everywhere, especially in lower-income *barangays* (districts or villages) characterized by narrow streets and small buildings. Manila's colorful and sculptural streetlights appear in various states of maintenance and are often repaired in a makeshift way. Lightbulbs installed by residents illuminate dark alleys in dense urban settlements. Street vendors sell their goods at night under the light of existing streetlights, using the poles as support for displaying goods. Other vendors bring their own battery-powered LED lamps or rent electricity from neighboring residents at exorbitant premiums. But not all of these ad hoc constructions and services originate with residents. In many cases, they are initiated by local neighborhood administrations, the barangay councils. While having no formal role in electricity provision, the council still tries to address its constituents' infrastructural concerns. Repairs are executed with the help of local artisans. Likewise, lighting for the scarce public amenities—such as small religious shrines or gathering spots—is co-produced with the community. If dark alleys require illumination, the council negotiates with residents to place a lightbulb in front of their house. In some cases, when a family cannot afford electricity, the council connects

Fig 3: Barangay chairperson Arleen G. Braga with an example of the co-production of streetlight provision with residents. Photograph courtesy of the author.

their household to the streetlight power supply. The council's unbureaucratic approach to public service provision illustrates that the traditional modernist dichotomy between a formal and an informal sector is incorrect. Informality is not something that exists outside the institutional realm but is an essential part of it, filling its gaps. The term "informality" is unproductive since it implies an irregular mode of action. Instead, informality reflects the most common way of negotiating and doing things, necessary when bureaucratic automatisms are insufficient.

Meralco attributes system loss to two reasons: outages in electric equipment including transformers and cabling, and electricity theft. Claiming that there is little it can do about power loss, the company focuses its efforts on preventing pilferage.[11] What goes unmentioned is the fact that the company is obligated to offer discounted lifeline electricity rates to low-income residents, which makes operations in certain neighborhoods less profitable. Unsurprisingly, the barangays with more lifeline customers are often the barangays designated by Meralco as high-system loss areas where the company focuses its campaign against power theft.

Electricity theft is a hazardous activity that can have catastrophic effects for the whole barangay. When too much power is drawn from a single transformer, the transformer can overheat, which has led to disastrous fires in densely packed neighborhoods. Even if such an extreme event fails to occur, the transformer will eventually break under additional load and leave the whole area without power. When this happens, the utility company intervenes and dictates the rules for restoring power. Typical demands include covering all open bills and paying the costs of repair and new installations. When Meralco restores power in a high-system loss area, it introduces a different delivery mechanism. Meters are no longer attached to individual buildings but are clustered on a tall pole, the elevated metering cluster (EMC). This measure moves power out of reach of pilferers and prevents power from jumping through an automatic mechanism that drops power as soon as any additional load is detected. Currently, surveyors use binoculars for their bimonthly meter reading of EMCs, which, in the first phase, contained regular meters. In a second phase, Meralco has started to deploy smart meters, which send data continuously to the distribution utility. In addition to consumption, these meters collect information about customer appliances and electric consumption to detect bottlenecks in the system and make it easier to identify power theft. Dedicated to this purpose, the company has sponsored several master's theses and dissertations on signal analysis.[12]

The cluster poles are highly visible elements that change the urban land-scape. Each of the meters on a pole is connected through an orange cable to its respective household, which is often more than a hundred meters away from the pole itself. The many additional wires cause visual clutter that has prompted the power commission to step in with regulatory action, limiting the previously unlimited number of wires admissible per EMC. While EMCs are a highly visible signifier of class, residents view them more favorably—as a sign of a functioning community connected to power. The poles are often located right next to the barangay gate, which typically features the portraits of barangay council members, surrounded by other political advertisements. Infrastructure thus serves as a material medium of communication, one that is especially relevant before local elections when urban services such as sewers, flood canals, streetlights, and elec-tricity are widely contested.

Fig 4: EMC cluster at the gate of Barangay 849.
Photograph courtesy of the author.

Meralco's smart meter initiative is not a generic smart city project installed on a vague promise of efficiency. Its role has to be understood in the local context of improvisational practices and the politics of infrastructure governance. Here, improvisation means the coincidence of planning and action—taking advantage of locally available resources—often driven by an urgent need.[13] Claude Lévi-Strauss's related concept of bricolage is useful here too. It refers to making do with whatever is at hand—the ad hoc recombination of half-finished elements to create a new solution that is often just good enough rather than optimal.[14] Practices of improvisation and bricolage are ubiquitous. Residents appropriate the hardware of the power grid and engage in ad hoc repair, maintenance, and service provision; they also rent electricity to other tenants and street vendors. Street-level bureaucrats try to improve service delivery in their respective neighborhoods by mobilizing the local resources that are available. The distribution utility introduces initiatives such as the EMC without much coordination with the local government. Finally, the public authority responds to the EMC initiative by regulating its impact on the urban environment and the social welfare of the public authority's constituents.

New infrastructures and platforms such as smart meter initiatives and the construction of EMCs are a result of improvisational governance, which unfolds through interactions between actors: the regulatory authority, the city and its local representatives, the residents, and the private electric utility company. These actors do not always follow a shared and mutually agreed-upon plan but instead respond to each other's actions in a musical "call and response." Unlike the case of jazz improvisation, the goals of the participants are not always aligned and often conflicting.

The process of platform building is an act of bricolage rather than an exer cise in large-scale anticipatory system planning. Practices of improvisation are not endemic to the rapidly urbanizing cities of emerging economies but are equally present in "rich" cities with developed systems of infrastructure and governance. Improvisational governance exists not only in cities such as Manila but also in cities across the United States and Europe, where companies—like those behind shared mobility apps, dockless bicycles, and electric scooters— follow the principle "deploy first, negotiate later," rapidly reshaping public space with new services and forcing cities to react with regulations after the fact.[15]

The metaphor of the platform is problematic, as it implies a system whose properties can be defined in advance and that remains stable once in operation. Such a perspective fundamentally misunderstands how platforms emerge and evolve. As social media platforms show, the system is defined by the practices of its users. The platform is never stable; it is always caught in an intermediate state of negotiation. Interventions usually take place locally rather than systemically.

Improvisation and bricolage lead to a different understanding of platform. Organizational theorist Claudio Ciborra describes the platform organization as a shapeless entity where explicit structures are transient but informal relationships are stable. Here, the platform is in a perpetual indeterminate state, comprising a collection of half-articulated solutions that can be recombined and reassembled in response to current needs.[16] The metaphor of the computing platform empha- sizes specific structure, while in the framework of the platform organization, things need to stay undetermined. The platform is a paradoxical entity. Every open data or citizen feedback system requires specific categories, binding proto- cols, and structures. However, in the larger time frame, these structures are always provisional, subject to renegotiation or redefinition through the practices of users.

While the infrastructural bricolage of Manila is highly legible, the improvisa- tional aspects underpinning smart urban platforms are less visible. The countless iterations and adjustments to software architecture, protocols, and interfaces leave less obvious traces in the physical environment. But the invisibility is also intentional. The aesthetics of platform interfaces, from the Uber app to the Google search engine, suggests a system of elegant simplicity, rationality, and effectiveness—a well-oiled system that would degrade attempting to control it through policy-making and regulation. Under the minimalist surface, however, these platforms are as messy as all other sociotechnical systems, as Amazon ironically acknowledges by naming its crowdworking platform, the Mechanical Turk, after the fake, eighteenth-century chess-playing robot operated by a human hidden inside. Like the human chess player hidden inside the historical automaton, platform application programming interfaces and smart algorithms are often merely a veneer masking a hidden dimension of human "muddling through," a persistent part of urban governance.

NHUBER is associate professor at
niversity in the fields of art and design
. He holds a PhD in urban planning
tts Institute of Technology. His
... .ocuses on the relationship between design,
technology, and governance. He is the author of *Waste
is Information* (MIT Press, 2017), works as an advisor to
the United Nations, and has published books on urban
data, accountability technologies, and urban informatics.

1   The case study discussed in this essay is based
on the "improstructure" project conducted in
collaboration with Katja Schechtner and includes
arguments from Dietmar Offenhuber and Katja
Schechtner, "Improstructure—An Improvisational
Perspective on Smart Infrastructure Governance,"
Cities 72 (February 2018): 329–338.

2   Dan Hill, "The Street as Platform," *City of Sound*
(blog), February 11, 2008, http://www.cityofsound.
com/blog/2008/02/the-street-as-p.html.

3   On Uber and Airbnb, see Geoffrey Parker,
Marshall Van Alstyne, and Sangeet Paul Choudary,
*Platform Revolution: How Networked Markets Are
Transforming the Economy and How to Make Them
Work for You* (New York: W. W. Norton, 2017); David
S. Evans and Richard Schmalensee, *Matchmakers:
The New Economics of Multisided Platforms* (Boston:
Harvard Business Review Press, 2016).

4   Benjamin H. Bratton, *The Stack: On Software
and Sovereignty* (Cambridge, MA: MIT Press, 2016);
Nick Srnicek, *Platform Capitalism* (Cambridge, UK:
Polity Press, 2017); Tarleton Gillespie, "The Politics
of 'Platforms,'" *New Media & Society* 12, no. 3 (May
2010): 347–364.

5   Christopher Kelty, "Geeks and Recursive Publics:
How the Internet and Free Software Make Things
Public," in *Beyond Habermas: Democracy, Knowledge,
and the Public Sphere*, ed. Christian J. Emden and David
Midgley (New York: Berghahn, 2014), 99–118.

6   Alberto Escalada Jimenez, Adrian Dabrowski,
Noburu Sonehara, Juan M. Montero Martinez,
and Isao Echizen, "Tag Detection for Preventing
Unauthorized Face Image Processing," in *Digital
Forensics and Watermarking: 13th International
Workshop, IWDW 2014, Taipei, Taiwan, October 1–4, 2014,
Proceedings*, ed. Christian Kraetzer, Yun Q Shi, Jana
Dittmann, and Hyoung Joong Kim (Cham, Switzerland:
Springer, 2014).

7   Edd K. Usman, "Meralco Smart Meters to Enable
Predictive Repairs, Rich Consumption Data," *Rappler*,
November 23, 2017, http://www.rappler.com/
technology/news/189359-meralco-smart-meters-
consumption-breakdown-predictive-repairs; Ashley
Theron-Ord, "Meralco Plans to Install 3.3m Smart
Meters by 2024," *Smart Energy International*, August
25, 2016, https://www.metering.com/regional-news/
asia/meralco-3-3m-smart-meters-2024.

8   Adam Greenfield and Nurri Kim, *Against the
Smart City* (New York: Do Projects, 2013).

9   Lantau Group, "Global Benchmark Study of
Residential Electricity Tariffs," May 2013, https://
slidex.tips/download/global-benchmark-study-of-
residential-electricity-tariffs.

10   Marlyne Sahakian, "Energy Consumption and
Cooling in Southeast Asia," in *Keeping Cool in Southeast
Asia: Energy Consumption and Urban Air-Conditioning*
(Basingstoke: Palgrave Macmillan, 2014), 27–59.

11   Usman, "Meralco Smart Meters."

12   Orlee Laguitan, "Electrical Power Theft Detection
and Wireless Meter Reading" (BS diss., University of
the East, 2014).

13   Miguel Pina e Cunha, João Vieira da Cunha, and
Ken Kamoche, "Organizational Improvisation: What,
When, How, and Why," *International Journal of
Management Reviews* 1, no. 3 (September 1999):
299–341, https://doi.org/10.1111/1468-2370.00017.

14   Claude Lévi-Strauss, *The Savage Mind* (Chicago:
University of Chicago Press, 1966).

15   Farhad Manjoo, "How Tech Companies
Conquered America's Cities," *New York Times*, June
21, 2018, https://www.nytimes.com/2018/06/20/
technology/tech-companies-conquered-cities.html.

16   Claudio U. Ciborra, "The Platform Organization:
Recombining Strategies, Structures, and Surprises,"
Organization Science 7, no. 2 (1996): 103–118.

Aleppo, Syria: Urban Destruction Beyond Winning the War

Laura Kurgan, Grga Basic, and Eva Schreiner

94

In spring 2011 Syrians all over the country took to the streets in peaceful protest to demand the removal of authoritarian president Bashar al-Assad. Their protests were met with violent repression, and the unrest escalated to armed conflict. The Syrian revolution-turned-war is still ongoing at the time of writing this essay. Aleppo, formerly Syria's largest city and commercial center, was one of the war's main battlegrounds from 2012 to 2016.[1] To better understand the multisided urban warfare in the city and to grasp the scale of Aleppo's destruction, the Center for Spatial Research constructed an open-source, interactive, layered map of the city at the neighborhood scale.[2] Using high-resolution satellite imagery from before and during the conflict, the map documents forms of urban damage, shifting front lines and battlefield positions, civilian responses to conflict, and the effects of warfare on the city's storied cultural heritage. The map is a platform, with multiple sources of data, for narrating what happened to and in Aleppo—and it is also an experiment in ways of conjoining mapping software, imagery, and data from both participants and observers in order to understand conflict at the urban scale. In the case of Aleppo, an ancient and historic city, what started as a project to document the destruction of memory allowed us, ultimately, to produce a memory of destruction.[3]

To create the map, we had to devise methods for viewing and analyzing the conflict from a distance. Although we were in contact with residents and activists in the city throughout our research, our work was necessarily remote. One of the virtues of that necessity was the development of tools and methods for the long-distance study of an urban battlefield. We strove not to displace perspectives and analyses from the ground but to explore how the remote view allowed us to aggregate dispersed spatial information and thus enabled the map's users to draw connections not always visible at close range. Over three years, from 2014 to 2016, we gathered and analyzed numerous data sources and sets to create the map's many layers. We spatialized and preserved video material from a set of reliable YouTube channels presenting work by local activists and news organizations in the city. Collaborating with geographer Jamon Van Den Hoek, we experimented with using freely accessible, low-resolution Landsat imagery to detect changes in the urban fabric of Aleppo every two weeks during the war. This work, in turn, guided specific investigations using higher-resolution but more expensive satellite imagery, which we purchased from private satellite companies. This process allowed us, as well, to fill in some of the gaps in the damage data generated by the Operational Satellite Applications Programme (UNOSAT) of the United Nations Institute for Training and Research (UNITAR), released once a year during the war, in 2014, 2015, and 2016.

Violent conflict produces all sorts of casualties, sometimes intentionally and sometimes collaterally. With NGOs and other researchers doing the important work of documenting, monitoring,

36°15'0"N

36°13'0"N

REBEL CONTROL

36°11'0"N

Moderately Damaged

Severely Damaged

Destroyed

10'0"E   37°12'0"E   37°14'0"E

Fig 1: Overlaid on a 2016 satellite image of Aleppo, the UNITAR-UNOSAT damage data depicts the location and intensity of the destruction that occurred between 2012 and 2016. Background satellite imagery from WorldView-2. © 2016 DigitalGlobe, Inc. Unless otherwise stated, all images produced by and courtesy of the Center for Spatial Research.

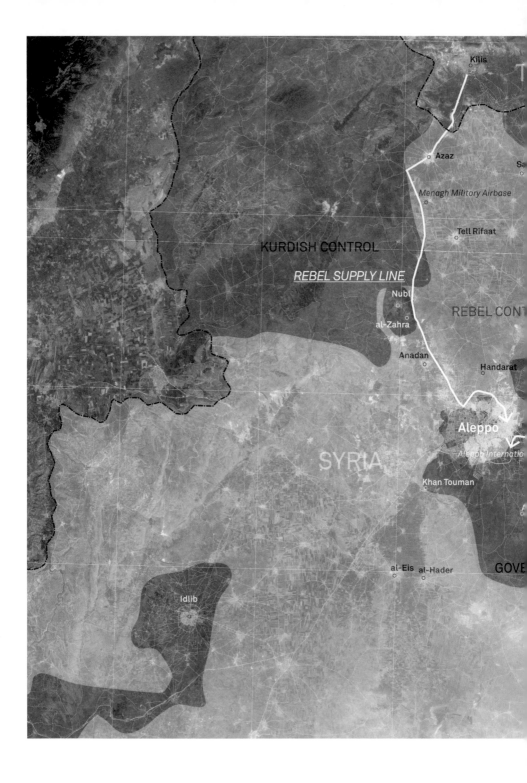

Fig 2: Aleppo's autonomous supply infrastructure—
which was organized around a single road,
with rebel forces in the north and government
forces in the south—explains, in part, the city's
internal division between 2012–2016.

Aleppo, Syria: Urban Destruction Beyond Winning the War

and researching civilian mortality, internal displacement, and refugees, or investigating the detention and torture of activists and fighters, we chose to focus on urban damage at various stages of the war. From its outset in July 2012, through four years of territorial stalemate, to the final siege of the city between August and December 2016, our map traces patterns of urban damage. It asks what these patterns reveal of the tactics and strategies of designed destruction, of organized violence that often exceeds the bounds of "proportionality" and "military necessity" (as problematic as those criteria can sometimes be). As a platform, the map not only confirmed what we knew about damage in well-known places such as the historic Citadel of Aleppo but also helped direct our attention to less prominent and now obliterated districts in the city, such as the so-called "informal" neighborhoods of Salah ad-Deen and Ashrafeyeh. By chasing clues provided by the map and its data layers, by tracing military operations, and, crucially, by connecting these processes to pre- and postconflict economic, social, and legal developments, we began to grasp the ways in which the extraordinary vandalism and brutality of war in Aleppo are connected to the everyday depredations of state power in Syria.

Compared to other major cities in Syria, where demonstrations and violent responses by the police and security forces were widespread, Aleppo was relatively calm in the first year of the war. It wasn't until the summer of 2012—when rebel fighters, predominantly recruited from the city's immediate environs, entered Aleppo—that the city was consumed by armed conflict and soon split in half, with the western side under government control and the eastern side becoming rebel territory. For four years, until summer 2016, the borderline between east and west barely moved, solidifying Aleppo as a divided city.[4]

How can we explain the front line's relative stability? An analysis of the map suggests that one determining factor was the specificity of Aleppo's transportation and supply infrastructure, which regulated both daily life and military operations in the city during the four years of conflict.

One of the first clashes between government forces and rebel fighters took place in Salah ad-Deen in the city's southwest.[5] Intense fighting in the neighborhood continued over the course of two months, with control of the area shifting between state and rebel forces.[6] The neighborhood ultimately fell into rebel hands and became one of the Free Syrian Army's first strongholds. The fact that fighting first erupted in Salah ad-Deen is not coincidental: it is strategically located next to one of the main roads into Aleppo from the south, the supply route that linked government troops to regime strongholds in the rest of the country. The road furthermore allowed access to the country's major weapons manufacturer, Defense Factories, located just south of Aleppo near the town of as-Safira.

Assad's army succeeded in containing rebel forces within Salah ad-Deen, and this containment sufficed to defend the army's southern supply line throughout the war. The regime was able to maintain the supply of resources even when rebel forces took control of a portion of the Damascus-Aleppo highway between Aleppo and Homs in March 2013—forcing Assad's troops to shift their main supply corridor to the so-called "southern axis," a narrow road connecting Hama and Aleppo via as-Safira and Kanasir.[7]

With southern access roads firmly in the hands of the regime, rebel forces established an entirely separate supply system into Aleppo from the north, where most armed rebel groups operated along a corridor from Kilis (in Turkey) to Azaz and Aleppo.[8] A twenty-eight-mile-long front line between the Al Nusra Front and ISIS formed parallel to this road, stretching from the Turkish border all the way to Aleppo.[9] Therefore, while government forces and their allies operated close to Aleppo, attempting to tighten the circle around the city, rebel groups engaged a much larger territory spanning the areas north of the city to the Turkish border. In many ways, it was the access to resources that fueled and secured the division of the city into two relatively stable parts. Relying on completely independent supply infrastructures meant that both sides were focused on maintaining and fortifying their defenses rather than on enlarging their territories within the city.

Minor interruptions notwithstanding, these two main supply corridors endured until July 2016, when, along the northern supply route, Castello Road was captured by regime forces, cutting rebel forces off from their main thoroughfare and supply line. With this operation, the government effectively won the battle for Aleppo, as procuring supplies became less and less feasible for the rebel groups.

Using Landsat imagery in combination with high-resolution imagery and YouTube videos, we can see that the targeting of Castello Road began in May 2016. The road was within reach of regime artillery fire by July 7 and was finally taken by government forces on July 17.[10] This period of intense fighting is further evident in the UNITAR-UNOSAT damage data, which shows the destruction of Ashrafeyeh in summer 2016. Ashrafeyeh, a rebel-held neighborhood in close proximity to Castello Road, exhibits one of the highest damage rates of all neighborhoods in the dataset. This regime advance ushered in what became known as the siege of Aleppo.

This military victory could have been an opportune moment to reach a political solution, but all attempts failed. A cease-fire between the Syrian government and a US-supported coalition of Syrian opposition groups, brokered by Russia and the United States in September 2016, was poorly adhered to and lasted only several days.[11] Instead, the subsequent fighting, which lasted

37°4'0"E   37°6'0"E   37°8'0"E

36°15'0"N

KURDISH C

36°13'0"N

GOVERNMENT CONTROL

al-Jamiliyeh

Sayf ad-Dauleh   Bustan al-Qaser

36°11'0"N

Salah ad-Deen

al-Ansari Mashhad

as-Sukkari

36°9'0"N

37°6'0"E   37°8'0"E

First Clashes

Fig 3: The first clashes in July 2012, which took place mostly in eastern Aleppo, quickly established a divided city of rebel- and government-held neighborhoods. Background satellite imagery from WorldView-2. © 2012 DigitalGlobe, Inc.

High Resolution: **March 23, 2016**

High Resolution: **June 11, 2016**

Fig 4: These two images show traces of the government capture and control of Castello Road in summer 2016, using Landsat pixel value change overlaid onto high-resolution satellite images in March and June 2016. What can be seen in June 2016 is major damage to the Castello Road overpass as well as to buildings in the surrounding area. Background satellite imagery from WorldView-2. © 2016 DigitalGlobe, Inc.

until December 2016, resulted in the systematic destruction of eastern Aleppo through heavy government shelling, barrel bomb air attacks, and finally a major ground offensive beginning on November 27. Moving roughly north to south, Assad's regime destroyed and seized neighborhood after neighborhood.[12]

By December, the rebel-held part of Aleppo was reduced to a small pocket in the southwest of the city—in the Salah ad-Deen neighborhood. It was in this neighborhood that the first clashes between regime and rebel forces had taken place in 2012; and it was from here that the green buses, evacuating the final remaining groups of rebel supporters to other provinces, left the city in 2016. Aleppo's war thus began and ended in precisely the same neighborhood.

The strategic military target—the rebels' supply infrastructure—had long been captured when eastern Aleppo was almost completely flattened in the five-month-long siege. Potential conclusions from this outcome are further complicated by looking at what exactly was damaged. The systematic destruction took place almost exclusively in the city's so-called "informal" settlements. A 2009 report, commissioned by the Syrian government and produced by the German Agency for Technical Cooperation (Gesellschaft für Technische Zusammenarbeit, or GTZ), designated twenty-two of Aleppo's neighborhoods as "informal." Using that report, addressed in more detail below, we can see a strikingly consistent pattern of damage across satellite images from 2012 to 2016: 53 percent of all damage was registered in "informal" settlements, with the majority of the rest occurring in the Old City. 88 percent of all damage was registered in the rebel-held areas of eastern Aleppo. Both Salah ad-Deen and Ashrafeyeh were listed as "informal" neighborhoods in the 2009 report—and both have been reduced to rubble.

Suggesting a direct, causal relationship between the labeling of these areas as "informal" in 2009 and the destruction of them in 2016 would simplify complex historic processes. What our spatial analysis of warfare in Aleppo does show, however, is the central role these neighborhoods played in the course of the war—and surely will play in any so-called postwar reconstruction.

In April 2018, the Syrian government adopted Law 10, a new property law creating designated zones for reconstruction across Syria. Presented as an urban planning measure and as "progress" toward a "modern postconflict Syria," the law has been strongly criticized for authorizing the confiscation and redevelopment of property without due process or compensation and for constituting a major obstacle to the return of displaced Syrian residents.[13] In fact, Law 10 radically extends a previous provision, Decree 66, from September 2012. Limited to the Damascus province, that decree allowed the government to "redevelop areas of unauthorized housing and *informal* settlements."[14]

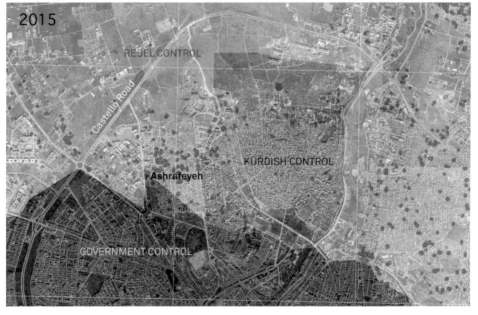

Fig 5: These three images depict damaged-building data produced by UNITAR-UNOSAT's zooming in on Ashrafeyeh in 2014, 2015, and 2016. Comparison of data from these three dates shows the drastic increase in the number of destroyed buildings in the neighborhood adjacent to Castello Road. Because this data was published only three times during the conflict, with points marking damage but not date of damage, we used biweekly low-resolution Landsat imagery to detect incremental change. Background satellite imagery from Pleiades-1A and WorldView-2. © CNES_2015, distribution AIRBUS 93 DS, France, and 2016 DigitalGlobe, Inc., respectively.

NOV 27, 2016

DEC 06, 2016

NOV 28, 2016

DEC 07, 2016

Fig 6: Sequence of maps (pages 108–111). After months of siege warfare, regime forces finally seized control of eastern Aleppo by destroying one neighborhood after the other from November 27, 2016 to December 23, 2016.

The duplicate maps for December 12, 2016 show the regime's advances over the course of the day. Data on areas of control from The Carter Center. Background satellite imagery from WorldView-2. © 2016 DigitalGlobe, Inc.

Aleppo, Syria: Urban Destruction Beyond Winning the War

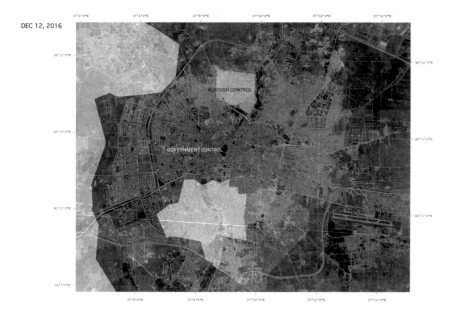

DEC 12, 2016

KURDISH CONTROL

GOVERNMENT CONTROL

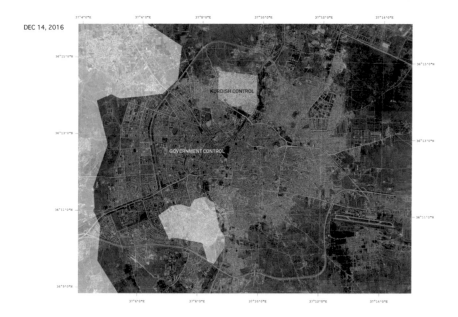

DEC 14, 2016

KURDISH CONTROL

GOVERNMENT CONTROL

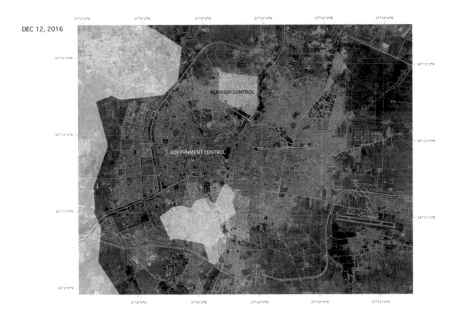

DEC 12, 2016

KURDISH CONTROL

GOVERNMENT CONTROL

DEC 23, 2016

KURDISH CONTROL

GOVERNMENT CONTROL

Based on these provisions, the decision about which areas will be expropriated and redeveloped lies in the hands of the Assad family and those close to the regime. Critics have pointed out that Decree 66 and Law 10 have been and will continue to be used to crack down on dissent in specific areas and as a punitive measure after revolts. In 2012, for example, the neighborhoods designated for redevelopment under Decree 66 comprised exclusively areas with strong opposition support.[15] Furthermore, the laws constitute a transfer of assets, tax-free, to private companies—rewarding and further enriching those who stood with the regime throughout the conflict. In March 2012 new legislation was introduced that allowed the establishment of real estate financing companies; a decree in May 2015 granted all units within the state the authority to form private investment companies; and in the following year, a new law permitting private companies to make deals with the government to manage state assets was set in motion.[16] Together, this legal regime creates lucrative investment opportunities for businesspeople close to the government—consolidating and reinforcing the patrimonial nature of the Syrian state.

Law 10 cannot be seen as a "postwar" development for the reconstruction of war-torn areas. As an extension of a 2012 decree, signed at the very beginning of escalating warfare, and based on a process of real estate privatization that had been underway long before fighting began, this legal framework complicates the notion of war as a period of violence with a designated start and end. It blurs the temporality of war. From this point of view, the Syrian civil war constitutes one particularly devastating episode in a longer process of state violence and resource allocation. Ways of knowing the war-torn city thus require a frame that is broader than merely mapping military operations: violent conflict works hand in hand with seemingly mundane but often weaponized processes of urban planning and policy-making—in other words, processes of politics ("by other means").

Most important for our purposes, Decree 66 and Law 10 focus exclusively on "unauthorized housing and informal settlements." Generally, the term "informal settlement" designates areas where residents either reside on land they do not own—land that is usually owned by the state—or build on land they own but lack the planning permission to do so. Encompassing vastly different social and economic classes, these areas generally experience substandard provision of services such as water, electricity, transportation, or sanitation; however, "informal" here does not necessarily imply the slum-like conditions that the term might imply elsewhere. From 2003 onward, the Syrian government sought to identify these areas and made them the focus of central planning initiatives. Assad's regime introduced numerous policies and laws for upgrading and legalizing "informal" housing, while also instituting increasingly drastic measures against illegal construction. Yet a government report estimated that in 2011 up to 50 percent of Syria's population lived in "informal" housing.[17] Current developments around Decree 66 and Law 10, both focusing on developing precisely these areas, are hence the continuation of policies almost two decades old.

In Aleppo, roughly half of the city's 2.4 million inhabitants lived in the twenty-two designated "informal" neighborhoods before the revolution turned into civil war. As used in the 2009 GTZ report, the term "informal" blankets different economies of informality: some neighborhoods, though not all, are comparatively poor; many, though not all, are provided with official infrastructure. In fact, one of Aleppo's "informal" neighborhoods is the relatively wealthy suburb of Khan al-Assal, where "large weekend villas, many with swimming pools," dominate the landscape. Khan al-Assal is included on the list of "informal" settlements alongside two Palestinian refugee camps administered by the United Nations Relief and Works Agency.[18] The designation of "informality" authorized the report's intention for these neighborhoods: to "minimize their growth" and "upgrade" their "social, economic and environmental conditions."[19]

It was in these often disadvantaged areas that early protest movements began across Syria and, in 2012, where rebels found their support base in Aleppo. This was not a coincidence. These neighborhoods tell a complex history of Syria: from the colonial legacies of Ottoman and French governance to the processes of class formation; from the role of the peasantry in Hafez al-Assad's rise to power to the growth of the state apparatus and its rigid real estate zoning practices during the Baʿth Party rule; from the establishment of a tight state-business network through Bashar al-Assad's "neoliberal" reforms to the role of the army and security apparatus in enforcing this network.[20] "Informal" settlements further mirror patterns of migration following the Iraq War beginning in 2003, which displaced half a million Iraqis to Syria, where they joined Palestinian and Lebanese refugees already residing there. There was also a sharp increase in internal rural migration to these neighborhoods, partly tied to a drought that began in 2006 and to the Syrian government's agricultural policies and corruption, which transformed the drought into a humanitarian catastrophe.[21] Therefore, studying the complexity of these neighborhoods beyond their designation as "informal" is necessary to understand the two forms of sanctioned destruction and conflict in Syria: the continuous emphasis on these neighborhoods in planning documents like Decree 66 and Law 10 and in the violence that occurred on the ground.

It is through the processes of mapping and spatial analysis that we can appreciate how essential these "informal" neighborhoods were to the war in Aleppo—and how essential they continue to be in its aftermath. After five years of warfare, it is these neighborhoods that lie in ruin. The elaborate communal, economic, and material threads that for centuries underpinned the social fabric of

Fig 7: Stills from drone video produced in December 2016 depicts the evacuation of rebel supporters from Salah ad-Deen, as well as the neighborhood's destruction following regime bombings. The footage was produced by an activist who was part of the Aleppo Media Channel, whose video archive we have stored and mapped. Content produced by this group often made it into the reporting of international news networks, sometimes without credit. The Center for Spatial Research has written extensively about this and other drone videos and also communicated with the videographer: "The View from Above, by Design," Conflict Urbanism: Aleppo, Center for Spatial Research, Columbia University, June 7, 2019, http://c4sr.columbia.edu/conflict-urbanism-aleppo/view-from-above.html. Stills from Aleppo Media Channel Drone Video, "Aerial Photography of the Evacuating of the Besieged Residents of Aleppo from Their Homes towards the Western Countryside of Aleppo," YouTube, December 15, 2016, https://www.youtube.com/watch?v=qwQOc0tSGI4.

Aleppo have been cut. The initial class divides between the wealthier western quarters and the poorer eastern neighborhoods of the city have grown even more stark. The questions of land ownership, real estate speculation, and housing shortages—which determined the issues around "informality" and were already prominent before the outbreak of military violence—continue to consolidate the economic, political, and spatial division of Aleppo's residents. The recent developments in reconstruction have replicated previous patterns, strengthened the power of the regime, and further marginalized Syria's disenfranchised population. It is safe to say that the future of Aleppo, and maybe Syria as a whole, will be determined in its "informal" neighborhoods.

There are numerous other cities in Syria that could be investigated with this kind of approach—from Daraa and Damascus to Hama, Homs, Idlib, and beyond. Our research on Aleppo constitutes merely one exemplary case of extraordinary violence among many. However, only by connecting the exceptional violence of warfare to the more mundane, everyday violence of life and law in an authoritarian regime can we understand the events unfolding in Aleppo during the four and a half years of conflict as well as in its aftermath. And it is through precisely this lens that we need to continue to study the urban developments in Syria's formerly largest city, where war continues to be fought by other means.

37°4'0"E 37°6'0"E 37°8'0"E

36°15'0"N

Ashrafeyeh
Ashrafeyeh - Bani Zeid   Sheik
Ashrafeyeh 1

36°13'0"N

GOVERNMENT CONTROL

36°11'0"N

Ansari Gharbi
Ansari Village
Haret el

36°9'0"N

Sheikh Seie
Sheik

37°6'0"E 37°8'0"E

Fig 8: This map of the 2016 UNITAR-UNOSAT damage data shows that just over 50 percent of damage in Aleppo occurred in the neighborhoods designated "informal" by the GTZ. Damage in those neighborhoods is highlighted in black. Background satellite imagery, WorldView-2 © 2016 DigitalGlobe, Inc.

LAURA KURGAN is an editor of this volume.

GRGA BASIC is a designer, cartographer, and educator with transdisciplinary expertise in resilience, media, and urbanism. He is currently an associate research scholar at Columbia University's Graduate School of Architecture, Planning, and Preservation. His cartographic representations have been exhibited at the Venice, Hong Kong, Shenzhen, and Rotterdam Architecture Biennials.

EVA SCHREINER is a PhD candidate in architectural history and theory at Columbia University's Graduate School of Architecture, Planning, and Preservation. Her dissertation concerns German imperialism in the Ottoman Empire around 1900, with a particular focus on agriculture, finance, and religion. This research is supported by the Social Science Research Council's International Dissertation Research Fellowship. She is also working with the Center for Spatial Research on the project "Conflict Urbanism: Aleppo."

1   Based on estimated numbers of internally displaced people and dispersed refugees, Aleppo can no longer be considered Syria's largest city.

2   "Conflict Urbanism: Aleppo," Center for Spatial Research, Columbia University, http://c4sr.columbia.edu/ conflict-urbanism-aleppo/map/ index.html.

3   In his book *The Destruction of Memory: Architecture at War*, Robert Bevan focuses on the ways in which the demolition of cultural heritage is a specific type of weapon of war as well as a crime against humanity (in the form of a crime against cultural memory). In our work at the CSR, we have inverted this concept to create a memory of destruction, a document of memory.

4   "Aleppo Conflict Timeline— 2012," The Aleppo Project, https:// www.thealeppoproject.com/ aleppo-conflict-timeline-2012.

5   "Syria: Assad Regime Launches 'Savage and Barbaric' Assault on Aleppo," *Telegraph*, August 8, 2012, http://www. telegraph.co.uk/news/worldnews/ middleeast/syria/9460836/ Syria-Assad-regime-launches- savage-and-barbaric-assault-on- Aleppo.html.

6   "Syria Crisis: Rebels Lose Key District of Aleppo," BBC, last modified August 10, 2012, https://www.bbc.com/news/ world-middle-east-19192413.

7   "Aleppo Conflict Timeline—2013," The Aleppo Project, https:// www.thealeppoproject.com/ aleppo-conflict-timeline-2013.

8   Jeffrey Bolling, "Backgrounder: Rebel Groups in Northern Aleppo Province," Institute for the Study of War, August 29, 2012, http://www. understandingwar.org/sites/ default/files/Backgrounder_ RebelGroupsNorthernAleppo.pdf.

9   "State Forces Progress North of Aleppo," *Al Jazeera*, July 15, 2014, https://www. aljazeera.net/home/getpage/ f6451603-4dff-4ca1-9c10- 122741d17432/5ebe12a2-80e6-42f4- a4fa-2fcc315ea045 (in Arabic).

10   A more in-depth study of this process, which also explains our methods in more detail, can be found on our website: "Remote Sensing Urban Conflict," Conflict Urbanism: Aleppo, Center for Spatial Research, Columbia University, http://c4sr.columbia. edu/conflict-urbanism-aleppo/ remote-sensing.html.

11   "Syria's Civil War: US and Russia Clinch Ceasefire Deal," *Al Jazeera*, September 11, 2016, https://www.aljazeera.com/ news/2016/09/syria-civil-war- russia-clinch-syria-deal- 160910031517683.html; "Syrian Opposition Figure Says Ceasefire Never Took Hold," Reuters, September 19, 2016, https:// www.reuters.com/article/ us-mideast-crisis-syria-opposition- idUSKCN11P240.

12   "Syrian Forces Tighten Grip on Besieged Aleppo," *Al Jazeera*, December 3, 2016, https://www. aljazeera.com/news/2016/12/ syrian-forces-gains-rebel-held-east- aleppo-16120306540293o.html.

13   "Q&A: Syria's New Property Law," Human Rights Watch, May 29, 2018, https://www. hrw.org/news/2018/05/29/ qa-syrias-new-property-law; Aron Lund, "Dispossession or Development: The Tug of War over Syria's Ruined Slum Dwellings," *New Humanitarian*, July 4, 2018, https://www.thenewhumanitarian. org/analysis/2018/07/04/ dispossession-or-development- tug-war-over-syria-s-ruined-slum- dwellings.

14   Ajib Nadi, "The Project of Decree 66 behind al-Razi: A Pioneering Experiment on the Road to Reconstruction," SANA, December 26, 2017, https://www. sana.sy/?p=683277 (in Arabic, emphasis our own); also see Joseph Daher, "The Syrian Reconstruction Question, Issues and Dynamics," *Fondation pour la Recherche Stratégique* (January 2018): 1–22, https://www.frstrategie.org/ web/documents/programmes/ observatoire-du-monde-arabo- musulman-et-du-sahel/ publications/en/22.pdf.

15   Valérie Clerc, "Informal Settlements in the Syrian Conflict: Urban Planning as a Weapon," *Built Environment* 40, no. 1 (2014): 34–51, https://halshs. archives-ouvertes.fr/halshs- 01185193; Tom Rollins, "Decree 66: The Blueprint for al-Assad's Reconstruction of Syria?," *New Humanitarian*, April 20, 2017, https://www.thenewhumanitarian. org/investigations/2017/04/20/ decree-66-blueprint-al-assad-s- reconstruction-syria.

16   Samar Batrawi, "Drivers of Urban Reconstruction in Syria: Power, Privilege and Profit Extraction," *Clingendael CRU Policy Brief* (January 2018): 1–11, https://www.clingendael.org/sites/default/files/2018-01/PB_Drivers_Urban_Reconstruction_Syria.pdf; Hazem Sabbagh, "President al-Assad Issues Law on Public-Private Partnership," *SANA* (January 2016), https://sana.sy/en/?p=66150.

17   Robert Goulden, "Housing, Inequality, and Economic Change in Syria," *British Journal of Middle Eastern Studies* 38, no. 2 (2011): 187–202, https://doi.org/10.1080/13530194.2011.581817; also see Clerc, "Informal Settlements in the Syrian Conflict."

18   German Agency for Technical Cooperation, *Informal Settlements in Aleppo: Rapid Profiles of All Informal Settlements in Aleppo* (Aleppo: Urban Development Project, 2009), 113, 49, and 57.

19   German Agency for Technical Cooperation, *Informal Settlements in Aleppo*, 3. Despite this being a stated goal, the report lacks concrete policy recommendations.

20   Goulden, "Housing, Inequality, and Economic Change in Syria"; Joseph Daher, "The Political Economic Context of Syria's Reconstruction: A Prospective in Light of a Legacy of Unequal Development," *European University Institute: Middle East Directions Research Project Report*, no. 5 (December 2018), http://cadmus.eui.eu/bitstream/handle/1814/60112/MED_2018_05.pdf; Bassam Haddad, *Business Networks in Syria: The Political Economy of Authoritarian Resilience* (Stanford, CA: Stanford University Press, 2012); Robin Yassin-Kassab and Leila Al-Shami, *Burning Country: Syrians in Revolution and War* (London: Pluto Press, 2016); Yassin Al-Haj Saleh, *The Impossible Revolution: Making Sense of the Syrian Tragedy* (London: Haymarket Books, 2017).

21   Raymond Hinnebusch, "Syria: From 'Authoritarian Upgrading' to Revolution?," *International Affairs* 88, no. 1 (January 2012): 95–113; Yassin-Kassab and Al-Shami, *Burning Country*, 32–34.

Ether and Ore: An Archaeology of Urban Intelligences

Shannon Mattern

120

We are, in many regards, living in exceptional times. Yet few of the transformations and revolutions we've witnessed over the past three years have seemed progressive. We have a petulant baby in the Oval Office. The Cold War has returned. Evils and neuroses long thought buried have resurfaced. Walls and moats, fists and firebombs are our diplomatic tools. Science is suspect. If anything, we've been living through a populist lesson in historiography: history certainly is not a unidirectional march of progress.

With so much hope lost on the national front and in the global community, many have invested in the *city* as a potential locus of progressive action: the sanctuary, the bulwark of sustainable practices, the place where mayors and municipal institutions can make a difference. And they can do so thanks in part, ostensibly, to efficient algorithmic governance, empirical data-driven endeavors, and their commitment to digital equity, civic tech, and open data initiatives.

Yet in some cases, despite our broader historiographic reckonings, the proponents of these programs—particularly their corporate partners—practice a willful amnesia. Narratives of innovation and disruption depend upon a convenient disregard for the past—or a marshaling *of* that past to rewrite a history that positions their work as its apotheosis. Thus our contemporary ways of knowing cities rely to some degree on deliberate, if perhaps subconscious, forms of *un*knowing or revisionism.

But there's a rich material body of precedent to draw upon. Cities, including many far afield from our contemporary data hubs and R and D labs, embodied networked smarts and forms of ambient intelligence well before we implanted sensors in the streets.[1] Yesterday's cities—even our earliest human settlements— were just as smart, although theirs was an intelligence less computational and more material and environmental. For millennia, our cities have been designed to foster "broadcast"; they've been "wired" for transmission; they've hosted architectures for the production and distribution of various forms of intelligence and served as hubs for records management; they've rendered themselves "readable" to humans and machines; they've even written their "source code," their operating instructions, on their facades and into the urban form itself. They've coded themselves both for the administrative technologies, or proto-algorithms, that oversee their operation and for the people who build, inhabit, and maintain them.

Acknowledging these histories is more than just a rarefied academic concern. There is more at stake here than historiography. Systems of knowledge are inscribed in the built world. And these knowledge regimes are often shaped, contained, preserved, and distributed through the prevailing media technologies of their time. Technologies inform and are informed by urban epistemologies—and together they're made manifest in the material city: "technology mediates the ways that knowledge, power, and culture interact to create and transform the cities we live in."[2]

And we're not just talking about modern computational technology, as many media historians and urban and cultural historians have acknowledged. Archaeologists can also tell us a lot about the history of the city as a mediated environment—and, furthermore, they can expand our understanding of what has the potential to serve as a medium or even what constitutes urban data. Archaeologists have found communicative potential in brick walls, stone structural elements, dirt mounds, bone tools, and even cities writ large. By examining how cities themselves have served as media (and how they've been mediated) across time, we'll see how media materialize in and through urban practices and processes—how they are the products of their urban environments and their human creators and users—and how those urban processes themselves are agglomerations of various media: stones and bones, streets and circuits, plazas and people.[3]

I invite you to join me in digging backward in time to examine how various historical—or what we might reductively call "old"—media forms have been given *urban* form: how their logics and politics and aesthetics have scaled up into the city. Let's start with some relatively recent technological resonances. Since the mid-nineteenth century, many cities' atmospheres have been charged with electric and electromagnetic telecommunications: telegraph and telephone wires and radio waves.[4] New communication systems remade cities around themselves: they incited the erection of new towers and broadcast buildings—from grandiose structures shrouded in mythology to humble shacks—and they frequently darkened the streets with their tangle of wires. While the city offered up a vast listening public and consumer base for broadcasters and service providers, the *material* city presented both material opportunities and barriers to their operation: its skyscrapers may have been ideal perches for antennae, but they also impeded the signals' dissemination.

Frank Lloyd Wright and Le Corbusier imagined that these new technologies would transform urban morphology, allowing for greater decentralization. Yet many historians suggest that those telecommunications technologies had both centripetal and centrifugal effects: concentrating businesses near the telecom exchange buildings, where customers could quickly access financial data and avoid signal attenuation, while also allowing for the dispersion of manufacturing and shipping facilities. They permitted company employees to settle along the streetcar lines, where they were only a phone call away from the downtown business office. There's even some speculation that the phone made the skyscraper a functional place of business: without a mediated means of communicating between floors, we would have needed countless bays of elevators to shuttle messengers delivering memos by foot. So many elevators, in fact, that they would have eaten up the floor plate.

Architectural historian Emily Bills argues that even Los Angeles—whose sprawl has been so often attributed to cinema and cars—owes its morphology to the telephone, which she calls "the first form of infrastructure to efficiently and effectively bind the greater Los Angeles area into a comprehensive multi-nucleated whole."[5] While early telephone networks, organized in a hub-and-spoke model, connected the city's downtown to its outlying agricultural areas, they didn't connect those agricultural communities to each other. Farming communities and growers' associations needed to share information with each other about weather, harvests, freight, and other business concerns—so they created their own phone lines, and communities grew around them. Farm-grown phone networks thus seeded Los Angeles's further decentralized development.

We might say that telecommunications' topology of derricks and switches and wires and exchanges reflected a market epistemology—a way of knowing and activating the city to facilitate the dissemination and operationalization of business information and to satisfy new domestic and commercial telecom customers. Of course, this market-driven way of knowing the city isn't new: the fact that the

Fig 1: Radio tower, Schenectady, New York.
From Frederick E. Drinker and James G. Lewis,
Radio: Miracle of the Twentieth Century
(Washington, DC: National Publishing, 1922), i.
© Underwood & Underwood.

Ether and Ore: An Archaeology of Urban Intelligences

Fig 2: Stockholm telephone tower, circa 1890.
Courtesy of Tekniska museet.

city has served as a mediated space of exchange—of goods and services and information—has long impacted its material form and its inhabitants' lives.

New technologies exposed those inhabitants to new sensory experiences: new ways of listening in public, new ways of knowing their cities through *sound*. Brian Larkin writes about the arrival of colonial radio in Nigeria in the 1940s; loudspeakers installed outside the emirate council office, the public library, the post office, and other public places brought music and words, uttered in British accents, intended to win Nigerians over to the "power and promise of modern life."[6] For centuries, in the Islamic world, the call to prayer and, more recently, recorded sermons have resounded—mixing with the urban din, providing a means of spiritual orientation for the faithful, and, particularly in spiritually diverse cultures, inciting debates over spatial and sound politics. After centuries of dispute over the heights of minarets and the position of the muezzin who issues the call, some cities, responding to complaints of noise pollution, have decreed that those calls be broadcast via radio rather than cast into the urban air.

The urban infrastructures of telecom have proven themselves quite adaptable, retrofitable, for an Internet age and a terrain of connected devices. The new topologies of ethereal cellular communication and arrays of connected things still rely on networks of wires and poles and other material (often metal) gadgets. Our bodies can flow through the city streets with "seamless" coverage, never suffering a lost connection, because of a byzantine assemblage of hardwired antennae bolted to rooftops and facades, knit together with millions of seams, beaming imperceptible but still very much material waves at all that

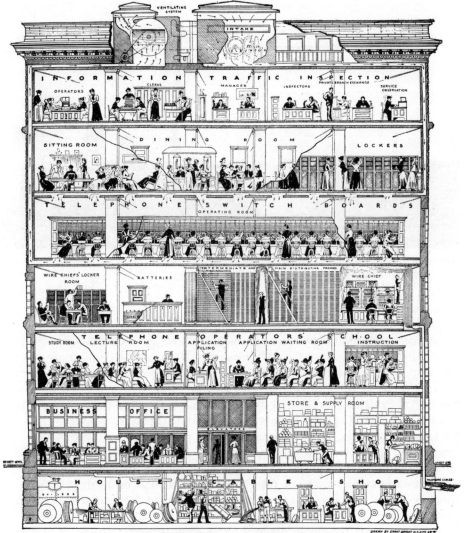

SECTIONAL VIEW OF A TELEPHONE BUILDING

A Typical American Central Office Building, Showing the Efficient Arrangement of the Various Departments

Fig 3: Sectional view of a telephone building, circa 1900. From Henry Chase Hill, *The Wonder Book of Knowledge* (New York: J. C. Winston, 1921).

populates the streets below. We inhabit a data space defined by various levels of intersecting protocols that direct our connections, facilitate or close off access, and thus subtly shape the geographies—both informational and physical—we are then able to explore.

Amid such indecipherable, proprietary, and even exploitative co-optations of the electromagnetic spectrum, we find some communities staking a claim to their own frequencies. While pirate radio was particularly prevalent in the 1960s,

Fig 4: Rooftop pirate radio transmitters in London. Still from a short documentary by Palladium Boots for its Exploration film series. "London Pirate Radio," YouTube, March 25, 2015, https://www.youtube.com/watch?v=1E0yqCPd5PY. © VBS.IPTV.

we see today, around the world, a resurgence of low-powered radio: resolutely local stations, often committed to homegrown music and to community news that, in conflict zones, become a lifeline. Even these informal broadcasts still rely on the city as an infrastructure. As Matthew Fuller writes of London's tower blocks: "The thicker the forest of towers, the more antennae perched above the city, the more the Radiant City, botched, radiates."[7] In such "botched" cities, where so much of the world's population lives, pirate radio sounds out the disjuncture, mismatch, time slippage, grafting, and hacking that characterize urban survival. The city might be "botched" or "broken up," as Fuller says, but still, it resounds. Improvisatory *resounding* and *listening* constitute its way of knowing. Wired or unwired, concentrated or dispersed, smooth or striated, the media city hums as it has for millennia.

Let's turn back the clock. Whereas today some governing bodies find it more efficient and convenient to delegate the work of listening and decision-making to the machine—allowing an algorithm to impartially churn through the ethical and moral dimensions of governance—such matters of computation were once matters of deliberation or decree.[8] Cities have historically provided space (either deliberately or accidentally) for the verbal articulations of democracy or dictatorship and for the vocal and bodily performances of public demonstration. Through archaeoacoustics, we can understand how ancient Athens's law courts, stoas, and auditoriums, each with their own geometry and materiality, cultivated orators' delivery and their audiences' engagement. Even the philosophers' "ideal city" itself often called for a particular infrastructure for the exchange of information: Aristotle prescribed a city that would contain no more people than could hear a herald's voice. Archaeologists and classicists, in seeking to understand how the Roman forum functioned acoustically as a space for speech and pageantry, have acknowledged that their own ways of knowing these ancient cultures rely on much more than the verbal script, as did the ancients' means of engaging with the content of a proclamation or a eulogy. These were multisensory affairs. The forum and other public spaces "created a formal tableau" that assigned status to different sensory experiences: the smells of bodies and food, the heat of the sun, the visual and textural cacophony of statuary, and the epigraphy that covered those public artworks and buildings.[9]

Despite both ancient and contemporary planners' attempts to create cities as spaces of formal and visual order and acoustic harmony—spaces known through reason and rationality—we also know our cities to be terrains of cacophony and, at times, productive chaos. Voices of demonstration and collective dissent have long punctuated urban soundscapes, transforming streets and squares into resonance chambers for protest—places where counterepistemologies are produced. The particular material properties of those urban gathering spaces and their codes of operation also inform how collectives form and how voices are heard. Sites of infrastructural convergence are symbolically rich, often reinforcing the political messages of the people demonstrating there. But gatherings also often coalesce in underutilized, marginal spaces—*terrains vagues*—where, Saskia Sassen argues, threatened and otherwise "invisible" groups can "become present to themselves" and to others unlike them.[10]

In 2004, when the Nepalese civil war prohibited the public gathering of large groups of people, artist Ashmina Ranjit choreographed a procession of black-clad performers, directing them to walk silently in pairs through the streets of Kathmandu. In the procession, one member of each pair would drop to the ground in feigned death; the other would draw her outline in chalk. While the performers did not speak, some carried radios broadcasting cries and wails across all FM stations and the state-owned Radio Nepal: "Recorded and transmitted through the radio," Laura Kunreuther explains, "the sounds of mourning"— "mothers' sobs" symbolically lamenting the violence and loss in rural villages— "were transposed and remediated from their usual familial setting to a public, national one... The anonymity of crying became a means to create the *sense* and sensibility of public cohesion." It was a cohesion built from the convergence of broadcast and architectural acoustic infrastructures.[11]

Jane Webster notes that "individuals at all levels of ancient Roman society"— including slaves—made literary and nonlinguistic figural inscriptions, both painted and carved, on the city's surfaces.[12] These inscriptions have long served to codify architectural functions, proclaim power, mark territory, evoke beliefs, profess allegiances, direct ritual, announce laws, and identify those who are welcome and unwelcome. The Islamic world has a particularly rich epigraphic tradition. "In a largely aniconic culture"—that is, one that forbids the creation of images of sentient beings—Yasser Tabbaa explains, "public inscriptions were by necessity one of the primary visual means of political and religious expression and one of the few ways for a dynasty to distinguish its reign from that of its predecessor."[13] The aesthetic properties of those public texts—their color, materiality, and form—have played a key role in how and what they communicate. These scripts function haptically rather than merely visually. For instance, the floriated Kufic script, sometimes ornamented with gold and glass mosaic, was "deliberately ambiguous": it was both boldly visible and incomprehensible, seemingly inclusive and transparent but ultimately obfuscatory.[14] This urban code was thus encrypted.

Roman and Islamic inscriptions—an early form of urban markup, we might say—were often encoded on the humblest of geological substrates. And today

Fig 5: Epigraphy near the Qalawun complex,
Cairo, 2009. Photograph by Christopher Rose.

many urbanites have come to recognize that even their seemingly immaterial digital media are resolutely material—that their virtuality and seeming artificiality are dependent upon natural geologic components—copper, coltan, tungsten, silicon. Urban history manifests this entanglement: mud and its material analogues (clay, stone, brick, concrete) have supplied the foundations for human settlement and forms of symbolic communication, and they have bound together our media, urban, architectural, and environmental histories. Some of the first writing surfaces, clay and stone, were the same materials used to construct ancient city walls and buildings, whose facades also frequently served as substrates for written texts. The formal properties of those scripts—the shapes they took on their clay (or, eventually, parchment and paper) foundations— were also in some cases reflected in urban form: how the city molded itself from the materials of the landscape. Written documents have always been central to the operation of cities: their trade, accountancy, governance, and culture.

Think of all the other print-based forms of urban media that embody urban epistemologies and that "program" the material city: newspapers and their columns; filing cabinets and the enormous file of the skyscraper itself; early architectural treatises and their prescription of particular, repeatable spatial forms; "legible" building facades and urban forms; and libraries full of books. These media represent entire chapters of technological and urban history that we simply don't have time to explore here—but they, too, profoundly impact the way cities are designed, built, administered, experienced, and understood. We've been predicting a paperless era for decades, but print is still here: independent bookstores are experiencing a renaissance, our cities host vibrant niche publishing cultures, and the exchange and display of print materials in public spaces affords many urban dwellers a means of carving out a commons amid increasing corporatization and "platformization."

As we focus increasingly on digital and data-driven media technologies, it's important to recognize that cuneiform tablets and epigraphy are data too. That the old and the analog are still present and active. They are, as Raymond Williams explains, "residual": "formed in the past but still active in the cultural process, not only and often not at all as an element of the past, but as an effective element of the present."[15] We're still talking and listening and reading and writing and printing and filing. Our cities, past and present, mediate between various manifestations of intelligence—legal codes and copper cables, inscriptions and imaginaries, algorithms and acoustics, public proclamations and system protocols. They're both old and new, clay and code. A city that *knows* its dependence on both ether and ore is better equipped to accommodate temporal entanglement and epistemological plurality. And more capacious, historically attuned *ways of knowing* our cities—and of generating and operationalizing urban intelligences—produce cities that are ultimately much smarter, or *wiser*, than the sum of their intelligent parts.

SHANNON MATTERN is a professor at the New School for Social Research. She is the author of *Code and Clay, Data and Dirt* (University of Minnesota Press, 2018), *The New Downtown Library: Designing with Communities* (University of Minnesota Press, 2017), and *Deep Mapping the Media City* (University of Minnesota Press, 2015). She also contributes a regular long-form column about urban data and mediated infrastructures to *Places Journal*. You can find her at wordsinspace.net.

This essay was adapted from Shannon Mattern, *Code and Clay, Data and Dirt: 5000 Years of Urban Media* (Minneapolis: University of Minnesota Press, 2017); Portions were originally published as "Of Mud, Media, and the Metropolis: Aggregating Histories of Writing and Urbanization," in *Cultural Politics* 12, no. 3 (2016): 310–331. © Duke University Press. All rights reserved. Republished by permission of the copyright holder, Duke University Press.

1   This paragraph is adapted from Shannon Mattern, *Code and Clay, Data and Dirt: 5000 Years of Urban Media* (Minneapolis: University of Minnesota Press, 2017), xi.

2   I draw here on the description of the conference that inspired this volume of essays: "Ways of Knowing Cities," Columbia University, February 9, 2018, https://www.arch.columbia.edu/events/816-ways-of-knowing-cities.

3   Mattern, *Code and Clay*, xxiv.

4   Much of the next seven paragraphs is adapted from Mattern, *Code and Clay*, chapter 1.

5   Emily Bills, "Connecting Lines: LA's Telephone History and the Binding of the Region," *Southern California Quarterly* 91, no. 1 (Spring 2009): 28.

6   Brian Larkin, *Signal and Noise: Media, Infrastructure, and Urban Culture in Nigeria* (Durham, NC: Duke University Press, 2008), 50.

7   Matthew Fuller, *Media Ecologies: Materialist Energies in Art and Technoculture* (Cambridge, MA: MIT Press, 2005), 15–16.

8   Much of this paragraph and the next is adapted from Mattern, *Code and Clay*, chapter 4.

9   Diane Favro and Christopher Johanson, "Death in Motion: Funeral Processions in the Roman Forum," *Journal of the Society of Architectural Historians* 69, no. 1 (March 2010): 15.

10   Saskia Sassen, "Does the City Have Speech?," *Public Culture* 25, no. 2 (April 2013): 217.

11   Laura Kunreuther, "Democratic Soundscapes," *Avery Review* 21 (January 2017), http://averyreview.com/issues/21/democratic-soundscapes.

12   Jane Webster, "Less Beloved: Roman Archaeology, Slavery, and the Failure to Compare," *Archaeological Dialogues* 15 (June 2008): 118. Much of this paragraph and the next is drawn from Mattern, *Code and Clay*, chapter 3.

13   Yasser Tabbaa, *The Transformation of Islamic Art during the Sunni Revival* (Seattle: University of Washington Press, 2001), 54.

14   Yasser Tabbaa, "Review of Islamic Inscriptions by Sheila S. Blair; Writing Signs: The Fatimid Public Text by Irene A. Bierman; Islamic Ornament by Eva Baer," *Ars Orientalis* 29 (1999): 182.

15   Raymond Williams, *Marxism and Literature* (New York: Oxford University Press, 1977), 122.

Data Driven: Managing Care and Dis(re)member-ing in the Knowing City

Anita Say Chan

How does the Internet come to know—and remember—you? Interrogating this apparently simple question is central to studying the promise of how networked environments are being reconfigured into intelligent "sensing" spaces. And the question has as much to do with how city infrastructures are being remade into "knowing" ecologies and self-ordering infrastructures as with how everyday urban actors are being repositioned as "knowing" navigators. Navigators and information managers who, empowered with dynamic data channels, information feedback loops, and real-time app updates, come to sense themselves as "inhabitants of information systems"—hailed to manage an ever-mutating complex of urban systems that can at last be revealed, even if only momentarily, as verifiably "useful" and untroublingly "reliable" manifestations of urban form.[1]

It has been the work of corporate "smart city" vendors—whether IBM, Cisco, Google, or Uber—through marketing materials and projections, to naturalize such framings of user empowerment and personalization via "datafied" ecologies. Central to this work has been the simultaneous muting of the more pernicious aspects of how the Internet comes to know and remember you—aspects that acknowledge the degree to which the tools and infrastructures of surveillance capitalism have been set to mine the abundance of human experience (and to invade privacy) as raw material for new, opportunistic practices of commercial extraction, prediction, and sales.[2] With the excesses of surveillance capitalism now inserted into the everyday architectures all around us, it should be taken as no small matter that every citizen or human *user* today is expected to be comfortable with being tracked and remembered (or re-membered) by the spaces—public and private alike—through which their routine and ordinary activities take place. Neither should it be taken for granted that users have come to accept the roles and responsibilities that come with navigating such intelligent architectures—with all their requirements for information management and continual input. After all, such ecologies, designed and deployed to store and recall individual data trails, histories of information requests, and individual terrains and maps of use, rely on data feeds and user input to operate—and ultimately to work toward fortifying the capacity of IT companies to predict and modify human behavior. In the words of a software engineering director at a leading "Internet of things" company on the new opportunities offered by these "economies of actuation": "It's no longer simply about ubiquitous computing... Now the real aim is ubiquitous intervention, action, and control. The real power is that now you can modify real-time actions in the real world. Connected smart sensors can register and analyze any kind of behavior and then actually figure out how to change it."[3]

How then might we explain the ever-more common shift away from the fundamental tenets of liberal individualism, such as the right to (or the default expectation of) privacy, the right to free will and the ability to express and exercise free, unfettered choice? Algorithmic infrastructures—as a contemporary response to the perceived demand for heightened securitization—have undoubtedly played a central role in this shift. Media theorist Wendy Hui Kyong Chun has underscored the increasing reliance on computational code as the primary means to anticipate and avoid crisis. Code, today, automates safe living. She writes:

> If "voluntary" actions once grounded certain norms, technically-enforced settings and algorithms now do, from software keys designed to prevent unauthorized copying to iPhone updates that disable unlocked phones, from GPS tracking devices for children to proxies used in China to restrict search engine results... [Today], software codes not only save the future by restricting user action, they also do so by drawing on saved data and analysis... They thus seek to free us from danger by reducing the future to the past, or, more precisely, to a past anticipation of the future.[4]

The temporal work involved in "knowing" users to avert crisis—whether the source of that crisis is internal or external—has not been minor. Indeed, as diverse international privacy rights groups have observed, it has involved the plumbing of users' data trails, the analysis of social networks, and the tracking of platform activity and life events, minor and major—all to identify patterns and alert users to potential future emergencies. Crises, as Chun writes, "cut through the constant stream of information differentiating the temporally valuable from the mundane [and] offering users a taste of real time responsibility and empowerment."[5]

This essay builds on such analyses of the affective politics of datafied ecologies and environments. It explores the range of desires and needs that exceed the conventional liberal frames of individual empowerment, responsibility, and personalization, which have been central mantras of smart city discourse and have largely been credited for fostering the spread and acceptance of datafied architectures.[6] These affective and hope-infused imaginaries have become outgrowths of today's smart cities and datafied environments despite their all-too-evident challenge to both the privacy and the sovereignty of the free, rational-decision-making individual that is heroically celebrated by liberalism. Cities and urban environments, as sensible ecologies, also reveal a parallel dimension to the temporal work of coded ecologies, demonstrating how networked environments have not only reordered the experience of time and event to avert or mitigate crisis but have also redefined spatial orientation, refiltered geography and the experience of co-location, and transformed the condition of feeling lost or simply out of place. Such functions—which are attendant to an individual's personal sense of orientation, subjective sense of location and identity, and experience of security or of being cared for—underscore the degree to which the user experience of vulnerability and care has become central to datafied ecologies and their continued widespread acceptance.

Without a doubt, the "crisis of care"—which feminist scholars such as Nancy Fraser have used to underscore the growing "pressures from several directions that are currently squeezing a key set of social capacities: those available for birthing and raising children, caring for friends and family members, maintaining households and broader communities, and sustaining connections more generally"—has something to do with this.[7] So too does the move towards, what Feminist science and technology studies scholar Maria Puig de la Bellacasa calls, a "commodification of care."[8] The marketplace has expanded to the extent that its goods are now key resources (for some, *the* key resources) available and relied upon to "maintain, continue, and repair our world [including our bodies, ourselves, and our environment] so that we can live in it as well as possible."[9] When rendered online, these forms of social reproduction, whether involving family care or the most mundane forms of "retail therapy," now entail a predictive and personalized understanding of need or future need.[10]

Today, online maps, search engines, and other datified platforms promise to anticipate, recognize, recall, and respond to a user's changing needs, desires, and requests. And even if such processes of recognition are automated, once filtered and rendered visible on a datafied platform, an individual user at least avoids going entirely unknown and unseen. Having offered up their data for processing, the user no longer runs the risk of being categorized or rendered wholly irrelevant—instead they become a body or a source that can now be examined, assessed, compared, valued, and calibrated against the bodies of other users.[11] Indeed, in a context where crisis at the global and local scale has become the norm—and where care, stability, and continuity are growing scarcities, and where the expansion of uncertainty has come to be a defining condition of the contemporary moment—it's little wonder that prediction and fixed outcome emerge as new fetishized objects.

One doesn't need to be in South Korea's Songdo, in the depths of Silicon Valley, or in the heart of self-driving-car-enabled zones—discrete sites that prototype proximate futures and aspirational smart city functions—to witness how datafied platforms and interfaces work to remind users that they never have to feel lost, abandoned, or delinked from proximate sites or objects of value.[12] Google announced this condition when it launched the new version of its maps application—and pronounced the end of the single, standardized map and the beginning of endlessly responsive, customizable geolocation. The company enthused: "What if we told you that during your lifetime, Google could create millions of custom maps... each one just for you? In the past... a map was just a map... What if, instead, you had a map that's unique to you, always adapting to the task you want to perform *right this minute?*... a mapping experience that helps you find places you never would have thought to search for."[13] Not unlike PageRank, Google's online search algorithm that has dominated the market by taking hundreds of "signal" inputs from each user—from where you logged in, to what browser you used, to what you searched for—Google Maps can now recall your past navigation patterns, predict your future navigation needs, and determine the kinds of sites you'd like (or should like) and the kinds you'd dislike (or that should be deprivileged, avoided, hidden, or removed from your navigation stream altogether).[14] Such shifts embody what Google CEO Eric Schmidt believed users want out of a data-driven product: a Google that can "tell them what they should be doing next."[15]

The anticipatory—and indeed prescriptive—function of Google products is key here. It is, in fact, fundamental to the logic of data-driven decision-making and tech-industry governance that this function claims to not only enhance user experience—present and future alike—but also to extend a model of individual care optimized by new data-driven market products. Such products promise to enact, amplify, and even automate a certain practice of real-time responsiveness to the personal, subjectively assessed needs of an individual user evidenced via the continuous channeling of tailored recommendations and content, and the delivery of prescriptive information feeds and recommended actions that, throughout the course of a day, shift according to the changing contexts and dynamic needs of individuals.

Mediated by the experience of portable screens, personal devices, and a network of apps, data-driven care is designed to feel as if it unfolds according to a newly optimized (hyper)attentiveness to the individual—one that perfectly recalls past patterns of data use and also responds in real time to present use. The all-too-familiar mantra of "personalized Internet content" projects an idea of user experience determined by assessing a discrete individual's digital profile (a singular but growing asset). Such a focus, however, disguises a core dependency of data-driven computational systems: that an assessment of any individual profile and any discrete "personalized" determination of individual need can be made and rendered meaningful only for systems designed to predict and assess user profiles and behavior when compared to the larger pool of data collected around *other* user profiles.

For commercial platforms, data-driven computational assessment is generally undertaken with the promise that new forms of value creation (like "membering") and computationally recognizable patterns of predictive association are possible. The user who might now be "valuable" within the real-time assessments of new data-driven systems is actually only relatively valuable in comparison to other users in the system—users who, in the same process, are simultaneously re-membered and determined as relatively "unvaluable." In such a way, any act of individual data assessment—and any experience of care and responsiveness within a data-driven system—relies at once on an assessment of a collective pool of data profiles, a comparative processing of value within the collective set of profiles, and a determination (almost always invisible to the individual user) of one's value, worth, or relevance relative to (but always lesser than) the "valued" user. Analyzing an individual's data profile thus always involves an assessment of a collective of user profiles, where analysis impacts more than a single user and where value can be rendered only in relation to, and at the expense of, the devaluation of other users within the system.

That operations of dynamic content personalization rely, quietly, upon socially stratifying and fundamentally polarizing functions has troubled other actors within the Internet media ecology.[16] Upworthy founder Eli Pariser has warned that these forms of "massaging" user experience via information manipulation, redoctoring, and the explicit omission of data and the suppression of difference—or exclusion of sites projected to conflict with the predicted tastes and profiles of individual users—amplify the polarizing effects of "filter bubbles." These reengineered information ecologies, explicitly designed to keep a user locked inside and occupied by their own interests, are thus spaces of "invisible auto-propaganda": "indoctrinating us with our own ideas, amplifying our desire for things that are familiar and leaving us oblivious to… [the] territory of the unknown."[17]

With the specter of fake news, disinformation campaigns, computational propaganda, and the supposedly unexpected rise of extreme right-wing parties gripping Western democracies today, filter bubbles have turned into objects of global debate. So too have questions about the relationship of big data to empiricism, whether or not the explosion of limitless data streams brings us closer to the totally indexed and interconnected reality that was promised. These concerns ushered in the "end of theory," notoriously celebrated by *Wired* magazine's Chris Anderson over a decade ago.[18] Since then, new questions have emerged about whether big data ecologies and data-driven platforms (like Facebook or Google Maps) amplify the general spread of "news" feeds and information "signals"—via their own work to identify, capture, and process data trails drawn from individual users—or instead intensify the general spread of disinformation, turning the content of news feeds into new channels of attention-demanding noise. Under data-driven logics that leverage personalized content to keep users locked into sites at all costs, even a news feed can be retailored to serve functions other than to inform. As long as they heighten or provoke user engagement, personally tailored news feeds and data streams can bury and silence signs of other realities for individual users—including ones that might have defied the soothing comfort of ready-made explanations and the already known preconceptions of the self-empowered navigator.

Publicly, social media companies have started to acknowledge the effects of filter bubbles. Mark Zuckerberg's 2017 Humanitarian Manifesto was released just before Google announced changes to its "featured snippets" function after reports that the feature gave prime placement to search results that spread and inflame fake news.[19] But while industry giants continue to insist that they are necessary to solve the social polarization of networked ecologies, their continual self-references—in the case of Facebook, for instance—to acting in the interest of a presumed shared "global community," so that "*our* community can have the greatest positive impact on the world," reveals a certain key conceit.[20] Such a projected self-image is one that presumes they *already* represent the force best positioned to bring about "the greatest positive impact on the world." For broader publics, it begs the question: is it possible for leading Internet companies to move beyond their own built and reinforced filter bubbles, and instead imagine worlds where varied unknowns, unpredicted but embodied others—*not* their own platforms, enterprises, and predictive algorithms—might serve as the central connective forces and key operants fostering alternative and creative reworldings?

DATA CONDUCT AND TRAINING IN THE ENTERPRISE CITY

There is little question that Silicon Valley's self-projections have fundamentally shaped the self-awareness of actors in a diverse range of global innovation zones and urban start-up ecologies. The data-driven start-up and code academy Laboratoria, founded in Lima, Peru—which has been celebrated within global tech sectors for its work transforming professional education and training women from at-risk zones in Latin American cities to be employment-ready coders in just six months—offers a key case in point and illustrates the affective promise of datafied urban ecologies today to manage vulnerability, portion out a version of care, and orient the individual vis-à-vis others. Code academies like Laboratoria have grown quite rapidly since they began to appear in IT circles just a few years ago.[21] And since then, they have made headlines for responding to the reported global crisis of a shortage of coders and for demonstrating the market viability of accelerated educational ventures, which, unlike university degree programs, can teach and graduate employable programmers in as little as two or three months.

At a recent graduation ceremony in Lima for one of Laboratoria's latest cohorts, the company's motto on the power of code to transform—both individual students and urban ecologies alike—was palpable. The event, hosted in a packed auditorium in the manicured tourist district of Miraflores, opened with the familiar, triumphant soundtrack from *Star Wars*, with text flashing on the screen: "in a galaxy far far away, the students of Laboratoria were called upon to 'transform' code work." It was followed by a virtual three-minute video of a morphing network graph representing the class's collective activity in their shared GitHub repository—a code-based archive representing all lesson work and coded commits over the course of the six-month boot camp. The video represented, in other words, six months of collective student activity compressed into a three-minute network visual. The first minute's steady whirls of movement mesmerized the audience, which was largely made up of family members from neighborhoods hours (and, in some cases, days) away from the upper-middle-class district of Miraflores. In the video's final seconds, the graph suddenly burst into rapid whirls visualizing the two hackathon events that had been organized during one month in the summer of 2017 as a way for students to temporarily work and connect with Laboratoria's network of over four hundred regional companies. The back-to-back, all-night events of onsite competition (intensified by the potential of earning employment) were now captured in the flurry of data streams before the audience.

Data-driven start-up companies like Laboratoria have worked to prototype the presumed "proximate future": ubiquitously connected environments that, now empowered with new tools, can work to optimize results in the artificially intensified and temporally compressed space of the urban boot camp. And while Laboratoria's work hinges on reputed capacities for managing thousands of user profiles—to weed out thousands of applicants per cohort and mine information pools for signals that best identify viable talent and enable the company to rapidly, even automatically, respond to individual need—the company has also been touted for being "more than the typical code academy"; for being a start-up venture that has worked to know its applicants, and the city ecologies where they are based, differently.

Since its founding five years ago, all of Laboratoria's students have been young women, and most of them have been first-generation degree earners from economically challenged sectors in Lima—the city's most peripheral districts and *pueblos jovenes* (or new settlement zones) where families from the Andes, remote jungle regions, and dispersed indigenous communities have often migrated and settled. For such learners, two-hour-long commutes to class (in a single direction)—weaving through Lima's traffic and vast cultural and economic divides—are routine. And these commutes mark only the first among many layered complexities that Laboratoria's students are required to navigate on a daily basis in order to invest in and train for their futures.

Mariana Costa Checa, the twenty-nine-year-old cofounder of Laboratoria, neatly sums up its work to redefine the city in another way:

> What we try to do is go out and find talent where nobody else is looking for it. So we try to identify young women who

haven't been able to access quality education or job opportunities, because of economic limitations, and train them to become the most awesome web developers they can be… and [then] connect them with employment opportunities in the tech sector.[22]

The work of "filtering out" talent and tapping into the "undertapped" potential in the city is what has made Laboratoria a celebrated entity in the world of social enterprise today, earning it, in its short existence, multiple international awards in the technology and development sectors. It won the 2014 Kunan Prize for social entrepreneurship and the 2016 Google RISE Award; it was recognized by MIT *Technology Review*; and it has received millions of dollars in support from venture capital sources like Google, Microsoft, and Telefónica, and from Peru's national government.[23] Laboratoria notably earned a $1.8 million Inter-American Development Bank investment to support the growth of projects in Chile, Mexico, and Peru over three years and, in 2016, gained prominent global visibility as one of only three awardees at the Global Entrepreneurship Summit—an annual conference hosted by the White House to bring together entrepreneurs, lawmakers, and investors from around the world, moderated by Facebook's Mark Zuckerberg and then US president Barack Obama.[24]

All of this recognition has accelerated the expansion of Laboratoria's start-up sites. The company expanded to three new cities—Mexico City, Santiago, and Arequipa—and by summer 2017, it was slated to open three more offices, in Bogotá, São Paulo, and Guadalajara. With a total of seven sites, Laboratoria anticipated being able to expand its operations to accommodate ten thousand graduates per year across the network. To achieve its promised growth projections, the venture will have to grow graduation rates exponentially—more than ten times over—to roughly 1,400 students per site each year.

This frenzied growth occurs in the context of what Herman Marin, one of the charismatic cofounders of Laboratoria, underscores as a key shift in the age of big data: the importance of optimally managing space and time. Data-driven conduct, after all, means new possibilities for micro-attention to constant feedback loops and an experience of the self that is embedded within fluid and interactive spaces—even when off-line. Marin explicitly coaches students on how to best use time and space, even the smallest microunits of time and the most compact, temporary sites for work (such as a bus seat or a standing zone as a mobile office space). "It's a fact that a person takes about 26 minutes to recover when there is an interruption in work. That is a huge problem because imagine if you're interrupted three or four times… we are talking about an hour, or two hours of lost work and productivity that you fail to develop. And employers lose an opportunity to continue creating value… and obviously there are ways to limit that... to learn to manage my time well, and organize my work space."

These comments underscore how one's consciousness of time and space can get parsed and microsegmented to the tempo of local decisions, data points, and moments of *potentially* impactful action. While products of good decision-making might once have required months to identify, under logics of data conduct, it seems, even a minute can be used badly. As Marin advises, self-organization should start "before starting your work day... or maybe even the night before, when you have the opportunity to quickly check emails... or to try to coordinate in advance with the people you want to try to connect with the next day... [since] there are already people and things that are happening without you... and [you don't want them to have to] depend on your being there."[25]

But it's his next tip that I find most unexpected: "Another important strategy is to use commute time... and go from home to work in a more productive way... And there are a lot of things that can be done... like trying to use that space to be able to have meetings... today a lot of jobs work remotely... so you can have meetings on the phone... or use your phone for other digital conferencing that you could do during the commute... For many of us, commute times are long, right? More than an hour?... So that time can be used to accomplish things at work, and do not wait until you get there... It is [just] a matter of organizing."

For all Laboratoria's celebrated data management, and for all of Marin's own micro-attention to time and space, both seem to have entirely lost sight of the bigger picture. They miss, in fact, what even the most novice first-time visitors to Lima might notice: that the micro and public buses that the city is infamous for, and which are the most common and popular forms of transportation used by the vast majority of Limeñans (and almost all of Laboratoria's students) to traverse the city, are almost inconceivable as spaces for workplace activity in almost every way.

When Laboratoria's students reference a routine commute of two hours, this typically means two hours standing, with one hand gripping a handrail for balance and the other gripping a bag. Commuters are pressed together side by side, and most commutes require transferring between multiple bus routes. The reality is that there is never a still, uninterrupted stretch of time. And even if a seat by miracle is free, the cacophony of rush-hour traffic—the mix of horns, motors, and insistent hollers of drivers announcing their routes—would surely challenge the most productive worker. In many ways, Marin's imagination of the city as a site to reinvent where and how one works, at all times, is a vision that can't be separated from class.

Marin's own commute to work consists of a fifteen-minute walk through the picturesque, upper-middle-class neighborhood of Miraflores to Laboratoria's office space. In spite of the personal coaching and data collection Laboratoria undertakes to get to know its students, it does not seem impossible that its blindness to the basic complexities of life for the majority of its students is something that is itself *predesigned*. Could it be that the company's message around the power of individual training—empowerment through access to the right information and choices around technology—is sustainable only as long as it *can* keep attention away from the real and varied local complexities that differently shape the lives and daily work experiences of its students? As long, in other words, as it can manage *its own* management of time and attention across space, and keep too much care from accruing around the real lives and diverse lived experiences of the individual students who enter its classrooms?

Maria Puig de la Bellacasa's caution against the ready plumbing of "care-based solutions" as automatic antidotes to contending with conditions of risk is relevant here:

> More profound and preoccupying beyond this moral marketing gloss is how neoliberal governance has made of caring for *the self* a pervasive order of individualized biopolitical morality. People are summoned to care for everything but, foremost, for "our" selves, our lifestyle, our bodies, our physical and mental fitness, or that of "our" families... [meanwhile] those considered as traditional carers—women generally—or as typical professional carers—nurses and other marginalized unpaid or low paid care workers—are constantly moralized for not caring enough.[26]

Puig de la Bellacasa offers a way to work towards rejecting "unproblematic visions of care—whether as an exploit of higher ethical beings, a marketable productive activity, or even a recuperated morality." It offers a way to think about "caring obligations that could enact nonexploitative forms of togetherness," obligations that have not yet been imagined.[27] These comments reveal how powerful the unsullied narrative of individual care under a model of "transformation through code" is—and how easily it can be used to speak in the interest of a future city and future user spatialized and temporalized under the logic of a now data-driven innovation economy. As much as the work of sensor-connected environments is to manage urban infrastructures and systems as a privileged measure of the "knowing" city, it is also to manage, filter, and discount users' personalized information pools. With them, platforms take action on signal- and value-creating information, at once designating and creating categories of "noise" and non-value-generating information that can be "un-known" and "dis-remembered." And while awareness of certain aspects of human experience might be omitted in the interest of (supposedly) creating new efficiencies of care and value, such omissions are now virtuously pursued as a necessary, even indispensable means of managing ever-more pressing needs for care that respond to the urgent demands of scale, space, and speed in the data-driven innovation economy.

Laboratoria expresses the affective politics and products of datafied ecologies and environments, and reminds us of the appeal (or at least the tolerance) of the functions of the smart and surveillance-readied architectures we are routinely asked to accept and navigate as part of daily life. It is not merely the promise of recognition (as an empowered navigator) but also the possibility of attending to individuals in need of orientation, subjective recognition, or security. If users appear to offer themselves or their experiences up to the surveillance architectures of datafied ecologies and the filters of assessment, examination, and value extraction that mark them, they do so, perhaps, not only to shore up or amplify their own individual assets but also to avert the risk of being unrecognized, unknown, or irrelevant. Laboratoria thus serves as a reminder of what is at stake in recentering and refocusing on the human—communities, citizens, and users alike—in analyses of smart cities and architectures. In understanding how networked environments are being reconfigured into intelligent "sensing" spaces, the focus should not be solely on the technologies and technical infrastructures that order and expand today's ubiquitous computing and sensing environment but rather should be centered around the very human communities, citizens, and users upon which the enactment and performance of those architectures rely. Laboratoria reveals, in other words, the lab-like function of smart cities as urban prototypes—that if there are indeed objects being tested under the conditions of the smart city, they are not necessarily the dispersed urban sensors being implemented but the new human relations or modes of governance reengineered at the interface of surveillance architecture's new spatialized ecologies.

ANITA SAY CHAN is associate professor at the School of Information Sciences at the University of Illinois. She holds a PhD in history and anthropology of science and technology studies from the Massachusetts Institute of Technology.

1   Laura Kurgan, *Close Up at a Distance: Mapping, Technology, and Politics* (New York: Zone Books, 2013).

2   Shoshana Zuboff, *The Age of Surveillance Capitalism: The Fight for a Human Future at the New Frontier of Power* (New York: PublicAffairs, 2019).

3   Zuboff, *Age of Surveillance Capitalism*, 293.

4   Wendy Hui Kyong Chun, "Crisis, Crisis, Crisis, or Sovereignty and Networks," *Theory, Culture & Society* 28, no. 6 (2011): 92.

5   Chun, "Crisis, Crisis, Crisis," 92 (emphasis mine).

6   See Orit Halpern, *Beautiful Data: A History of Vision and Reason since 1945* (Durham, NC: Duke University Press, 2014); and Anthony M. Townsend, *Smart Cities: Big Data, Civic Hackers, and the Quest for a New Utopia* (New York: W. W. Norton, 2013).

7   Nancy Fraser, "Contradictions of Capital and Care," *New Left Review* 100 (July/August 2016): 99. More broadly, see Nancy Fraser, *Fortunes of Feminism: From State-Managed Capitalism to Neoliberal Crisis* (New York: Verso, 2013).

8   Maria Puig de la Bellacasa, *Matters of Care: Speculative Ethics in More Than Human Worlds* (Minneapolis: University of Minnesota Press, 2017).

9   Joan Tronto, *Moral Boundaries: A Political Argument for an Ethic of Care* (New York: Routledge, 1994), 103.

10   Carole M. Cusack and Justine Digance, "'Shopping for a Self': Pilgrimage, Identity Formation, and Retail Therapy," in *Victor Turner and Contemporary Cultural Performance*, ed. Graham St. John (New York: Berghahn Books, 2008), 227–241.

11   Michel Foucault, "The Correct Means of Training," in *Discipline and Punish: The Birth of the Prison* (New York: Vintage Books, 1995), 170–195.

12   See Chamee Yang, *Remapping Songdo: A Genealogy of the Smart City in Korea* (PhD diss., University of Illinois at Urbana-Champaign, 2019); and Paul Dourish and Genevieve Bell, *Divining a Digital Future: Mess and Mythology in Ubiquitous Computing* (Cambridge, MA: MIT Press, 2011).

13   "Meet the New Google Maps: A Map for Every Person and Place," Google Maps Blog, May 15, 2013, https://maps.googleblog.com/2013/05/meet-new-google-maps-map-for-every.html (emphasis mine).

14   Emily Badger, "Here's What Google Maps' Customization Might Mean in Practice," City Lab, May 29, 2013, https://www.citylab.com/life/2013/05/public-space-danger-new-google-maps/5736.

15   Holman W. Jenkins, "Google and the Search for the Future: The Web Icon's CEO on the Mobile Computing Revolution, the Future of Newspapers, and Privacy in the Digital Age," *Wall Street Journal*, August 14, 2010, https://www.wsj.com/articles/SB10001424052748704901104575423294099527212.

16   See Badger, "Google Maps' Customization"; Emily Badger, "The Potential Problem with Personalized Google Maps? We May Never Know What We're Not Seeing," City Lab, May 17, 2013, https://www.citylab.com/life/2013/05/potential-problem-personalized-google-maps-we-may-never-know-what-were-not-seeing/5617; and Eygeny Morozov, "My Map or Yours? Google's Plan to Personalize Maps Could End Public Space as We Know It," *Slate*, May 28, 2013, http://www.slate.com/articles/technology/future_tense/2013/05/google_maps_personalization_will_hurt_public_space_and_engagement.html.

17   Eli Pariser, *The Filter Bubble: How the New Personalized Web Is Changing What We Read and How We Think* (New York: Penguin Books, 2012).

18   Chris Anderson, "The End of Theory: The Data Deluge Makes the Scientific Method Obsolete," *Wired*, June 23, 2008, https://www.wired.com/2008/06/pb-theory.

19   For more on Facebook, see Mark Zuckerberg, "Building a Global Community," Facebook, February 17, 2017, https://www.facebook.com/notes/mark-zuckerberg/building-global-community/10154544292806634/%20Building%20Global%20Community. For more on Google, see Jennifer Calfas, "Google Is Changing Its Search Algorithm to Combat Fake News," *Fortune*, April 25, 2017, http://fortune.com/2017/04/25/google-search-algorithm-fake-news; Kevin Murnane, "Google Fights Back Against 'Fake News' Appearing in Search Results," *Forbes*, https://www.forbes.com/sites/kevinmurnane/2017/04/26/google-fights-back-against-fake-news-appearing-in-search-results/#a3b40b95d850; Michael Grothaus, "Google's Featured Snippets Are Spreading Fake News," *Fast Company*, March 6, 2017, https://www.fastcompany.com/4031809/googles-featured-snippets-are-spreading-fake-news; and Adrienne Jeffries, "Google Is Changing Its Search Algorithm to Combat Fake News," *Outline*, March 5, 2017, https://theoutline.com/post/1192/google-s-featured-snippets-are-worse-than-fake-news?zd=1&zi=zanxyurr.

20   Zuckerberg, "Building a Global Community."

21   "The Growth of Coding Bootcamps: 2017 Coding Bootcamp Market Size Study," Course Report, https://www.coursereport.com/reports/2017-coding-bootcamp-market-size-research.

22   Dan Colly, "How Latin American Women Are Cracking the Code to the Tech Sector," *Guardian*, December 1, 2016, https://www.theguardian.com/global-development-professionals-network/2016/dec/01/cracking-code-tech-women-latin-america.

23   See "Internet & Web—Mariana Costa, Innovators Under 35," *MIT Technology Review*, 2015, https://www.innovatorsunder35.com/the-list/mariana-costa; and Jimena Galindo, "A Conversation with Mariana Costa Checa, CEO & Co-Founder of Laboratoria," Global Americans, April 17, 2018, https://theglobalamericans.org/2018/04/conversation-mariana-costa-checa-ceo-co-founder-laboratoria.

24   Carolina Dalia Gonzales, "This Peruvian Entrepreneur's Startup Is Teaching Young Latin American Women to Code," Remezcla, July 11, 2016, http://remezcla.com/features/culture/mariana-costa-chica-laboratoria-women-code; Lisa Fischer, "Obama's Afternoon with Zuckerberg, Techies," CNN, June 24, 2016, https://money.cnn.com/video/technology/2016/06/24/obama-global-entrepreneurship-summit.cnnmoney/index.html. You can watch the summit on YouTube at https://www.youtube.com/watch?v=9EiFVA5PfL0.

25   Herman Marin, talk at Laboratoria attended by the author, July 14, 2017.

26   Puig de la Bellacasa, *Matters of Care*, 9.

27   Puig de la Bellacasa, *Matters of Care*, 23.

Right to the Smart City: How to Represent, Resist, or Disappear

B. Coleman

146

Thinking thought usually amounts to withdrawing into a dimensionless place in which the idea of thought alone persists. But thought in reality spaces itself out into the world. It informs the imaginary of peoples, their varied poetics, which it then transforms, meaning, in them its risk becomes realized.—Édouard Glissant, *Poetics of Relation*

THE RIGHT TO THE CITY

There is consensus on one front: everyone hates the word "smart" when talking about cities. I will hazard the statement that to critique the smart city is easy. At a moment when smart infrastructure is not simply being dreamed up in labs but is being installed across cities in the global North and South, we, as the inhabitants of these cities, have arrived at a threshold moment: we cannot live with a next iteration of a techno-deterministic design. Techno-determinism describes a narrow form of "smart," one defined as the automation of objects and processes, like a coffee maker that turns on and orders refill coffee pods on its own, or traffic lights that decide when to turn green based on real-time traffic conditions. Foremost, "smart" means the automation of decision-making by way of sensor-rich networked technologies that populate the world with an "Internet of things" and artificial intelligence.

These technologies in geolocated space affect a constitutional—and almost always invisible—change to the experience of public space as it has been constituted within a Western topos of free space from the Enlightenment to the liberal state. The examples of this change are legion even as they are so often framed within a white and masculinist designation of space: Rousseau's solitary walker, moving in his old age through the burgeoning metropole of Paris, the "capital city of the world"; Baudelaire and Benjamin's flaneurs taking in the spectacle of the same city two hundred years later; or the Situationist International's *dérive*, drifting through the industrialized, increasingly commercialized city and marking the end of the modernist era.

And the list goes on, particularly across European and Anglo-American discourses and territories. The examples hold in common a social imaginary that makes the notion of *freedom of movement* a key condition of the city (despite the fact that female and racial subjects are often excluded from this history of civic agency). Exclusions notwithstanding, this concept of a right to the city that includes the right to move freely has been a central paradigm until the relatively recent advent of the informational city. We face a global change of state with the new array of ubiquitous networked sensor technology. We have effectively entered a state of "technology of the surround," where the civic actor is subsumed by surveillance technology.[1] Under these conditions, the concept of an urban public transforms to mean a space of urban enclosure—where life on the street is extracted as a continuous source of data flow to feed the "smart."

In the 1970s, Henri Lefebvre and then David Harvey argued for a social construction of space, one specifically informed by the civic right *for all* to move through the city.[2] Their Marxist-inflected social science imagined an egalitarian "right to the city" that served as a corrective to the Enlightenment model, even as we have drifted away from such an articulation of "rights" today. "Neoliberalism" only begins to mark the fractious moment in the social contract we inhabit. We find aggravated engagement around identity, ideology, economic disparity. And now, in a time when the very idea of public space (as in public parks or streets)

and the idea of publics (as in a self-constituted civic body) are increasingly difficult to locate as a place or a concept, we drift further away from a sense of ethical
accountability or legal entitlement to a right to the city—a right that includes
a right to anonymity and a right to play. This is a squeezing of public space and
public life.

Just as the world of urban publics narrows, technology beckons again,
signaling new futures. Like Cupid's arrow, smart technology is irresistible; it
promises—as did the steam engine, the telephone, and the Internet—a solution
to current woes. And, of course, that promise of future technology is delivered
in mixed proportions with uneven effects. Considering the logic of "smart,"
we face a crossroads in terms of our design ethos: do we choose a privatized
world that builds on the business-technology models established by social media
giants? Or a civic model in the messy, noisy modality of the democratic? Are
there meaningful gradations between the two? What players are excluded from
both modalities?

Thinking of such gaps between publics and counterpublics, in working
toward a capacious "smart" city, I hail a third figure: the escape artist. In his
poetics of relationality, Édouard Glissant formulates the concept of *marronage*
as a nomadic or a drifting agency.[3] It is a figuration inspired by the stealthy black
escapee—the Maroon of colonial history—who disappeared across waterways
into the swamps of the Americas. For the purposes of imagining other futures
for smart cities, I take this Maroon as an archetypal prefiguration of the modern
urban escape artists to come—at least in the sense of undermining master plans.
For the direct purposes of comprehending what modality of "smart" city we
might engage, support, and enlist, the figure of *marronage* allows us to see an
adjacent right to the city that abandons virtually all framings of state and state
power for a fluidity of existence. It is a position that does not stand in opposition
to the Enlightenment trope of *freedom of movement* or counteract the revisionist
ideology of a *right to the city*; rather, it is a sly assertion of the right to play and
to disappear.

It is paramount that technology companies do not singularly determine the
trajectory of our world. In other words, we, as civic actors, have an opportunity
to intervene in how it will be built out. The examples that follow, for better
and for worse, speak to this "opportunity" as contingent on timing, on (self-)
activation, and on the capacity to live with risk. And it is this last condition that
is most often left out of the industry pitches to municipalities to implement
"smart" plans: with every increase in efficiency, there is also an equal and obfuscated escalation of public risk.

In this sense of "smart," as the advanced automation *and* disruption of
civic life, we might ask historical questions in a new light: What does policy
that facilitates civic participation look like? What does the ontology of smart
civic technology look like? These questions signal a shift from smart tech
to smart agent—a rebalancing of smart calibration to better include system
knowledge and actionability from a layered, located, and intersectional view.
Why not find out what the smart water pump "knows" in the form of a data
feed as well as what the resident of twenty years knows of flooding? This
means greater transparency and accountability for what we have programmed
our machines to do. It is also a call for greater civic responsibility. In asking
how we know the rationalist city, from Le Corbusier's "radiant" vision to the

promised kryptonite of big data, and how we know the playful city—that of the *dérive*, skateboarding, and underground dance parties—we ask a lot. It's a question that includes labor in its answer at every point: municipal, industrial, and civic. It is a question that also includes lightness: an air of exploration and risk for a future. Yet what choice do we have if we are going to make it right? The formulation of "right" as culturally generative and ethically normative might very well restart a utopian civic project in places that long ago abandoned it. I would claim *against the formulation of the utopic* a right to the possible even as it is not an instantiation of the perfect. Let's counter the machinic rhetoric of "efficiencies" that overwhelms smart city discourse with a right to representation, to resistance, and to disappear.

Fig 1: Signage outside Pakhuis de Zwijger,
Amsterdam. Photograph courtesy of the author.

CIVIC SMART CITY

In 2014 I was in Amsterdam for the inaugural meeting of the Smart Citizen Lab, a civic tech group hosted by the Waag Society. On the whole, the forty-some people gathered represented a progressive Dutch tech-activist sector: software engineers, musicians, inventors, and middle-aged rabble-rousers, all there to stick it to the man—in this case, the municipal government of the city of Amsterdam. Called to action by the Waag Society, the group assembled around a clear objective: to find measurements of environmental pollution (air, noise, etc.) for themselves and to compare those readings to government ones. In other words, as concerned citizens, they wanted to *see* for themselves.

Right to Representation: Positivistic Data, or What Does a Smart Citizen Lab Want?

The positivistic model of "seeing for oneself" underwrites much of the do-it-yourself (DIY) ontology. It is a mode of engagement that signifies a vernacular epistemology ("find this knowledge ourselves"). It is also an approach that asks for data to be knowable and accountable in a way that often belies complexity in the sense that it reduces all data to a calculus. In this case, complexity can be marked in the ways Amsterdammers know their city—through route, touch, sound, news, gossip, and so on. The possible ways of knowing go on forever, even though knowledge is never comprehensive, never "n=all." In relation to the framework of a finite scientific measurement, there is no generic account of a neighborhood.[4] Yet the Smart Citizen Lab desired an objective—affectless—measure of their environment in order to make it comparable to the city's data. And there is the crux of it: things must be rendered comparable, which also means they must be measurable by the same tool. Thus, the lab would need the same tools, reproducing the same measurement, in order to produce a counter-public data narrative (as with the counterpublic narratives of the Jakarta Urban Poor Coalition, discussed later)—and, as we shall see, it would need strawberries.

It is difficult to objectively produce standard environmental measurements that meet the criteria of scientific research labs—an issue with which the Smart Citizen Lab struggled. At the end of the year, as part of an organized self-review, the group concluded that while it had been awesome to get to know each other and hang out on a weekly basis, they had failed to capture any relevant data (except for some gauges measuring noise pollution, a form of pollution easier to capture than others). Hardware is hard, and socializing is not a smart city outcome, if the aim is positivistic proof. Beyond "it was cool to hang out," there was no finding—no way of knowing the city through its data. In terms of the diversity of possible, obtainable city data (and knowledge), the Smart Citizen Lab chose the most traditional, single-channel modality of expert measurement; based on that choice, the lab was obliged to replicate expertise in a modality that DIY efforts cannot always achieve. To a certain extent, DIY tech needs to be commensurate with official (scientific as state) tech to "properly" measure, which, of course, works to destroy the value of citizen data collection and analytics. This, however, is only the case if the data ontology is framed as the replication of authoritative knowledge as opposed to the amplification of local knowledge.

Thus we arrive at strawberries. In this data story, local berries served as an instrument in relational collaboration across sectors—a symbol of trust marking the condition of collaboration. In 2014 the Flemish periodical *Flanders Today* ran the headline: "Strawberry Plants Measure Air Quality."[5] Reporting on a partnership between StadsLab2050, a citizen-centric city lab, and Antwerp University's department of bioengineering sciences that stimulated the civic imaginary, the article consisted of an interview with project director Jelle Hofman. In it Hofman described distributing strawberry plants—playing the role of organic air-quality sensors—to five hundred people across neighborhoods in the city. Data from the strawberry plant leaves—which were planted by citizens in windows, along highways, and in other places—was then collected for lab analysis to render an air quality map of Antwerp.

With strawberries, local civic expertise—in terms of embedded and embodied knowledge of an area—influenced the formation of the dataset itself. By choosing the sites where the plants would sense air quality, the civic tech participants determined what material was (a) relevant and (b) collected for expert scientific assessment. That the instrument of collaboration was the strawberry plant—familiar to everyone involved and sufficiently sensitive as a sensor—made the project both more accessible in its method and successful in its outcome. The hidden mechanism that moved the project forward was the opportunity for trust between collaborators. The mutual dependence between civic (local) and scientific (expert) bodies in regard to how, where, and why to produce measurements (the complexity of *what* was being measured with environmental pollutants is a different topic) became a generative aspect in transforming data methods into actionable knowledge.

In this sense, the Smart Citizen Lab faced the challenge of addressing civic authority on its own terms: calibrated measurement without attention to a discursive context or metadata framework. These terms rely on a narrow definition of measurement that reifies authority and often obfuscates other epistemologies—a modality of a *right to representation* that works within the liberal democratic state (city) in a configuration of "citizen." Neither oppositional nor constitutionally subversive, this position frames much of the imaginary in regard to how a civic smart city is configured.

Examples of this mode of smart city are largely technology-driven and global-North-centric, sites that instantiate advanced automation in the built environment. In other words, the question in Amsterdam was never if networked sensors were a viable mode of measurement of a civic good but, rather, what information such sensors could gauge. Writ large, such technology represents the radical growth of both the surveillance state and a service state (not to be confused with the social welfare state). This is a territory undertheorized and overdetermined in terms of technological rollout, and it represents a primary hurdle that global North cities must address.

OPPOSITIONAL CITY

It is no coincidence that many of the strongest examples of "smart" civic action come from the urban poor of the global South. Because of the complex cocktail of environmental warming and global postindustrial markets, the poor of the equatorial South are, by necessity, moving to protect and shore up their neighborhoods from phenomenal and existential threats. Fighting against a system designed to erase them, all modes of resistance, traditional and innovative, have been brought to bear. In the case of Jakarta, the Urban Poor Coalition (UPC), with communications scholar Alessandra Renzi, has been working against the continued gentrification of the city, which, left unchecked, will lead to the increasing erosion of the *kampung* (slum), with flooding and other hazards. In short, as with Mexico City's quagmire, the free-market, modernist imaginary is actually built with concrete. Over years of postwar accretion, the weight of the concrete has *literally* been sinking the poorest neighborhoods of these cities.

In response to years of erosion, the UPC has developed a hack that uses official data, modeled by the real estate developers in Jakarta, as leverage against such gentrification plans. In her report on UPC activist work, Renzi describes a familiar global scenario: the aspirational Jakarta—in the form of extended malls and increasingly privatized environments for the moneyed—is rendered evidentiary (as a datum itself) in the publicly displayed models from which the actual construction will be built. She writes, "What follows here is a story of city making and struggle over land tenure and housing rights within the *model* of Jakarta. The struggle unfolds in a data-rich sociotechnical milieu where the becoming… of the city and its inhabitants is… importantly, enabled and intensified by data, algorithms, and software."[6] Renzi argues for an epistemology of "entangled data," where the power of data—both the quantitative (say, the measurement of water levels) and the representational (literally, the modeling of a gentrified Jakarta)—offers an opportunity for a counterpublic to emerge.[7]

It is important to note that the UPC does not contest the official measurement of flooding as reported by the state; in fact, it distinctly works within the data publics of the metric (in this case, I have coined the term "data publics" to address the emergent public of a physical location in relation to the informational layer of data that adheres to it). Rather, the UPC contests the interpretation: Which

Fig 2: Data visualization poster, "Why Jakarta Floods," by the Urban Poor Coalition, with Alessandra Renzi and Skye Moret-Ferguson. Courtesy of the Urban Poor Coalition.

branching path leads to neighborhoods under water? Which leads to continued territorial existence? Fundamentally, the UPC manifests a *right to resist*: this is a right spurred on by the oppositional city, often in the form of urban poor resistance to varied instantiations of a profound modernity of infrastructure, ethos, and aesthetic. The formation of this right rests in the space of publics, and it works within the discursive milieu of "publics" as a moment of exception— organized or informal—that refuses the domination of state power. In a sense, the UPC demonstrates the most legible form of counterpublic, which speaks to a right to the city, where the concentrated effort is toward extending existing rights to the disenfranchised.

Together, the UPC, Renzi, and designer Skye Moret-Ferguson weaponize the data of Jakarta as a means to other ends. Demonstrated graphically in the data visualization "Why Jakarta Floods: Current Solutions vs. Ideal Solutions," the discourse of entangled data speaks to the reappropriation of calculus by *kampung* dwellers as a mode of resistance against the architectural model of megacity globalization.[8] With the first panel of their three-part data visualization, they explicitly render the measure of the gentrified megacity. Phenomena such as waste management and reduction of ground-water pumping exemplify subcategories of the chart. Overall, the illustration points to a developer ethos that breeds the concrete-dependent terraforming on which the *Gesamtkunstwerk* of the climate-controlled total experience (from gym to entertainment complex to condo) depends. The design is meant to soothe and smooth the (affluent) user's experience.

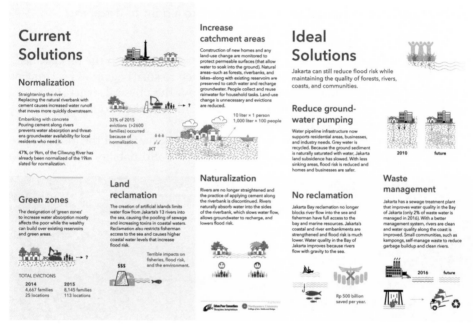

Fig 3: Data visualization poster, "Current Solutions vs. Ideal Solutions," by the Urban Poor Coalition, with Alessandra Renzi and Skye Moret-Ferguson. Courtesy of the Urban Poor Coalition.

This is the all-too-familiar globalized imagination of the city as gated full-service amusement park, which further stratifies wealthy and poor, user and service class. And in such constitutional bifurcation, we (meaning all) lose the magic of cities. We move away from the capacious imaginary and toward some abrupt version of "smart." In demarcating "Current Solutions" versus "Ideal Solutions," the UPC opens points of resistance (located activism, distributed knowledge, etc.) to the foregone conclusion of a model that would literally erase their neighborhoods and devalue their livelihoods. The UPC research scaffolds itself on the fundamental question of values and politics: do municipal and private developers design spaces that include—or even elevate—the urban poor?

The UPC demonstrates a primary strategy that frames a *right to appear* as a modality of a right to the city. As I have argued in other contexts, the right to appear—as part of a public—is related to a right to the civic.[9] It is a historical claim to citizenship inscribed as the right to appearance in public, with contingent constrictions regarding for whom that right is sustained.[10] By reappropriating the civic data of Jakarta in an act of opposition, the UPC reverses a means of "control and dispossession"—instead proposing "Ideal Solutions" to the problems presented by continued development. As a located community, the *kampung* makes itself visible (via census data) and argues for a right to the city through resistance. As Renzi and collaborators point out, it is a strategic maneuver to preserve life: "For good or bad, data about the *kampung* and its inhabitants places them on the map where they are otherwise invisible."[11] This is a strategy that works within the global urban imaginary to carve out (or preserve) a place in a sociotechnical milieu. The focus is directed toward the power of appearance. How then does this relate to a right to disappear?

KINETIC CITY

Writing about Mumbai, architect Rahul Mehrotra speculates on the protagonist of the smart city, articulating a shift from smart tech to smart agent in his concept of the "kinetic city": "Smart cities will not be about the physical structure of smart cities (yes, we can use technology). Smart Cities will be about smart agents, which can transform the imagination of the urban."[12]

Ground-up civic agency is implicit in such an imagination of the global South as a right to many things: public space, privacy, affordability. These are also

Fig 4: Rahul Mehrotra and Felipe Vera, "Nothing Is Forever, Nothing Is Sacred," *Ephemeral Urbanism: Cities in Constant Flux*, 15th International Architecture Exhibition, Biennale Architettura, 2016.

Photograph by Laurian Ghinitoiu. Courtesy of RMA Architects.

the qualities promised by the public-private consortiums that deliver the global North vision of the smart city. How is it possible to reconcile these two states that seem to be saying the same thing? A key difference between the normative framework of "smart" for the global North and the emergent kinetic one for the global South is the monumental versus the fluid, the recipient of services versus the agent of action. How is it that a city such as Mumbai can express the idea of both a static architecture that, in form and symbolism, puts agents in their place and a relational architecture that works responsively with agents. As Mehrotra writes, "Today, Indian cities include two components occupying the same physical space: the static city and the Kinetic City."[13]

Right to Disappear: Pirate Modernity, or How to Stay in Motion

The difference in knowledge between the static city and the kinetic city might be simply a lack of imagination. In the static city, the civic imaginary understands itself to possess (or aspires to possess) robust modern infrastructure and analogous architectures of power. Under such a condition, there is less public action in the renegotiation of place. The details of Detroit's lack of potable water or the absence of public space for the immigrant population of the Paris *banlieues* are rendered local (as discrete problems) as opposed to being legible as symptomatic structural issues.[14] In contrast, "ephemeral urbanism" describes a kinetic city born of necessity and ingenuity, one that grants a *right to disappear*, a civic allowance to move freely—whether through the publics of central squares or by slipping through local byways. As a right to the city, the right to disappear provides opportunity and resilience beyond the right to public and counterpublics. It is also often the space of the poetic city, the opportunity of the chance encounter.[15]

The kinetic city, with its right to disappear, differs from the static city in its agentic ethos of the temporary and the deterritorialized. This is the layered city of the contingent and changing adoption of city space that has been the domain of marooned populations—the dislocated, the dispossessed, the subaltern classes— since the arrival of cities. It is the play of the trickster, the one who guards and transgresses boundaries, which we find in figurations such as Michel Serres's *Hermès* or Glissant's creole *marronage*.

Like the nautical figurations of Glissant's Maroon, Mehrotra invokes a "pirate modernity" that jettisons the idea of a "counterpublic." This is an important part of the kinetic city: the conceptual and experiential reframing of the static city moves toward stratagems of refusal and repair that do not emulate the anticolonial organizing of the 1960s and 1970s. In other words, the kinetic city offers knowledge of a stacked existence *in motion*. Things happen on top of each other across different temporal moments but increasingly in the same located space. An exemplary site of this pirate modernity is the town hall of Mumbai, which Mehrotra documents as an architectural spectacle in the traditional representation of the state and also as a site of kinetic disruption. He cites the Independence Day festival that occurs each year as an example of this stacked condition, a moment when people take the space over, bedecking it with decoration and costume.[16] In this layered site—one that overcomes the monumental, vertical architecture for a horizontal and generative one—the figure of the modernist radiant city is subsumed by "an elastic urban condition" that effects not a utopian grand vision but rather a "grand adjustment."[17]

Fig 5: Town hall of Mumbai. Photograph courtesy of A.Savin.

"One way ashore, a thousand channels."[18] In this manner, Glissant has termed the relationality of becoming. In quotidian terms, the activation of a civic imaginary may move in the same direction; nonetheless, the specificity of geolocated routes through the urban manifests with variation. Jakarta is not Amsterdam. Amsterdam does not equate to Mumbai. And yet, in moving across ways of knowing, as architects, aestheticists, and theorists, we must consider the comparative relay of epistemologies based on the variation of location, need, and desire—what we might learn from each other in the simplicity of such a statement and in the complexity of its application. In the critique of the smart city, it is no longer sufficient to identify critical issues, such as algorithmic inequality and data redlining.[19] At an ethical and an ontological level, the task at hand is the facilitation of smart agency. There is a crisis of contemporary publics and a retrenchment of civic rights that calls for such a relationality of becoming. The strategies of each city to represent, resist, or disappear speak to the local knowledge that can serve, with modulation, across different contexts. Procedurally, for such tenets of knowing cities—representation, resistance, or disappearance—to be substantially built into the infrastructure of how cities work is still a radical endeavor. It is an endeavor of the "civic" that offers an emergent understanding of cities as a public imaginary and as territory that is not exclusively charted within the visibility lines of a liberal democratic state. If the smart city can strive for outcomes such as access, equity, and play, then indeed a multilayered vision of a "right to the city" can shift to include smart technology and data as critical instantiations of the urban.

DR. BETH COLEMAN directs the City as Platform lab. She is a professor at the Institute of Communication, Culture, Information, and Technology and the Faculty of Information at the University of Toronto. She is the author of *Hello Avatar: Rise of the Networked Generation* (MIT Press, 2011).

1   Beth Coleman, "Technology of the Surround," *Journalism & Mass Communication Quarterly* 96, vol. 2 (June 2019): 360–362.

2   David Harvey, "The Right to the City," *New Left Review* 53 (September/October 2008): 23–40.

3   Édouard Glissant, *Poetics of Relation*, trans. Betsy Wing (Ann Arbor: University of Michigan Press, 1997).

4   Geoffrey Bowker and Leigh Star, *Sorting Things Out: Classification and Its Consequences* (Cambridge, MA: MIT Press, 1999).

5   Andy Furnière, "Strawberry Plants Measure Air Quality," *Flanders Today*, January 10, 2014, http://www.flanderstoday.eu/education/strawberry-plants-measure-air-quality.

6   Alessandra Renzi, "Entangled Data: Modelling and Resistance in the Megacity," Open! Platform for Arts, Culture, and the Public Domain, February 20, 2017, http://www.onlineopen.org/entangled-data-modelling-and-resistance-in-the-megacity.

7   See Nancy Fraser, "Rethinking the Public Sphere: A Contribution to the Critique of Actually Existing Democracy," in *Habermas and the Public Sphere*, ed. Craig Calhoun (Cambridge, MA: MIT Press, 1992), 123–143; and Michael Warner, "Publics and Counterpublics," *Quarterly Journal of Speech* 88, no. 4 (November 2002): 413–425.

8   Warner, "Publics and Counterpublics."

9   Beth Coleman, "Domestic Disturbances: Precarity, Agency, Data," in *Bodies of Information: Intersectional Feminism and Digital Humanities*, ed. Elizabeth Losh and Jacqueline Wernimont (Minneapolis: University of Minnesota Press, 2018), 391–408.

10   Hannah Arendt, *The Human Condition* (Chicago: University of Chicago Press, 1998).

11   Renzi, "Entangled Data."

12   Rahul Mehrotra, "Negotiating the Static and Kinetic Cities: The Emergent Urbanism of Mumbai," in *Other Cities, Other Worlds: Urban Imaginaries in a Globalizing Age*, ed. Andreas Huyssen (Durham, NC: Duke University Press, 2008), 205–218.

13   Rahul Mehrotra, "The Kinetic City: Emerging Urbanism in India," http://rmaarchitects.com/files/Kinetic-City_Essay-for-BSR.pdf.

14   See Mitch McEwen, "Watercraft: Water Infrastructure and Its Protocols of Sprawl and Displacement," in this volume; and Doina Petrescu and Constantin Petcu, "R-Urban Resilience," R-Urban, http://r-urban.net/wp-content/uploads/2012/01/R-Urban-resilience_Atlas.pdf.

15   Beth Coleman, "Let's Get Lost," in *Civic Media: Technology, Design, Practice*, ed. Eric Gordon and Paul Mihailidis (Cambridge, MA: MIT Press, 2015), 265–294.

16   Mehrotra, "Negotiating the Static and Kinetic Cities," 208. For an image of the town hall during Independence Day see page 210.

17   Mehrotra, "Negotiating the Static and Kinetic Cities."

18   Glissant, *Poetics of Relation*.

19   See Virginia Eubanks, *Automating Inequality: How High-Tech Tools Profile, Police, and Punish the Poor* (New York: St. Martin's Press, 2018); and Bill Davidow, "Redlining for the Twenty-First Century," *Atlantic*, March 5, 2014, https://www.theatlantic.com/business/archive/2014/03/redlining-for-the-21st-century/284235.

Minding the Gaps. Navigating Absences in the Zimbabwean Imaginaries

Tinashe Mushakavanhu and Nontsikelelo Mutiti

Zimbabwean history is a patchwork quilt made by a few and premised on a very strict and narrow genealogy of ideas. In order to unravel the complexities of Zimbabwean history, it is important to start by navigating this history from its street names, the names of "war heroes" and "liberators" that signpost Zimbabwe's cities. After independence in 1980, streets and buildings were renamed to reflect the new political reality: colonial figures were replaced with black heroes. Pioneer settlers such as Jameson, Selous, Rhodes, Speke, and Livingstone were dutifully replaced by a generation of black freedom fighters such as Chinamano, Chitepo, JZ Moyo, Silundika, and Tongogara. But these heroes are increasingly difficult to locate in the country's vaults of history. Apart from being street names, their autobiographies, biographies, and memoirs remain unpublished or elusive. They are acknowledged only as supporting figures to the heroes who currently occupy political office. The street in Harare, therefore, functions as a site of burial, a place where dead heroes are left to hang in public as silent witnesses—a common manifestation of the "dead archive." This dead archive is reactivated only periodically for political expediency; it suffers from a lack of narrative. These heroes cannot speak, but they are spoken for. Even though they are memorialized on street signposts, they have become footnotes in the history of Zimbabwe. In their silence, they have led us to search for them—to trace them (and ourselves) across the world, following their exilic wanderings through Asia, Europe, North America, and back to Zimbabwe. The war to liberate Zimbabwe extended to neighboring countries such as Mozambique and Zambia, to ideological and military bases in China and Russia, and to universities and seminaries in America and Britain. As a consequence of this global effort, the Zimbabwean archive is scattered and fragmented.

CODING HOME

In the summer of 2016, we started a series of conversations on the absences and gaps in Zimbabwean history with our contemporaries in Brooklyn, New York. The enduring questions were: At what point does national history begin and end? Who is telling these histories? There were no easy answers. The Zimbabwean national archive is threatened with extinction: many of the key books of Zimbabwe's literary canon, for example, are now out of print, and most young people have no way of knowing they even exist. We set up what we thought was a simple website to restore the Zimbabwean archive, to give visibility and easy access to an otherwise submerged canon. The project became a way to discover more about what has been written about Zimbabwe, and to interrogate the power to name and assign value. The portal, Reading Zimbabwe (readingzimbabwe.com), became a way to reimagine the country differently around the issues of memory, the afterlives of colonialism, and the forms of narrative that are commensurate to telling a nation's stories.

The project became a journey back to ourselves and a way to see what the Zimbabwean landscape (both material and ideological) looked like in terms of information, creative writing, and commentary about a nation, a big nation but one told through what Chimamanda Ngozi Adichie calls, the dangers of a single story. Robert Mugabe's hold on the Zimbabwean imagination for almost four decades necessitated a new set of questions, new practices and methodologies, to harness the inventiveness, the generative resilience, and the agility of Zimbabwean society. How does one talk about the history and the beauty of a

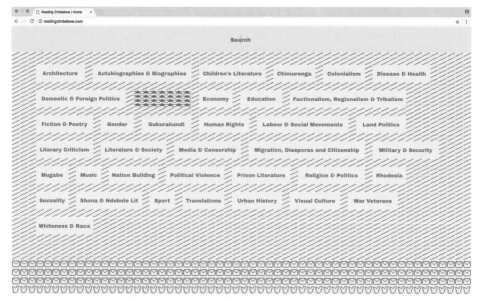

Fig 1: The navigation of readingzimbabwe.com is built in a mazelike system, reflecting the convergence of digital design and the built environment through categories that implicate the landscape of Zimbabwe in relation to power. Courtesy of Black Chalk & Co.

space with so many conflicting identities, so many different moments in time, so many interesting histories? We decided to start wherever we could.

Displacement from Zimbabwe became a creative force. Through travel, we became aware of home; through the journey away from it, we became a part of home by recovering its histories, its narratives, and its books. New York, our temporary residence, was life in a crowd. A modest brownstone on Halsey Street, in Bedford-Stuyvesant, became a cultural hub, a literary salon, for the exchange of ideas. We hosted *sadza* parties, opening our living room to friends and strangers, a motley crowd of creatives—visual artists, photographers, writers, filmmakers, musicians, journalists, and academics. There were no VIPs. Everybody was equal, held together by words, music, and food. And there was always drink to lubricate the gatherings. The conversations and laughter were animated, and they certainly drifted and echoed throughout Brooklyn back to Africa. We summoned the past through books. In this place, we could be ourselves completely. But as we mapped books about Zimbabwe, they became wholes unto themselves. They were intermingling stories, individual and collective, private and public. Not only in form, but in their direction, movement, development, and change. Each book changed something in us: each book made particular revelations and brought us news, discoveries, premonitions, promises, and sometimes disappointments.

As a project that grew out of nostalgia for home and place, Reading Zimbabwe became a means to explore the relationship between texts and maps, the mappability of literature, and, since we live in a milieu predisposed to deception, a means to uncover the lie of maps. The convergence of digital mapping and globalization has spurred a cartographic turn in literature. Reading Zimbabwe offers a systematic overview of an emerging approach to the study of African literature. It is a literary map but not merely an illustrative guide. It represents a set of relations and tensions that raise questions about representation, fiction, space, and knowledge production. Literary criticism, with its creative use of mapping words, and, above all, literary texts, with their imaginative ways of mapping worlds, should be reconsidered as relevant sources for cartographic theorization and mapping research.

The archive is, therefore, building where there has been a void. It is essentially the performance of frustration over an inability to locate ourselves in our national histories—a frustration that we turned into a tangible act of decolonization. Placing the archive online keeps this space open to a wider community and suggests that literary texts can productively be approached as sites of encounter, as well as sources for the observation of emergent cartographies. How do we inhabit historical time—that is, the sense of temporal entanglement, where the past, the present, and the future are not discrete and cut off from one another but rather live the simultaneity of that entanglement? How does one map this narrative?

While Reading Zimbabwe is a work in progress, or a living archive that is constantly growing and changing, it provides critical and creative potential for digital literary mapping. The architecture of the site, coded in its aesthetics, is primarily inspired by the ruins of Great Zimbabwe—an African kingdom that existed between the eleventh and fifteenth centuries and that the country was named after. Zimbabwe means "House of Stone." The kingdom's history is widely contested, and some claims to this history implicitly deny that African culture can be sophisticated. The minority white government of Rhodesia even put political pressure on archaeologists and researchers to refute that native African people constructed the monuments. We employ, therefore, a complex and symbolic cartography that challenges the colonial archive as much as it questions its memory, bringing many contradictory texts into dialogue with one another. Using books as our bricks, we seek to build paths and map directions to that past and other pasts, especially after we found ourselves displaced from Harare—the city of our birth—to New York. The quest for the landmarks of Zimbabwean history underpins this work of recovery and remembering.

Reading Zimbabwe is a way of making home and identity. The impetus to work on the project from New York, and not Harare, is in part a negotiation with the homelessness and placelessness that exile, voluntary or forced, creates. Reading Zimbabwe, therefore, adopts a participant model of provenance that expands who is considered a record creator or a memory keeper of a country's history to include everyone who has contributed to the record and has been affected by its action. This gives control and oversight to the very people treated as subjects of colonial government records with lesser claims to and rights over those records. Working from New York was the response to a simple provocation: the major historical records of Zimbabwe still reside primarily in Britain and the United States. We have to travel so far to engage with archives about ourselves.

As a platform and an intervention, Reading Zimbabwe is a processual space to think geographically about the texts and mapping practices that have imagined and theorized Zimbabwe for the past six decades. Our documentation starts with the early 1950s, when the first black Zimbabwean writers and intellectuals could write and publish books. In 2000 the government of Zimbabwe, out of desperation, decided to repossess land from minority white farmers and promised to give it back to landless black people. The reform did not forge strong connections or bonds to the land but instead resulted in increased displacement and migratory wanderings. With lucrative farms taken over by politicians, many Zimbabweans tired of the false promises and political rhetoric of change, left the country—moving across the Limpopo River to South Africa or flying to England and elsewhere—and thus became map-minded. Mapping as a means of survival became embedded within the Zimbabwean sociopolitical context. For instance, Brian Chikwava's novel *Harare North* (2010) imagines the geographic expansion of the Zimbabwean experience as it shifts and spreads globally. In Zimbabwe, London is regarded as an extension of Harare because of the many people who fled there to claim asylum during the brutal years of Mugabe's rule. London in the Zimbabwean imagination became an overseas province of Harare. A literary mapping such as Chikwava's intervenes in the perceptual, ideological, political, and practical orientation of place and experience. It rejects the colonial map and adopts the Deleuzo-Guattarian map: as "a rhizomatic ('open') rather than as a falsely homogeneous ('closed') construct."[1]

HOME MEANS NOTHING TO ME

Writer Dambudzo Marechera is both foundational to Zimbabwean radical thought and the privileged site of masculine intellectual self-fashioning. Our reading of Marechera's engagement with history, identity, and society is wayward. Engaging with the breadth of Marechera's work, which involves many formal and informal experiments of his own, facilitates new ways of

Fig 2: Home Means Nothing to Me, a mapping project that traces the last five years (1982–1987) of writer Dambudzo Marechera in Harare, after his return from exile in England. Courtesy of Black Chalk & Co.

reading Zimbabwe. His innovations in literary form challenge the lethargy enforced by the government through media propaganda and a politicized school curriculum. Criticism of the political class in Zimbabwe is often treated as treason—so many of Marechera's ideas have shaped student activism, unionism, and protest in contemporary Zimbabwe. His legend is part of the street lore in Harare. He spent the last five years of his life, between 1982 and 1987, sleeping on park benches, in office building doorways, or in city nightclubs. For a long time, we stood at the edges of Marechera's world. It is not easy to read Marechera without feeling disturbed or some combination of rupture and elation at the same time. We—as architect, graphic designer, writer—started moving through the city on foot, retracing his steps, and visiting and photographing the sites he inhabited.[2] What emerged was a map: a way of thinking *with* Marechera and also in critical relation to him. We worked with scraps from his fragmented archive. That's where our imagination of practice resides. That's where our hearts reside.

For Marechera, there seems to be something difficult about being in a place that he doesn't know and that doesn't know him. He finds himself disoriented. Sometimes that disorientation challenges the way he looks at things. His writing is a way of trying to figure out clues, to build up certain literacies in regard to the world around him. Writing becomes a way he builds home.

Marechera never had a strong relationship with Harare. It wasn't home. He was raised in a small town in Vengere Township, Rusape, and went to school in Penhalonga, Mutare. He lived in Harare for only a few months while attending the University of Rhodesia, before he got expelled for leading riotous student protests. His relationship with Harare actually started only when he came back from exile in 1982 after Zimbabwe's independence. He was coming back to a home that was never his home. What kind of home remains after war? The bulk of Marechera scholarship has misread him. There is a prevailing idea that his seminal book *The House of Hunger* (1978) is set in Harare. *The House of Hunger* is, in fact, set in Vengere Township, in the eastern part of Zimbabwe. Home Means Nothing to Me challenges this popular misreading. It looks for him in specific places. This map of Marechera is both faithful and fictional, necessarily so, because it plays with the mythology of the writer. We follow Marechera to the places where we know we can encounter him, through his own writings and through the ideas of him shared by others. On the map, Marechera the person leads us to Marechera the mythology. But both locate and attach Marechera to actual places. Something happened to Marechera after he had been stripped of his identity as a Zimbabwean and an African. After he won the Guardian Fiction Prize in 1979, he was suddenly described as "a universal writer," as an "international writer." He was no longer rooted in a place but uprooted. What narrative emerges when we relocate or replace Marechera in Zimbabwe? Harare and Zimbabwe merge in Marechera because of his own experience.

The spaces occupied by Marechera don't have definite borders. Cartography might usually work with hard boundaries to show the edges of a phenomenon— a place or the limits of a single element can be accurately described—but mapping a peripatetic figure like Marechera requires working with soft boundaries, with less accurate definitions of where the "edge" of a world in a particular piece of literature begins or ends.

After returning from exile, Marechera first lived in the country of his birth like a tourist—in a hotel and later on the streets. It was his own refusal to be trapped by the materialism that had corrupted the new political class in government and in boardrooms; most of the members of that class were his peers, friends from school and in exile. The title Home Means Nothing to Me is also a refusal to have one's biography pared down to the details of one's space and history. His writings illustrate the desire to transcend the limitations of a history, a space, a body, a psyche, and a soul. It is the desire to map one's way in the world without being circumscribed by it.

In the 1980s Robert Mugabe set in motion a genocidal ethnic cleansing known as Gukurahundi, a Shona term that loosely translates to "the early rain that washes away the chaff before the spring rains."[3] The North Korea-trained Fifth Brigade murdered tens of thousands of Ndebele people to quash a potential rebellion from rival politician Joshua Nkomo, widely known as Father Zimbabwe for leading the first waves of nationalism in the country from the 1940s onward. Mugabe—a Johnny-come-lately to nationalist politics who ascended to the highest office by any means necessary—managed to centralize the country around himself and around Harare. Zimbabwe became Harare. The Zimbabwean experience—politically, economically, socially, and intellectually—was centered around Harare. Even though Bulawayo, Zimbabwe's second city, has its own fascinating history, it has become peripheral to national identity—a footnote to the history of Zimbabwe. Yvonne Vera's oeuvre, however, challenges this singular city-country narrative. She places Bulawayo at the heart of Zimbabwe's cultural and political life in her six books, *Why Don't You Carve Other Animals* (1992), *Nehanda* (1993), *Without a Name* (1994), *Under the Tongue* (1996), *Butterfly Burning* (1998), and *The Stone Virgins* (2002). Locating Marechera in Harare, however, complicates these easy binaries. In the Zimbabwean imagination, Marechera is everyman. Through this map, we are forcing him, as an artist and a citizen, into a space that is repulsive to him. Is he a writer from Harare, or is he a writer from Zimbabwe?

Marechera himself says, "If you are a writer for a specific nation or a specific race, then fuck you."[4] He refused nationality and national identity. His alienation with Harare grew out of not finding a community of thinkers, an intellectual community that understood his creative project and vision. And so, at the end of the day, he identified with ghosts of the Beat Generation—they were his company during his itinerant existence in Harare. The journal section in *Mindblast* (1984), the last book he published while he was alive, summons the Beat writers—especially Allen Ginsberg, Jack Kerouac, and William Burroughs. He was lonely, and *Mindblast* was a cry of loneliness. While he might have been physically back in his community, in Harare and Zimbabwe, the community rejected him and shut him out. Yet it is out of this alienation, or this loneliness, that Marechera's narrative project emerges. All of his work, especially *The House of Hunger*, is about community—about what happens when a black community is under siege. Loneliness is a real thing that afflicts Marechera, and that contradiction, that tension, that exists between his loneliness and the communal aspects of his work assumes a personality of its own.

In 1984 Marechera decided to be a story doctor. This new enterprise got fabulous press in all the newspapers in Zimbabwe for the four days that he ran it early that year. For those four days, long queues of young writers, of curious

Fig 3: A postcard featuring Dambudzo Marechera reading in First Street Mall, Harare, during the inaugural Zimbabwe International Book Fair, held in August 1983; adapted from an image by Tessa Colvin. Courtesy of Black Chalk & Co.

young people, waited to see Marechera. It was a time of great dislocation; people had come back to the country after independence in 1980 with a lot of trauma from the war. Everyone had a story, but nobody knew how to share their story. The government of Zimbabwe under Mugabe suppressed and closed any outlets of free expression or dissent. Unlike in South Africa, in Zimbabwe there was no Truth and Reconciliation Commission, no process to face the psychological and damaging effects of war. Marechera assumed this role single-handedly; he confronted these problems by listening to people narrate harrowing stories of war. His office—which also had a mythical quality to it—had no furniture; it was carpeted, with a phone in the corner. Anyone could come and sit. Marechera was like a monk, like a spiritual master. He decided to build an institution outside official institutions. He understood the spiritual hunger of Zimbabwe, and that is why his legacy endures and resonates with many today.

Marechera's ghost still lurks in the streets of Harare because of *The House of Hunger*. The book has assumed prophetic power in the imagination of Zimbabwe's young people. It's as if through it, he foretold all the things that have happened and are happening in and to Zimbabwe now. In 2005 the House of Hunger Poetry Slam was established as part of the annual Harare International Festival of the Arts. It became a platform for young, radical poets to come together. The poetry slam took place at the Book Café, which was once the most vibrant cultural hub in Harare—a space where one could say anything, a space of freedom that evaded censorship even though there were rumors that state security agents were always present in the audience.[5] No performance was ever stopped. No one was ever arrested. In a way, a lot of the writing presented and shared at the Book Café was addressed to Marechera. Young poets were borrowing from him. His writings and thinking articulated their angst.

The Internet was our starting point as we worked backward to understand Zimbabwe and our place in it. Our interest in Reading Zimbabwe has less to do with the past than with the present. We are not concerned with mapping as a media of geographic locatability but rather as a figurative graphic that performs the role of corridors leading readers and audiences through virtual space. The platform, as a library and archive, connects content to audiences and audiences to each other. Reading Zimbabwe may be interpreted, at the same time, as an intersection where multiple ideas about literary and social practice, economics and politics, converge—producing new knowledge and agency. As we work through this multifaceted matrix, books enable us to map and reframe Zimbabwean identity. The project defies the limits of geography as it exists online. We are using maps not as metaphors but as analytical tools to understand the relationship between the geography of the world, knowledge production, and power. The interchange between literature and cartography demands that we ask questions about method and effect: How do we map narratives and their complex spatial structure? And what do we achieve by mapping literature? In other words, through this reflective exercise, we are able to see where and how real and fictional space overlap—or collide with each other, as in Marechera's case. By searching for some (provisional) answers, the horizon of a promising interdisciplinary research field becomes visible: a future literary geography.

TINASHE MUSHAKAVANHU is a writer, editor, and scholar from Zimbabwe. He holds degrees from English, Welsh, and Zimbabwean universities. He is invested in how the poetics of anarchy inform creative writing, digital media, and African literature. He is co-founder of Black Chalk & Co and principal co-investigator of Reading Zimbabwe. He is a postdoctoral fellow at WISER, University of Witwatersrand.

NONTSIKELELO MUTITI is a Zimbabwean-born visual artist and educator. She is invested in elevating the work and practices of Black people, past, present, and future, through a conceptual approach to design, experimental publishing and archiving practices, and peer-to-peer collaborations. She is co-founder of Black Chalk & Co and artistic director of Reading Zimbabwe. She teaches graphic design at Virginia Commonwealth University.

1   Graham Huggan, "Decolonizing the Map: Post-Colonialism, Post-Structuralism, and the Cartographic Connection," *Ariel* 20, no. 40 (October 1989): 29. Also see Gilles Deleuze and Felix Guattari, *A Thousand Plateaus: Capitalism and Schizophrenia*, trans. Brian Massumi (Minneapolis: University of Minnesota Press, 1987).

2   This project was a collaborative effort undertaken by Simba Mafundikwa (architect), Nontsikelelo Mutiti (graphic designer), and Tinashe Mushakavanhu (writer).

3   See *Report on the 1980s Disturbances in Matebeleland and the Midlands*, compiled by the Catholic Commission for Justice and Peace in Zimbabwe, March 1997, http://www.rhodesia.nl/ Matabeleland%20Report.pdf.

4   Flora Veit-Wild and Ernst Schade, *Dambudzo Marechera, 14 June 1952–18 August 1987: Pictures, Poems, Prose, Tributes* (Harare: Baobab Books, 1988), 3.

5   Harare's Book Café was permanently closed in 2015 after the death of its founder, Paul Brickhill.

Tracing the Diasporic Experience through the African Hair Braiding Salon

Nontsikelelo Mutiti

It was in Bedfordshire in the United Kingdom that I had the eureka moment. My older sister presented me with a set of black combs after our visit to a Nigerian-owned Black beauty supply store situated on the High Street. The packet contained ten combs and was identical to the set my mother had brought back from a trip to the United States in the early 1990s. Each comb was tucked away in its own pocket in the transparent plastic wrapper. The combs varied in size, shape, and number of teeth. More than useful instruments for personal grooming, these shiny black forms became the first point of connection to a constellation of objects, artifacts, and rituals that

Fig 1: Video stills from *Pain Revisited*, a collaborative audiovisual piece produced by Nontsikelelo Mutiti and Dyani Douze, 2015. The work is an exploration of Black female subjectivity. Courtesy of Nontsikelelo Mutiti.

would form my ongoing investigation into Black
hair aesthetics and diaspora. This essay is presented
in the form of vignettes: a series of reflections
through which I see myself and that connect me
to community through travel.

AFRICAN HAIR BRAIDING SALONS AND AFRICAN DIASPORA COMMUNITIES

My first visit to Harlem, New York, introduced me
to the African hair braiding salon. The space I sat in
as I waited for my cousin to have her braids undone
invoked the spaces at home in Harare, Zimbabwe.
This salon was run by a community of women from
Senegal and Guinea. We were all Africans but with
many differences between us. There is a television
sitting high up on the wall playing Nollywood movies
and a pile of patterned fabrics that one braider sells
to make extra money on the side. In this space, things
blend, edges fall away. We have a shared kinship
over our immigrant statuses, a shared understanding
of what it is like to have to build community and
routine out of fragments, remixed into something

Fig 2: A collection of hair
braider business cards handed
to Nontsikelelo Mutiti by
braiders in Harlem. Braiders
advertise their services
through one-on-one interactions on the streets of New
York. This is very different
from the word-of-mouth
referrals among community
members in Harare, Zimbabwe.
Courtesy of Nontsikelelo Mutiti.

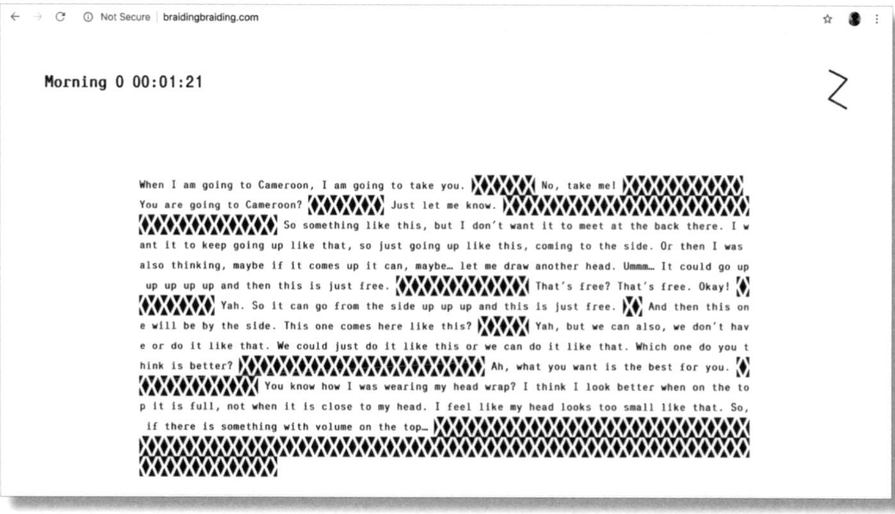

When I am going to Cameroon, I am going to take you. ▨▨▨(No, take me! ▨▨▨▨▨▨ You are going to Cameroon? ▨▨▨▨ Just let me know. ▨▨▨▨▨▨▨▨▨▨▨ ▨▨▨▨▨▨▨▨ So something like this, but I don't want it to meet at the back there. I w ant it to keep going up like that, so just going up like this, coming to the side. Or then I was also thinking, maybe if it comes up it can, maybe… let me draw another head. Ummm… It could go up up up up and then this is just free. ▨▨▨▨▨▨▨▨(That's free? That's free. Okay! ▨ ▨▨▨▨ Yah. So it can go from the side up up and this is just free. ▨ And then this on e will be by the side. This one comes here like this? ▨▨ Yah, but we can also, we don't hav e or do it like that. We could just do it like this or we can do it like that. Which one do you t hink is better? ▨▨▨▨▨▨▨▨▨▨▨▨▨ Ah, what you want is the best for you. ▨ ▨▨▨▨▨▨▨ You know how I was wearing my head wrap? I think I look better when on the to p it is full, not when it is close to my head. I feel like my head looks too small like that. So, if there is something with volume on the top… ▨▨▨▨▨▨▨▨▨▨▨▨▨▨▨▨▨ ▨▨▨▨▨▨▨▨▨▨▨▨▨▨▨▨▨▨▨▨▨▨▨▨▨▨▨▨▨▨▨▨ ▨▨▨▨▨▨▨

that resembles home. The transactions in this space stand in for familial relationships. A customer is a daughter, the braider an aunty.

Morning 0, an interactive online platform at braidingbraiding.com, documents my experience moving through Johannesburg in a neighborhood called Yeoville, where many African immigrants live. During one hair braiding appointment, I produced an audio recording that documented the full duration of my visit with the stylist. Transcribing and then editing audio is always a tricky process. How do you communicate the syntax to people who were not there, who might not understand? Sentence construction, emphasis, and exclamations that punctuate speech are nuanced and codified. Language, in a way, is like a map. The British inflection in my voice ties me to the colonial history of Zimbabwe even as I sit on a plastic chair in a salon in Johannesburg having my hair braided by Mama, our Cameroonian "aunty," and her assistant from Nairobi, Kenya.

Fig 3: A screenshot of the interface for Morning 0. Braidingbraiding.com documents a conversation between braiders and their client, artist and researcher Nontsikelelo Mutiti, in a salon in Yeoville, Johannesburg. The graphic patterns speak to the notion of repetition in both the aesthetics of braided hairstyles and the rule-based commands, or algorithms, that were used to build the website. Collaboration with Julia Novitch, 2015. Courtesy of Nontsikelelo Mutiti.

SPACE, IDENTITY, AND SOCIAL CODES

Moving through the world across geographic boundaries, negotiating my person between cultures, I become increasingly aware of the effect that space has on my identity. My appearance seems to shift depending on where I stand: appearance, the way that someone or something looks; or appearance, an act of participating or performing in a public event.

Negotiating one's place and stake in a community is an important aspect of immigration. Who is deemed an outsider, and how does one accrue membership or insider status to become the insider? What is the line between visitor or neighbor and acknowledged kinfolk? The Black beauty supply store and African hair braiding salon are spaces for self-styling, but they also serve as agents of assimilation. They provide the tools and services for the reproduction of Black hair aesthetics, a highly codified system based on values and ideas that reference historical notions of identity, beauty, and status. Presentation matters. It is a marker of how one wants to be perceived, a shape-shifting magic that we can access through these portals. Presentation as a gateway to access.

Fig 4: A sign in Tulse Hill in London. There is a notable presence of African and Caribbean immigrants in this neighborhood and in other adjacent neighborhoods such as Brixton. Courtesy of Nontsikelelo Mutiti.

Fig 5: Because hair salons are community spaces where people of similar cultures congregate, it is not surprising to find other services being advertised that fulfill specific community functions. This sign points to the reality of immigrant communities moving goods back and forth between their home country and host country—either goods for sale or gifts for family or personal items during a process of relocation. Courtesy of Nontsikelelo Mutiti.

HAIR BRAIDING AS A VISUAL LANGUAGE

The African hair braiding salon, the African food store, and the African textile trader are clear signs of the presence of a noteworthy and sizable African diaspora. These spaces can be found in immigrant communities in Australia, the United Kingdom, and the United States. On trips back home, between Zimbabwe and South Africa, I have come to consider the status of Africans who cross borders for work—who, like many of us living abroad, are economic refugees. The African hair braiding salon is a space that has the capacity to take up the skilled and the unskilled, any individual willing to learn the trade. Where there are kinfolk, there is work. Braiding as a simple, repetitive technique is quite universal, but the styles that one can construct using this simple, replicable set of operations is infinite. Not only is there a diverse range of possible aesthetics, but these styles also develop according to cultural meaning and trends reflected through media, and they can communicate ideas about status. Braiders working in a salon must learn and follow the trends specific to the community they are serving. Accompanying this knowledge are the terms used to name hairstyles. One must know the difference between a "pineapple," a "half equation," and a "fish tail." The "fish tail" in Harare is very different from the "fish tail" in Brooklyn. Language is central to the hair braiding experience.

Fig 6: Nontsikelelo Mutiti at a braiding appointment in a salon in Maputo, Mozambique. Because of the Portuguese influence on the country's culture, the hairstylists in the salon struggled to produce the braided hairstyle. Many salons in Maputo prefer to perform hair straightening processes that align with a European standard of beauty. Courtesy of Nontsikelelo Mutiti.

You can also map a genealogy of ideas onto the hair braiding salon: where do these hairstyles come from? An aspect of community technology is the generation of culture: from initiator to follower, ideas are transmitted and begin to take hold as norms and emblems of a group or social system. Modes of production, tools, and time become interwoven as trends appear, fade, and recur. The space of the African hair braiding salon, for me, is similar to the space of the graphic design studio: it is a place to respond to a prompt, to interpret, to iterate, and to create something new.

Fig 7: *RUKA (to braid/to knit/ to weave)*, an installation that served simultaneously as a design studio, a project space, and an African hair braiding salon. Produced by Nontsikelelo Mutiti during a residency at Recess art space in New York City, 2014. The space was programmed with film screenings, braiding workshops, and discussions. Courtesy of Nontsikelelo Mutiti.

LABOR

When you participate in the act of hair braiding, either as the sitter getting styled or as the braider, you have a heightened understanding of labor—of how time and technical skill come together to produce the experience (and not just the resulting hairdo). These aspects move the conversation past notions of craft and aesthetics. We can begin to delve into the idea of self-care and intimacy. Hair braiding demands proximity; it demands entering into one another's personal space. Trust and vulnerability become inextricably linked to activity and work.

Fig 8: Loose strands of hair extensions are commonplace in most cities. On the left is a piece of hair extension lying in a grassy patch in Harare, Zimbabwe. On the right is a tumbleweave encountered on a street in Richmond, Virginia. Courtesy of Nontsikelelo Mutiti.

HAIR BRAIDING AND CARTOGRAPHY

"Tumbleweave," a term made popular by the movie *Good Hair* (2009), is evidence of the reality of a Black body having moved through a space. The loose braid or tangled trail of a braiding extension or weave is a trace that creates a very real link between public space, like a sidewalk, and the more intimate African hair braiding salon or Black beauty supply store. Tumbleweave is always reinforcing a connection to Africa. Tumbleweave is a symbol of power and a symbol of presence.

The lexicon of hair braiding, much like that of typography, is continually evolving, responding to innovations in tools and absorbing new symbolisms and cultural references. I am constantly attempting to pull strands, various cultural signifiers, into a single braid. The term "threads" might conjure up images from the 1960s or 1970s, a time when the Black Is Beautiful movement had a palpable presence in the United States. Black hair aesthetics have been significant, so close to core values, a community currency that knits the references of black American life together with those from an African context. They articulate the reality of kinship and connection that continues to reinforce ways home for those of us in diaspora.

A War on Mobility: The Border Empire Strikes Back?

Maribel Casas-Cortés and Sebastian Cobarrubias

We are familiar with expressions such as "a war on drugs" and "a war on terror," but what about "a war on mobility"? Is anyone speaking about the realities of our world in this way? It is time to popularize a radical twist in the discourse and perception of international migration and the ways it is currently dealt with. This essay builds on the idea of a *war on mobility*, interrogating migration through the "war" being waged against it and through the territorial technologies exporting borders and monitoring movement *into* the European Union.

THE BORDER EMPIRE GOES GLOBAL

Migration control increasingly takes place beyond the borders of destination countries.[1] Migrants' journeys are traced using advanced technology and paramilitary deployments that target their supposed places of origin and possible routes of transit. The United States, the European Union, and Australia have increasingly displaced their respective border controls farther away from national limits, under the assumption that these countries are the destination for most migrants.

During the recent "refugee crisis," the European Union increased its bilateral agreements with "third," or non-EU, countries for the containment of migration flows—strengthening collaboration on border patrol, surveillance, and interception. These border cooperation projects between destination-transit-origin countries are fundamentally changing the spatial imaginaries and realities of borders and the practices used to maintain and enforce them. EUROSUR, the European Border Surveillance System, has begun to reinforce near-real-time data sharing on border movements through national coordination centers in EU member states and partner countries. To support these efforts, Frontex (a body that coordinates border management across and between EU countries), European national border guards, and independent think tanks, such as the International Centre for Migration Policy Development (ICMPD), are providing technical and training support to countries at and beyond the external frontiers of Europe.

These border policies, which involve acting beyond territorial lines and in coordination with third countries, constitute an approach to migration management called "border externalization." Externalization has become the predominant migration control policy in the European Union, implementing border work far beyond national borderlines. As a system for managing mobility, externalization coordinates tactics and cooperations at various scales—from retraining police and border forces and exporting biometric technology for national ID cards to intervening in third countries through paramilitary operations. Externalization not only *outsources* border work, meaning that a country, or group of countries, requests or coerces another country to police migration, as we have seen in the European Union's financing of Morocco to police both Moroccan emigration and African immigrants in Morocco who may (or may not) be en route to EU countries; it also establishes the ability of border and migration enforcement institutions of one country to intervene in another. Take, for instance, the joint coastal and land patrols developed between Spanish and Mauretanian or Spanish and Senegalese border institutions.

Border externalization fits with recent theoretical considerations on "moving borders," signaling how border work is not limited to the border itself or to traditional checkpoints but rather is constantly mobile, adjusting to migrants' ever-changing itineraries. Besides the impact on human life, critics have denounced the legality of stretching the border in this way and externalization's tendency to evade international law and national jurisdictions. While externalization has been expanding in recent years, its practices have a longer history. In fact, a genealogy of externalization can be traced as far back as the slave trade and slave suppression efforts, and to early attempts at imposing visa requirements prior to travel or carrier sanctions, both dating back more than a hundred years. A more contemporary outsourcing of border control has roots in the United States' interdiction of Haitian refugees in the early 1980s.[2]

The conventional understanding of migration control has been that each nation-state is in charge of its own borders at territorial lines and through visa applications in national embassies abroad. However, this traditional approach is considered incomplete among EU migration-policy circles. "Efficient migration management" requires that a nation-state goes beyond the place and time of the entry point. Transnational cooperation makes it possible to track exactly where the migrant is and is ostensibly going. This system of *remote control*, the *off-shoring and outsourcing* of borders, aims at tracing and managing the entirety of the migration journey.[3] Externalization thus manifests the spatial logics of a global strategy of mobility control. This is how "migratory routes management"—which was first expressed by the European Union in the Global Approach to Migration and Mobility in 2005 and which aims to track and intervene in migrants' trajectories throughout their journeys—has become a migration management concept and strategy.[4]

Enacting migratory routes management as a strategy, though, requires both important shifts in how and where the border is imagined and implemented and the identification of countries needed to operationalize this strategy. To this end, externalization has also entailed new spatial thinking and vocabulary (such as the "migratory route" as an object of management) as well as new cartographies that aid in visualizing the space of the border anew. The generation and deployment of data in relation to international mobility provides an impressive number of figures, statistics, and representations about human flows, many of which are visualized as maps of migratory flow and direction. In fact, migration maps are key to current migratory policies. These institutional cartographies chart entire migratory journeys (or purport to)— identifying potential points of control far beyond any given country's territorial limits—and thus signal both border externalization's neo-imperial pretensions and its social impact on cities within and outside the European Union.

The i-Map project, produced and managed by the International Centre for Migration Policy Development, is an important example of this attempt to reimagine the externalized border. The i-Map constitutes a thick visual archive of migratory movements presumably toward Europe. Since 2006 different versions of the i-Map (some more interactive and more detailed than others) have been available online. The i-Map clusters itineraries along major routes— indicated by thickened color lines—representing the common paths thought to be taken by irregular migrants from different locations. The map visualizes itineraries by linking "hubs" and "sub-hubs," such as cities or neighborhoods, mentioned in police interrogations with irregular migrants. Each hub has a hyperlink (not accessible to the public) with risk assessment information developed by Frontex, along with the European Union Agency for Law Enforcement Cooperation (better known as EUROPOL) and the United Nations Office on

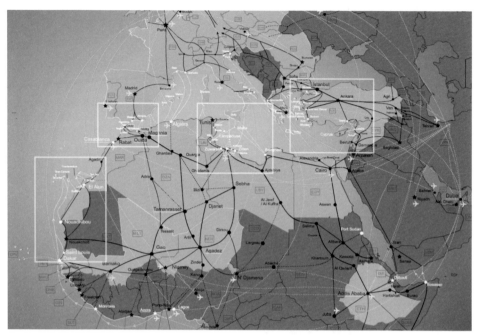

Fig 1: The i-Map, or the interactive map on migration, portrays global itineraries or migratory routes. Produced by the International Centre for Migration Policy Development, Vienna, 2012–ongoing.[5] Courtesy of ICMPD.

Drugs and Crime. These route lines are the predominant feature of the map, as opposed to national borderlines. By representing the entire route one travels, and thus visualizing the route as a transnational geopolitical concern, the i-Map constructs new forms of illegality, targeting border crossing before any border is crossed—making people *illegal* at the very time and place they decide to migrate.[6]

The European Union and its member states have instituted border policies that attempt to manage or limit migration long before a migrant arrives at or near official EU borders. One such series of operations is Operation Seahorse, coordinated by Spain in North and Western Africa and funded by the European Union.

Operation Seahorse established relations with border and coast guard authorities between multiple West African and EU countries with Spain acting as the primary mediator. These relations included conducting trainings, distributing equipment, and negotiating and conducting joint border patrols.[7] These were not simply one-off exchanges but rather multiyear police cooperation missions requiring new infrastructures and protocols to facilitate them. "System architecture" is one way the Spanish Civil Guard's border unit refers to the material buildings and technological support needed to operate these new border control projects (see figure 2). Multiple communication and control points across cooperating countries are articulated by two central nodes in Madrid and the Canary Islands (each box in figure 2). Although spanning five countries, this apparatus is considered one border architecture. According to Spanish police representatives, one of the key factors determining the success of these operations is the regular joint patrols consisting of coast guard forces from different countries (Cape Verdean/Portuguese, Mauretanian/Spanish, Senegalese/

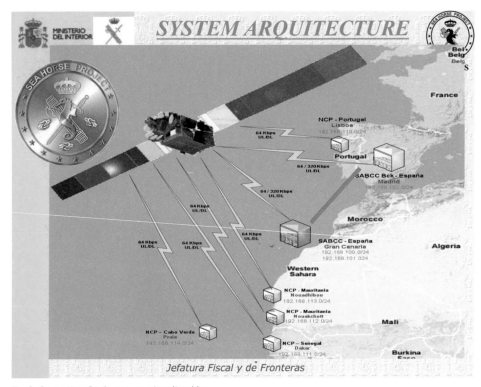

Fig 2: Operation Seahorse, as visualized by Spanish border authorities. PowerPoint by Servicio Fiscal y de Fronteras de la Guardia Civil, "Slide on System Architecture," Madrid, 2013. Courtesy of the Spanish Civil Guard.

Italian, and Senegalese/Spanish) along the West African coast (see figure 3). One can't help but wonder why such a robust transnational police and military framework—with its corresponding political and technological infrastructures— is necessary to detain wooden boats filled with low-income or unemployed fishers. Regardless of the motives, the efficacy, or the human consequences of border externalization, these emerging practices of migration control deeply reconceptualize border architectures.

EUROCENTRIC VISION OF MOBILITY?

While we were working on the lineage of the current EU migration regime, a controversial official document, by the EU Commission, proposing to divide the world into concentric circles caught our attention: the "Strategy Paper on Immigration and Asylum Policy."[8] The geographic imaginary in this document underpins the extraterritorial operations of Operation Seahorse; and it is a geographic imaginary that is fraught, literally, with Euro(con)centric tensions.[9]

During the Austrian presidency of the European Union in 1998, a geographical vision of managing mobility into Europe scandalized EU authorities. Perceived as an unnecessarily restrictive and discriminatory approach to migration, the official document released to the EU commission and council evoked a clear though rigid understanding of how mobility should be distributed in the world. This 1998 document classified worldwide territories and populations

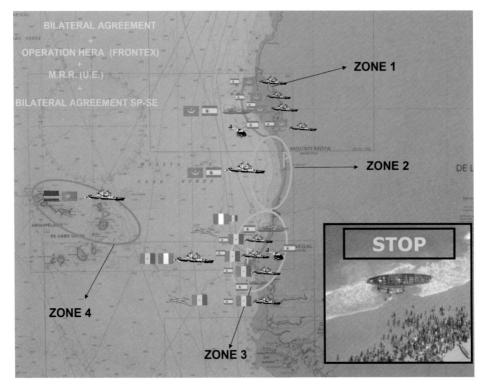

Fig 3: Operation Hera, as visualized by Spanish border authorities. PowerPoint by Servicio Fiscal y de Fronteras de la Guardia Civil, "Slide on Stop Operations," Madrid, 2013. Courtesy of the Spanish Civil Guard.

therein into four concentric circles. It mapped an idea of the world where everyone, in a sense, belongs and should remain in their respective circle, with few exceptions. Such a geographical imaginary centers the European Union and dictates who should move and who should not move around the world. Despite its rather Eurocentric and hierarchical approach toward human mobility, this managerial vision underpins current EU migration policy, especially its border outsourcing practices.

The policy itself was officially voted down in 1998, though some of its ideas were further pursued by the High-Level Working Group on Migration (HLWG) and individual member states of the European Union.[10] Slowly but surely this spatial vision has become an informal organizing framework for EU policy on migration management and the basis of restrictive migratory policies. This vision and its mapping of the world have not been fully achieved on the ground: plans and projects were tried; some succeeded, some failed. This is not a representation of the EU border regime as it actually exists. Yet the designation of spaces of the world beyond the European Union and their role in migration systems and border policy have, for the most part, remained intact.

As explicitly stated in the document, the goal was to go "global" and to replace the model of "fortress Europe." In this globalization of borders, mobilities were instead categorized and confined to four zones according to certain criteria. The 1998 document clearly designates zones of the planet where permissible or

Fig 4: A cartographic visualization of the EU Commission's "Strategy Paper on Immigration and Asylum Policy," a proposal toward inward migration presented during the Austrian EU presidency in 1998. "The Four Concentric Circles of Mobility," 2018. Circle 1 marks the desirable destinations and zones of mobility; Circle 2 highlights countries adjacent to the European Union considered almost as rest zones in the migrants' itineraries; Circle 3 highlights countries far away from the European Union but still considered "transit zones"; Circle 4 highlights countries considered as sources of population flows (the yellow stars reveal sites identified by Frontex as current sources of illegal migration). Courtesy of Tim Stallman.

less permissible human movement occurs. Entire groups of countries are slated as "secure" in their borders or as sources of problematic emigration, and yet the factors leading to any of these designations (accurate or not) are ignored. The first zone, represented as a circle, is formed by the EU member states, capable of fulfilling Schengen standards of control, and other countries that "do not cause emigration" but have become "target countries on account of their advanced economic and political situation."[11]

The second zone consists of "transit countries," which no longer generate emigration but "on account of a relatively stable internal economic and political situation accept only very limited control procedures and responsibility for migration policy." This circle comprises countries neighboring the Schengen/EU territory that have signed some form of association agreement with the bloc and "perhaps also the Mediterranean area." According to the report, these countries' systems of control should gradually be brought into line with the first-circle standards.[12]

The third zone is characterized by countries of both emigration and transit—that is, the Commonwealth of Independent States (CIS) area (the former Soviet Union), Turkey, and North Africa. These countries would be required to "concentrate primarily on transit checks and combatting facilitator [migrant smuggler] networks."

The fourth (outermost) zone is made up of countries of emigration apparently deemed beyond the reach of European "political muscle" (it mentions "the Middle East," China, and "black Africa"). These countries are encouraged to "eliminate push factors" of migration.[13]

The EU Commission's "Strategy Paper on Immigration and Asylum Policy" outlined a reward system for controlling, policing, and curbing migration—incentivizing a country to meet the obligations of its particular circle and assignment: "For example, the second circle must meet Schengen standards as a precondition for EU membership; for the third circle, intensified economic cooperation is linked to the fulfillment of their obligations; and the fourth circle, the extent of development aid can be assessed on that basis."[14] These maps make graphically explicit what many of us take for granted in our critiques: a problematic Eurocentric vision of migration.

This highly hierarchical and racialized Euro(con)centric vision of mobility contains several assumptions that, while problematic, persist: first, everybody intends to get to circle 1 (ignoring movement within and across circles—that is, South to South migration); second, nobody gets out of the European Union, and there is no movement from circle 1 to circles 2, 3, or 4 (ignoring increasing numbers of EU citizens fleeing the austerity crisis); third, circle 1 should command who moves where; and fourth, partner countries in circles 2, 3, and 4 have no other goals or approaches to the management of mobility. In this vision, a center assigns particular roles to distinct regions of the world for both producing and managing mobility. Individual governments are expected to control their own citizens—carrying out border control in certain ways and instituting specific regulations about how and where their populations can move.

Outraged by this vision of control and its Eurocentric assumptions, we have tried to share this research with broader audiences through exhibitions showcasing the numerous cartographies produced by border authorities—and migratory maps rarely available to the public—alongside our own representations of the problematic geographic imaginary embedded in EU migratory policy documents.[15] We decided to revisualize the European Union's geographical imaginary as a series of maps, in the hope that a compelling counternarrative about migration might become clear: that the proclaimed "problem" of migration is *not* about troublemakers from poor countries in the South fleeing in a massive exodus toward the United States and the European Union, changing the face of the world. This dusty EU policy document turns taken-for-granted assumptions of migration control upside down: the problem does not rely on those who are moving. Rather, the concern is the attempt to impose a scary plan to control human mobility worldwide.

While institutional migration maps deploy a certain professionalism and neutrality associated with expertise, they are driven by a restrictive logic of containment. Our maps, on the other hand, are the product of embodied, experiential, and activist knowledge(s) coming from those supporting and enacting a politics of freedom of movement. The examples of countercartographies show

Fig 5: The exhibition *It Is Obvious from the Map*, at REDCAT, Los Angeles, 2017. Courtesy of Sohrab Mohebbi and Thomas Keenan.

how controversial, problematic, and inaccurate institutional maps for migration control are. These countermaps enable alternative visions and practices of human mobility.[16]

"EMPIRE" TIMES

Border externalization appears to reproduce the colonial logic of "ordering" territories and populations, one that dates from the high imperialism of the late nineteenth century. Direct intervention on the part of the European Union in places of supposed origin and transit of migrant trajectories—through development projects, the creation of civil registry databases, international military deployments, or foreign police operations—has led to critical readings of externalization and border cooperation as a form of neocolonialism.[17] Processes of externalization imply more than a rollout of imperial power, if the agency of African nation-states, with their diverse and at times divergent reasons for participating in border cooperation with the European Union, is also taken into account.[18]

In the i-Map, Europe-bound migrations are represented in flashy migratory routes that erase African national borders. This is reminiscent of the boundary-making power that Europeans have historically exerted on the African continent since colonial times. This geographic imaginary embraced by the European Union and its member states portrays a displaced border space, which ignores and overrides African nation-state borders.[19] That imagining only makes sense in the historical context of a colonial erasure of previously existing polities and societies. Again, Africa becomes a kind of living space for Europe to design, order, and profit from.[20] In fact, we can see border externalization as the next chapter in the story told by migration and citizenship scholar Seyla Benhabib. In her writings on postcolonial migration, Benhabib observes:

Fig 6: The exhibition *Signs and Whispers*, at Galeria Nova, Zagreb, 2018. Courtesy of the What, How, and for Whom Collective.

This legacy of empire has come back today to haunt the [rich] countries of the Northern Hemisphere through the rise of transnational migrations. Transnational migrations also produce an uncoupling between territoriality, sovereignty, and citizenship but in ways quite different than colonialism. Whereas in the nineteenth and twentieth centuries, European imperialism spread forms of jurisdiction into colonial territories, which were shielded from democratic consent and control, contemporary migratory movements give rise to overlapping jurisdictions which are often protected by international norms… The Westphalian state which extended towards the rest of the world now finds that its borders are porous in both directions and that it is not only the center which flows to the periphery but the periphery which flows towards the center.[21]

The center again flows to the periphery in its attempts to border the same transnational migrations that emerged, at least in part, from the postcolonial condition. While migration may produce an "uncoupling between territoriality, sovereignty, and citizenship," shifting border policy is also contributing to this "uncoupling" in distinct ways. National affiliations based on exclusive loyalty to a single sovereign state have been shaken by international migration flows. With border externalization processes, "whose" border is "where" is also thrown into question. Confusion emerges in cases where, for example, a Spanish Gendarmerie officer intercepts someone in Senegalese waters. If that person claims asylum, which country must process that claim? Spain or Senegal? Overlapping jurisdictions undercut accountability, international norms, and human rights legislation.

THE BORDER EMPIRE TARGETS CITIES

While many studies of externalization focus on understanding its geopolitics and the transformations it entails in relation to law, sovereignty, and human rights, the urban dimension of externalization is often overlooked. What are the implications of externalization at the urban scale? While news headlines may focus on fences, coast guard patrols, or even desert traversals, metropolis and minor urban settlements have become a priority in the European Union's agenda for containing migratory flows. For remote border control, cities are considered hubs that facilitate human mobility. This is explicit in the migration routes management strategy and in the i-Map, which draws the route by connecting different cities and towns where migrants are thought to have traversed. Thus the route to be managed is a string of cities understood as migratory hubs. Depending on the time and the city along a route, border practices might include the facilitation of development projects that bring stable employment opportunities to those places; increasing police raids and the number of checkpoints asking for ID; or the rise of independent transportation services among different towns for deporting people. Given that routes and migration may shift over time, partly in response to externalization measures, the "hubs" or cities affected and how they are affected will change. All these practices constitute processes for making someone's movement undesirable and ultimately coded as "illegal." This production of illegal mobilities is unfolding ubiquitously, regardless of place, although it is occurring with increasing frequency and intensity at the urban scale.

These bordering practices have tangible effects on the urban fabric of cities where externalization is carried out. The city, in addition to its role in facilitating mobility through transportation infrastructures and facilities, becomes simultaneously antagonistic to mobility. This antagonism becomes apparent when the city serves as a site for increased police patrols, new policing equipment, the rolling out of ID cards for residents, EU-funded propaganda and billboards dissuading irregular migration, and even new buildings to house the International Organization for Migration and other migration-related bodies (who, at times, have become significant employers in the city). The urban landscape is thus transformed through this migration industry, or what anthropologist Ruben Anderson calls the "Illegality Industry."[22] In some cases, such as in Rabat (Morocco) and Nouadhibou (Mauretania), these transformations have led to increasingly segregated migrant landscapes. The pursuit of people who "might" be on their way to Europe and the adoption of restrictive migration policies by host African countries cooperating with externalization efforts are contributing to rising patterns of discrimination and ghettoization in places where these dynamics of urban spatial segregation were historically less frequent. This can occur through the stripping of legal residency from intra-African migrants and increased police attention toward those same migrant communities.

BORDERWARS AND ITS FRACTAL TECHNOLOGIES

In recapitulating externalization policies and their impact on cities, we offer a theorization of the mobility of borders and its underlying imperial politics of controlling (certain) people on the move. For this, we start by reciting the evocative statement "We did not cross the border, the border crossed us," which has become a rallying call for pro-migration activism beyond the US–Mexico context where it was originally voiced.[23] While counterintuitive, it points to the historical and ongoing contingent itinerancy of borderlines. It also speaks about the ingrained discriminatory character of a border mindset that believes that one's very self can be permanently marked as "border crosser" and thus "intruder," an inappropriate and usually undesired other.[24]

While border crossing constitutes a hot policy and scholarly concern, borders themselves are actively "crossing" over people, regardless of their geographical locations and kinship. Borders—as institutionalized practices of containing, filtering, and ordering populations—do not just take place at the territorial limits of countries. In fact, the act of arranging people into hierarchies of mobility is becoming a ubiquitous process and reality wherever one is. Thus, the message conveyed by "the border crossed us" uniquely captures the goal of current migratory policies and the ever-reaching regime of mobility control. In its pervasiveness, all of us are potential targets to be crossed by endless sets of reproducible borders. Both the imagination and the enforcement of migration control are intended to "cross"—as in traverse through—populations. This crossing *by* borders is conducted through the arbitrary containment, classification, and segregation of people who are both in place and on the move.[25]

Furthermore, borders are crossing territories far beyond the borderlines they supposedly contain. On the one hand, growing public budgets are subsidizing high-tech infrastructures for the tracking and interception of human movements at and *beyond* the borderline (such as with contraction of fences and externalization missions). On the other hand, institutionalized practices toward the bordering of bodies are taking place at and *within* the borderline through the proliferation of checkpoints inside the destination countries (the cross-checking of migration status with databases for other services like banking, driving, medical care, etc., and migrant detention). All of those practices within receiving countries speak to a parallel process of "border internalization." This double process points to a growing normalization and institutionalization of border work regardless of location, which, in turn, leads to concerning levels of racialized profiling, random incarceration, abuse during interrogation, and deportation. The question of mobility is further complicated when we consider populations and groups of migrants who have managed to enter into the European Union. As Martina Tazzioli and Claudia Aradau have argued, it is the settlement of refugees in EU cities that becomes the target of prohibition, meaning that mobility, in turn, becomes a weapon of displacement and precarity used to keep migrants constantly on the move.

We propose to embrace this twist in our understanding of borders: from stable lines to be crossed to institutional practices actively "b/ordering" populations in an endless war on mobility.[26] That is, borders as actively and consistently *crossing us* to the point that they dictate political allegiances, our corresponding entitlements, or lack thereof. Seen in this way, the powerful yet normalized device of mandatory membership and social stratification—

the national border—would scandalize many, regardless of ideological position. The rigid control of human movement into, out of, and within countries has often been associated with dictatorships attempting to maintain control within their despotic limits. Culturally, for many people, the control of people's movements—interrupting journeys and interrogating destinations and points of transit—is not well taken. People want to get through airport security quickly, travel for summer vacation, avoid traffic jams. Seen at this abstract level, the freedom of movement can be seen as a shared value regardless of political disagreements. Legally speaking, the *ius migrandi* (right to migrate) was codified in a protocol by the League of Nations in 1929, amid calls by the same international organization to abolish passports.[27] In fact, article 13 of the 1948 Universal Declaration of Human Rights, which established the right to *emigrate*, is merely an abridged version of the 1929 protocol. The rest of that protocol—that is, both the *right to immigrate* and the *right to reside*—was lost in the context of the Great Depression, World War II, and the emerging Cold War. Thus, our current world order keeps actively disregarding this deeply held cultural value and its tradition in international law to focus instead on a ferocious and publicly funded control of international mobility.

This questionable way of dealing with people and their movements is not only felt at the customs line (who gets fingerprinted and iris-scanned, who gets sent to the "interrogation room," who moves through the faster lines for citizens or Global Entry, etc.). Borders are reproducing in a fractal way, implementing their b/ordering logic of social control in unexpected ways and generating a controlled space with no outside. Fractals are patterns that are similar across different scales. Fractals are generated by repeating a simple process over and over again. Border fractals are thus a series of checkpoints, made out of smaller checkpoints, which are made out of even smaller checkpoints (border walls to visa regimes to databases cross-checking migration status, and so on). In the core of assumed destination or host countries, particularly in their cities, these fractals are reproduced through migrant detention, Immigration and Customs Enforcement (ICE) raids, and threats to employees using Social Security numbers that may not match the Social Security Administration records—a continuous pattern of contention, displacement, and stratification that is ever present and can seem invincible.

With externalization this fractal pattern spreads its work thousands of kilometers away from legal borderlines, where, for example, the "successful" (in police terms) monitoring of Spanish and Moroccan coasts is moved to similar processes of patrolling in West African waters, which is then followed by a move to conduct land border control in countries like Mali and Niger. In these efforts, urban nodes of transport become points for intervention. Port cities (like Agadir in Morocco or St. Louis in Senegal) become sites where all boats must be registered, all license numbers cross-checked with migration authorities, and all fuel sales registered with local police. Bus stations in cities like Agadez become surveilled sites with police impounding any vehicle believed to be used for transporting potential migrants. The borderline has moved both inward and outward of the territorial state's limits. The border empire is everywhere, or rather potentially anywhere. Such a spatial proliferation of bordering practices materializes a regime of mobility control that would scare anyone if it were the subject of the latest action movie: *Border Wars*, anyone?

BORDERS ADRIFT

Borders are on the move. This itinerant character might look similar to a Situationist "drift" at first glance, but it is not the itinerancy envisioned by the open-ended method of the drift. In stark contrast, these borders in motion follow orders from a center, ruled by experts and followed by military agencies. A political will lies behind border drifting: the desire to control human mobility.

The politics driving current migration management is encapsulated in a text message sent by a sub-Saharan migrant who tried to swim the fifteen kilometers between the African and the European continents through the Strait of Gibraltar: "There is an ongoing war on migrants."[28] A few decades ago, a regular ID would have been enough to enjoy a safe trip by ferry from Africa to southern Spain, but now he and many others are prohibited from ferry travel and must embark on the more treacherous South-to-North route. This war on mobility is spatially and culturally infecting the globe. Given the displacement of migratory control practices from national lines to points along the migratory journeys, following and incriminating migrants from beginning to end, the war against mobility has become global: urban and not urban; in centers and peripheries, mobilizing both space and time. In this scenario of borders "drifting," where are the members of the "resistance" to such a border empire? We want to believe that resistance is also everywhere. Indeed, those moving regardless of administrative paperwork, zigzagging in unexpected motions, embody the ongoing challenge to the ubiquitous presence of the border regime. Still—and this question is yet to be explored—how does one position oneself *outside* and *against* this war on mobility?

Thanks to Sohrab Mohebbi and Thomas Keenan, curators of the exhibition *It Is Obvious from the Map*, presented at the Los Angeles–based art gallery REDCAT. We value their passionate interest in the EU border regime and their pursuit of making its intricacies accessible to the broader public. Also, we highly appreciate the advice of REDCAT's editor, Jessica Loudis, who carefully reviewed the original version of this text to make it as clear as possible. Finally, thanks to cartographer Tim Stallman for working with us to visualize the geographic thinking behind some of the key EU documents defining current migration policy. Last but not least, thanks to all of those who keep moving across borders, with or without required paperwork, for challenging the current border system.

MARIBEL CASAS-CORTÉS is an interdisciplinary scholar working at the intersection of border studies, cultural analysis, and critical theory. She was recently awarded a research position in Spain following a Hunt Fellowship, which enabled her to work on a monograph on social movements and precarity in southern Europe, affiliated with the University of North Carolina at Charlotte. She holds a PhD in cultural anthropology from the University of North Carolina at Chapel Hill and has published in journals such as *Citizenship Studies*, *Rethinking Marxism*, *Cultural Studies*, and *Anthropology Quarterly*.

SEBASTIAN COBARRUBIAS is currently an ARAID research professor in the Geography Department at the University of Zaragoza, Spain. His research interests include border studies, social movements, and critical cartographic theory. He holds a PhD in human geography from the University of North Carolina at Chapel Hill and has published in journals such as *Antipode*, *Political Geography*, and *European and Urban Regional Studies*.

1   This section is based on our multisited research project on "Border Externalization by the EU," funded by the National Science Foundation 2010–2014. We also draw from the graphics we gathered for the exhibition *It Is Obvious from the Map*, curated by Thomas Keenan and Sohrab Mohebbi in Los Angeles and Zagreb.

2   For more on this, see "New Keywords: Migration and Borders," which is a collaborative publication produced by more than a dozen migration and border studies scholars that consists of key concepts in current research and that establishes the parameters of a common language in critical migration and border studies. Maribel Casas-Cortés et al., "New Keywords: Migration and Borders," *Cultural Studies* 29, no. 1 (2014): 55–87.

3   Aristide Zolberg, "The Archeology of 'Remote Control,'" in *Migration Control in the North Atlantic World: The Evolution of State Practices in Europe and the United States*, ed. Andreas Fahrmeir (New York: Berghahn Books, 2003), 195–223; Ruben Zaiotti, ed., *Externalizing Migration Management: Europe, North America and the Spread of "Remote Control" Practices*, Routledge Research in Place, Space and Politics (New York: Routledge, 2016); Luiza Bialasiewicz, "Off-Shoring and Out-Sourcing the Borders of Europe: Libya and EU Border Work in the Mediterranean," *Geopolitics* 17, no. 4 (2012): 843–866.

4   Maribel Casas-Cortés, Sebastian Cobarrubias, and John Pickles, "Riding Routes and Itinerant Borders: Autonomy of Migration and Border Externalization," *Antipode* 47, no. 4 (2015): 894–914.

5   This is a static visualization of the migration routes published by the ICMPD in 2014. The most recent version of the i-Map is accessible only with a username and password. You can request access at https://ec.europa.eu/knowledge4policy/online-resource/interactive-map-migration-i-map_en.

6   Maribel Casas-Cortés, Sebastian Cobarrubias, and John Pickles, "B/Ordering Turbulence beyond Europe: Expert Knowledge in the Management of Human Mobility," in *Mapping Migration, Identity, and Space*, ed. Tabea Linhard and Timothy Parsons (Cham, Switzerland: Palgrave Macmillan, 2019), 257–281; Sebastian Cobarrubias, "The i-Map and the Cartopolitics of 'Migration Mangement' at a Distance," *Antipode* 51, no. 3 (2019): 770–794.

7   Figures 2 and 3 are from PowerPoints used by the Spanish Civil Guard. These presentations demonstrate the rationale of externalization as well as how the border is imagined spatially in this type of border operation.

8   Council of the European Union, "Strategy Paper on Immigration and Asylum Policy, from the Austrian Council Presidency to the K4 Committee," 1.7.98, 9809/98 CK4 27, ASIM 170, limite (1998), http://archiv.proasyl.de/texte/europe/eu-a-o.htm. Note: This refers to the initial leaked draft. Subsequent drafts have the following codification: 9809/1/98, Rev 1 Limite, CK4 27, ASIM 170; and 9809/2/98, Rev 2 Limite, CK4 27, ASIM 170.

9   A detailed study of this EU document can be found in our piece, "Concentric Circles in the EU's External Migration Policy? Dissecting Colonial Logics in the Ordering of Territories and Mobilities," in *The Critical Handbook on Migration Geographies*, ed. Kathryne Mitchell, Reece Jones, and Jennifer Fluri (London: Edgar Ellen, 2019), 193–205.

10   The HLWG was set up at the end of 1998 as part of an initiative of the Netherlands, which was president of the EU at the time. The HLWG is a strategic analysis group with representatives from various member states tasked with drafting "action plans" on migration and border policy vis-à-vis non-EU countries. It was under the auspices of this group that the strategy paper continued to have influence in official circles.

11   Council of the European Union, "Strategy Paper on Immigration and Asylum Policy" (points 60 and 116).

12   Council of the European Union, "Strategy Paper on Immigration and Asylum Policy" (points 60 and 118).

13   Council of the European Union, "Strategy Paper on Immigration and Asylum Policy" (points 60 and 119).

14   Council of the European Union, "Strategy Paper on Immigration and Asylum Policy" (point 61).

15   For more information, visit REDCAT, https://www.redcat.org/exhibition/it-obvious-map, and Galeria Nova, http://www.whw.hr/galerija-nova/izlozba-signs-and-whispers.html.

16   Many of these maps are now part of the itinerant art collection first launched in Los Angeles and later hosted in Zagreb: *It Is Obvious from the Map!* Maribel Casas-Cortés and Sebastian Cobarrubias, "'It Is Obvious from the Map!': Disobeying the Production of Illegality beyond Borderlines," *Movements: Journal für kritische Migrations und Grenzregimeforschung* 4, no.1 (January 2018): 29–44.

17   Mark Akkerman, *Expanding the Fortress: The Policies, the Profiteers and the People Shaped by EU's Externalisation Programme* (Amsterdam: Transnational Institute, 2018); Sara Prestianni, "The Dangerous Link between Migration, Development, and Security for the Externalisation of Borders in Africa" (Rome: ARCI Reports, 2018), https://www.arci.it/documento/the-dangerous-link-between-migration-development-and-security-for-the-externalisation-of-borders-in-africa-case-studies-on-sudan-niger-and-tunisia; Tony Bunyan, "Analysis: The EU Goes to War with African 'Elite,'" *StateWatch Bulletin*, 2016.

18   Paolo Gaibazzi, Stephan Dünnwald, and Alice Bellagamba, *EurAfrican Borders and Migration Management: Political Cultures, Contested Spaces, and Ordinary Lives* (New York: Palgrave Macmillan, 2017).

19   This erasure of African national borders is far from the call to "scrap the borders" that Achille Mbembe makes in a recent impassioned plea: "The next phase of Africa's decolonisation is about granting mobility to all her people and reshaping the terms of membership in a political and cultural ensemble that is not confined to the nation-state." Freedom of movement within Africa becomes a "cornerstone of a new pan-African agenda": "To become a vast area of freedom of movement is arguably the biggest challenge Africa faces in the 21st century. The future of Africa does not depend on restrictive immigration policies and the militarisation of borders." Achille Mbembe, "Scrap the Borders that Divide Africans," *Mail & Guardian*, March 17, 2017, https://mg.co.za/article/2017-03-17-00-scrap-the-borders-that-divide-africans.

20   Peo Hansen and Stefan Jonsson, *Eurafrica: The Untold History of European Integration and Colonialism* (New York: Bloomsbury Academic, 2014).

21   Seyla Benhabib, "Twilight of Sovereignty or the Emergence of Cosmopolitan Norms? Rethinking Citizenship in Volatile Times," *Citizenship Studies* 11, no. 1 (February 2007): 19–36. The quote appears on pages 23–24.

22   Ruben Andersson, *Illegality, Inc.: Clandestine Migration and the Business of Bordering Europe*, California Series in Public Anthropology 28 (Berkeley: University of California Press, 2014).

23   The origin of this slogan comes from people in the US Southwest, often of Mexican descent—both migrant and not—expressing the fact that much of the Western United States was once part of Mexico. In fact, Texas, New Mexico, Arizona, and California were seized by the United States in the Mexican–American War of 1846–1848. Pointing to the irony of labeling Mexican citizens in the US Southwest as foreigners and illegal trespassers, the expression has been attributed to everyone from writer José Antonio Burciaga to actress Eva Longoria to the band Aztlan Underground. It is widely popular because it communicates the notion that geopolitical borders are imposed on peoples that have lived in those places prior to those dividing lines.

24   Besides being used for immigrant rights, the slogan has resonated among indigenous movements, Palestinian solidarity groups, and anticolonial and racial justice struggles, all working against institutional racism and practices of exclusion.

25   See Martina Tazzioli, "Governing Migrant Mobility through Mobility: Containment and Dispersal at the Internal Frontiers of Europe," *Environment and Planning C: Politics and Space* (April 2019); and Claudia Aradau and Rens van Munster, "Governing Terrorism through Risk: Taking Precautions, (Un)Knowing the Future," *European Journal of International Relations* 13, no. 1 (March 2007): 89–115.

26   "B/ordering" as developed by critical migration scholars of the Nijmegen School, relates well to this notion of borders themselves as actively crossing over people. This piece embraces this understanding of borders as complex filters that classify populations under an apartheid logic through the triple function of bordering, ordering, and othering. See Henk van Houtum, Olivier Thomas Kramsch, and Wolfgang Zierhofer, *B/Ordering Space* (Aldershot, UK: Ashgate, 2005); Henk van Houtum and Ton van Naerssen, "Bordering, Ordering and Othering," *Tijdschrift voor economische en sociale geografie* 93, vol. 2 (December 2002): 125–136.

27   Speranta Dumitru, "When World Leaders Thought You Shouldn't Need Passports or Visas," *Conversation*, September 27, 2016, http://theconversation.com/when-world-leaders-thought-you-shouldnt-need-passports-or-visas-64847.

28   As quoted in Emmanuel Blanchard et al., eds., *Guerre aux migrants: Le livre noir de Ceuta et Melilla*, Collection "Arguments et Mouvements" (Paris: Syllepse, 2007).

"Hostile Environment"(s): Sensing Migration across Weaponized Terrains

Charles Heller and Lorenzo Pezzani

In May 2012, the then UK home secretary Theresa May announced in an interview the introduction of new, groundbreaking legislation in the field of immigration control. The aim of these new measures, she declared in language that was described as "uncharacteristically vivid," was "to create here in Britain a really hostile environment for illegal migration."[1] "Work is under way," she further explained, "to deny illegal immigrants access to work, housing, and services, even bank accounts."[2] Two successive immigration acts, passed in 2014 and 2016, translated this announcement into law—making access to various public and private services (such as medical care, education, housing, or banking) and the ability to work conditional on immigration status and requiring governmental agencies to share the data they routinely collect with immigration enforcement agencies. Since then, a vast range of public servants such as doctors, teachers, and university lecturers as well as private citizens (landlords, bank employees, and driving instructors) have been tasked with carrying out immigration checks and thus surreptitiously have been turned into border-control agents. One might say that with this legislation, the border has infiltrated everyday life in ways that, while far from being new, have become unprecedentedly pervasive. The whole space of the state as defined by national borders has turned into a "hostile environment" for those without the right papers.

Fig 1: As part of the hostile environment policy, in the summer of 2013, the UK government sent vans around six London boroughs threatening those living in the United Kingdom illegally with arrest and asking them to "voluntarily" leave the country. © Rick Flinder.

The process of making (mainly urban) space unlivable for some bears an eerie resemblance to the ways in which other, more "natural" environments have been turned into hostile spaces for migrants. From the arid lands of the Sonoran and Sahara Deserts, to the rugged mountain passes of the Alps or the area between Iran and Turkey, to the oceans encircling Australia, the United

States, Europe, and the Arabian Peninsula, migrants have in the last few years been forced to traverse more and more inhospitable and hazardous terrains—in the hope that the risk of injury and death they will face might deter them from attempting the crossing.[3] In these cases, it is the very geophysical characteristics of the environment that have been enlisted and harnessed as crucial tools of border control.

This process is particularly visible in the Mediterranean Sea. Since 2011, and in the context of a project called Forensic Oceanography, we have critically investigated the militarized border regime imposed by European states across this maritime zone, analyzing the political, spatial, and aesthetic conditions that have led to more than thirty thousand migrant deaths *recorded* over the last thirty years.[4] Together with a wide network of NGOs, lawyers, scientists, journalists, and activists, we have produced maps, videos, visualizations, and human rights reports that attempt to document and challenge the transformation of the Mediterranean into the deadliest crossing in the world: the epicenter of those "landscapes of deaths" represented by global borders.[5] In these works, we have argued that while these terrains might already in some way constitute "natural boundaries" due to their geophysical characteristics, it is through very specific practices, protocols, and laws that these characteristics have been weaponized against specific categories of people and these environments rendered hostile to them.

It is from this angle, perhaps, that we might start to think about the administrative procedures that are being mobilized in urban areas in the United Kingdom in conjunction with what is happening across these "natural" environments, connecting what happens in these remote and difficult-to-access border zones with the very cities where most people live and work. The bordering practices that are at work across these different sites are an expression of a form of power that operates not by disciplining specific subjects but rather by intervening in the milieu—understood as a socionatural space—they inhabit or traverse, as Michel Foucault has already noted in some of his later work on biopolitics.[6] The French philosopher had begun to theorize a form of governance through the milieu—what he called, echoing his notion of governmentality, "environmentality"—as his analysis of biopolitics shifted from a historical to a more contemporary context. In nothing more than a few scattered notes, Foucault described the then budding forms of neoliberalism as "an environmental type of intervention" rather than a subject-based or population-based distribution of governance.[7]

How can we forge a conceptual optics that would allow us to understand the border enforcement mechanisms operating in London and in the middle of the Mediterranean together, as different but intimately related expressions of the same logic and of its expansive, multiscalar reach? What role do sensing technologies, by creating selective conditions of (dis)appearance, (in)audibility, and (in)visibility, play in this context? And, last but not least, how could this perspective lead us to rethink conventional understandings of both environment and displacement, connecting questions of and struggles for migration, borders, climate change, and the commons in new ways?

THE NATURE OF BORDERS

The idea that borders are somehow the political expression of naturally existing, geophysically determined boundaries is a well-known trope of the modern era, one that often "formed part of a constitutive myth of the state" and served to legitimize and rationalize the territorial claims of the then emerging European (empire-)states.[8] One of the most cited expressions of this theory comes from France, where the state-building process was underpinned by the "idea that 'geography determined French policy': that, since the sixteenth if not the twelfth century, France had undertaken a steady and consistent expansion to reach the Atlantic, Rhine, Alps, and Pyrenees."[9] These, according to a famous dictum attributed to Cardinal Richelieu, were "the limits that Nature had traced," a divine vision that the French state was called upon to fulfill.

This vision has received widespread and sustained critique at least since the nineteenth century, when a "new generation of geographers set out to relativize the role of physical geography (topography in particular) in the comprehension of human territoriality."[10] In her widely read 1911 textbook *Influences of Geographic Environment*, Ellen Churchill Semple argued that among the many different types of "natural boundaries" that "set more or less effective limits to the movement of peoples and the territorial growth of states," "the sea is the only absolute boundary, because it alone blocks the continuous, unbroken expansion of a people."[11] Yet, in another passage, she also recognized that the "mobile forces in the air and water" could be "domesticated" to increase people's "powers of locomotion" and bring different populations into contact.[12]

What Semple's excerpt points to is that while, as highlighted by Elisabeth Grosz's notion of "geopower," geographic environments are certainly endowed with "forces contained in matter that precede, enable, facilitate, provoke, and restrict 'life,'" we also need to account for how political practices shape the ways in which this geopower operates, empowering some forms of mobility and restricting others.[13] Critical to this understanding is what we might refer to as a "relational" understanding of sociality, one that frames the human and non-human as mutually constituted in and through sociopolitical relations and that straddles the nature/culture divide.[14] From this perspective, we can see, for instance, how the materiality of oceanic spaces (the liquidity of water, the architecture of waves, the seasonality of meteorological conditions, etc.) and the invention of new means of navigation (as well as the policies that determine who can and cannot access them) interact to make the sea "oscillate between states of fluidity, enabling the passage of people, forms, and ideas and states of solidity, blocking passage under given political and historical circumstances."[15]

DESIGNING HOSTILITY

A central aim of our work has been to reveal how the Mediterranean Sea's geopower has been mobilized in the context of border control to constitute a perilous liquid mass. This process not only makes migrants' journeys extremely precarious, threatening to swallow their lives at any moment; it also functions to distance migrant death from the eyes of the European public and to shirk any responsibility for these deaths by presenting them as "natural," ultimately shifting the blame onto the sea itself.

This process of weaponization can hardly be understood if the analytical frame remains exclusively focused on the space of the sea alone. As Maribel

Casas-Cortés and Sebastian Cobarrubias argue in this volume, contemporary border control must be thought of as a series of concentric circles whose reach extends well beyond that of the physical manifestation of the border (understood as a linear demarcation separating sovereign states).[16] Among the factors that have most prominently contributed to making the Mediterranean crossing dangerous is the increasing denial of visas to citizens of the global South since the end of the 1980s, in conjunction with the consolidation of freedom of movement within the European Union. As a result, a growing number of migrants were illegalized—barred access to safe and legal means of transportation and forced, in turn, to cross the sea on increasingly more unseaworthy and overcrowded vessels.

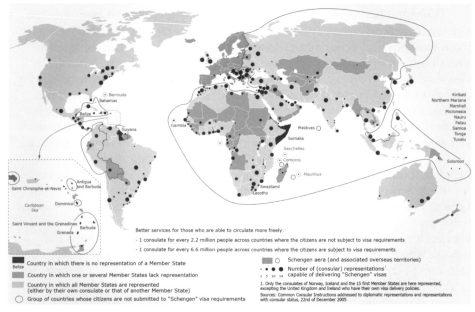

Fig 2: "At the front lines of the Schengen zone." From *Atlas of Migration in Europe: A Critical Geography of Migration Policies* (Oxford: New Internationalist, 2013). Courtesy of Olivier Clochard, Migreurop.

But it is also the space of the sea itself that has been transformed. Complex and overlapping jurisdictions at sea play a fundamental role in creating the conditions that structurally lead to the death of migrants. At sea, border crossing is a process that can last several days and that extends across an uneven and heterogeneous territory that sits outside the exclusive reach of any single polity. At sea, the spatial imaginary of the border as a line without thickness dividing isomorphic territorial states is stretched into a deep zone "in which the gaps and discrepancies between legal borders become uncertain and contested."[17] As soon as a migrants' boat sets off, it passes through the many jurisdictional regimes that crisscross the Mediterranean: from the various areas defined in the UN Convention on the Law of the Sea to Search and Rescue Regions, from ecological and archaeological protection zones to areas of maritime surveillance. At the same time, it is caught between legal regimes that depend on the juridical status applied to those on board (refugees, economic migrants, illegals); on the rationale of the operations that involve them (such as rescue and interception); and on many other factors.

These overlaps, conflicts of delimitation, and differing interpretations are not malfunctions but rather structural characteristics of the maritime frontier that have allowed states to simultaneously extend their sovereign privileges through forms of mobile government and elude the responsibilities that come with it.[18] For instance, the strategic mobilization of the notion of "rescue" has allowed coastal states to justify police operations on the high seas, yet the overlapping and conflicting Search and Rescue Regions have also led to recurrent cases of nonassistance to migrants in distress.[19] In contrast to the trope of the sea as a lawless zone, whose liquidity would make it impossible to draw stable boundaries, here it is not the absence of law but rather the proliferation and spatial entanglement of different legal regimes across the maritime border— what we might call, as Keller Easterling has, its "disposition"—that has created an "unfolding potential," an "inherent agency" that "makes certain things possible and other things impossible," ultimately producing large-scale violence.[20]

Fig 3: Map of maritime jurisdictions in the Mediterranean, based on data compiled by Marineplan (www.marineplan.es) and the International Maritime Organization. Courtesy of Forensic Oceanography.

While these policy and legal transformations created the overall conditions in which migrants' deaths occur on a structural basis, the sea has been made more or less deadly through specific operational shifts. In particular, operational areas of different maritime activities (search and rescue operations but also border control and military operations) have been drawn and redrawn over the course of the last few years. For instance, as we have documented in a report published in 2016 titled "Death by Rescue," EU agencies have sought to use the shrinking of operational areas and the resulting increased risk for migrants as a means of deterrence—even though well aware that this would lead to an increase in the number of fatalities.[21] As explicitly stated in a document produced by Frontex, the European Border and Coast Guard Agency, cutting back rescue operations "could become a deterrence for facilitation networks and migrants… taking into account that the boat must now navigate for several days before being rescued or intercepted." These different practices disclose a specific form of liquid violence that operates at the European Union's maritime frontier—one that operates in an indirect way, not only *at* sea but *through* the sea, *mediating* between state policies and practices on the one hand and the bodies and lives of migrants on the other.[22]

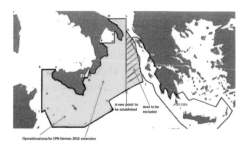

Fig 4: Evaluation of operational area shifts. From a document titled "Concept of Reinforced Joint Operation Tackling the Migratory Flows towards Italy: JO EPN-Triton" (Frontex, 2014), 9.

What emerges quite clearly from these examples is the process of *design* at work in the becoming hostile of deserts, oceans, and mountain ranges as borderlands. It is through this process that these environments are transformed into *terrains*. As Stuart Elden has effectively pointed out, the term "terrain" designates "a relation of power, with a heritage in geology and the military, the control of which allows the establishment and maintenance of order."[23] Paraphrasing him, we might say that hydrology and policing strategies conspire in the Mediterranean to create the conditions in which (b)ordering occurs.

SENSING PRACTICES WITHIN AND AGAINST THE BORDER

Media and sensing technologies play an essential role in the transformation of the sea into a hostile terrain. The selective conditions of (dis)appearance, (in)audibility, and (in)visibility they impose on the sea are intimately linked to its weaponization. Contrary to popular representation of maritime territory as an empty expanse, the sea appears today as a technologically mediated space thick with events and complex relations between people, environments, and data. For instance, the coasts of the Mediterranean as well as state-operated vessels are equipped with radar that scan the horizon by sending out high-frequency radio waves that can reveal objects within a certain radius. Automated vessel-tracking data for large commercial ships or for fishing boats is sent out by a transponder on board via very high frequency radio and captured by coastal or satellite receivers, providing a view of all registered vessels out at sea. Optical as well as synthetic aperture radar satellites generate images by "snapping" the surface of the sea according to their orbiting trajectories and are used to detect unidentified vessels or track pollution. Meteorological and oceanographic sensing devices collect data about air and water temperature, wind, currents, and the like.

This vast sensorium, which constantly records, transmits, stores, and broadcasts information about what happens at sea for many different purposes, has come to play a very important role in the context of policing cross-Mediterranean migration insofar as states use it to shed light on acts of unauthorized border crossing. Different feeds are assembled within maritime surveillance rooms with the aim of achieving the most complete "integrated maritime picture" possible. Through this assemblage emerges what Karin Knorr Cetina has called, with reference to financial markets, a "scopic system": "an arrangement of hardware, software, and human feeds that together function like a scope: like a mechanism of observation and projection."[24]

Fig 5: Finmeccanica PowerPoint slide from "Dal VTS al VTMIS" (Rome: Finmeccanica, 2007). The graphic presents the Vessel Traffic Management and Information System (VTMIS), a model for the assemblage of multiple remote sensing technologies to produce an integrated maritime picture.

However, despite the optimistic promises of full-spectrum visibility that are ubiquitous in state agencies and surveillance companies' communiqués, the Mediterranean's scopic system does not produce a totalizing panoptic view but rather operates a form of incomplete and patchy surveillance. This is due in part to the conflict between information quantity and resolution, which makes it difficult for these sensing technologies to monitor vast areas closely enough to detect small vessels used by migrants. But it is also a consequence of the "stubborn materiality" of the ocean, where the work of detection is affected by the presence of waves, fog, etc.[25] From this perspective, we can see how sensing practices "emerge, take hold, and form attachments across environmental, material, political, and aesthetic concerns, subjects and milieus… shifting from an assumed human-centered set of perceiving and decoding practices, to extended entities, technologies, and environments of sense."[26] These environments are not simply the inert background instrumentalized by border control; they participate in and come to matter to practices of border enforcement, enhancing or inhibiting detection capabilities depending on, as detailed above, meteorological as well as sociotechnical conditions.

Aware of the uneven nature of these surveillance efforts, the control of the European Union's maritime frontier tends to focus on what a security consultancy company called CIVIPOL has defined, in a report to the European Commission, as "focal routes… which account for more than 70 percent–80 percent of detected cases of illegal immigration by sea" and whose locations are dictated by geography: "straits or narrow passages where Schengen countries lie close to countries of transit or migration: the Straits of Gibraltar, the Sicilian Channel, Adriatic Sea, the Dodecanese island channels, the Canary Islands Channel and the Gulf of Finland."[27] These nodes of logistical tension are ones where "the surveillance required is highly intensive, detailed, and semi-permanent in virtually constant areas."[28] However, rather than stopping the inflow of illegalized migrants, CIVIPOL itself acknowledges that "when a standard destination is shut off by surveillance and interception measures, attempts to enter tend to shift to another, generally more difficult, destination on a broader and therefore riskier stretch of water."[29] This splintering and funneling of migration routes toward longer and more perilous areas is one of the main mechanisms leading to migrants' death on a structural basis, de facto turning the sea into an unwilling killer. In this lethal mechanism, the effect of border control at the maritime frontier echoes what has long been observed in the US–Mexico border desert as the strategy of "prevention through deterrence," which was adopted by US border guards as early as 1993. By deploying massive numbers of agents along the sections of the border that are easiest to cross, usually around urban areas, migrants are pushed to cross in deserts and other inhospitable areas, often leading to cases of death. "Prevention through deterrence" thus most fully (and most explicitly) acknowledges the ways in which the desert's environmental characteristics have been deployed for the enforcement of political borders.[30]

Our work has attempted to reverse the process by which surveillance technologies are used to weaponize terrains—using them instead to challenge the deadly effects of border control. This is perhaps most clearly exemplified in the ways satellite imagery and drift modeling were used in the frame of our investigation of the "left-to-die boat" case.[31] In this incident, seventy-two passengers were left to drift for fourteen days despite repeated contacts with ships and helicopters in an area closely monitored by tens of military assets deployed in the context of the 2011 military intervention in Libya, which led to the slow death of sixty-three people.[32] By combining a satellite image taken at the time of the event with a spatial model that mapped the trajectory of the drifting on the basis of wind and current data recorded by various meteorological and oceanographic sensors, we were able to establish that the bright pixels in the image were large ships located in the vicinity of the migrants' boat just as it had run out of fuel. All vessels in the area had been informed of the distress of the migrants as well as the boat's position and could have easily rescued them—yet all chose not to intervene. Instead, they abandoned them to the wind and currents. While their act of nonintervention transformed the sea into an unwilling killer, our project sought to turn it into a witness of sorts.

Satellite imagery and drift modeling are just some of the many techniques we have used to offer an alternative reading of the ocean and of this dramatic event. This reading has meant mobilizing against the grain the vast and technologically mediated sensorium that is often used for the purpose of policing illegalized migration, repurposing it to produce evidence of a crime of nonassistance. Instead of replicating the technological eye of policing and its untenable promise of full-spectrum visibility, we exercised what we called a "disobedient gaze," one that redirected the light shed by the surveillance apparatus away from illegalized migration and back toward the act of policing itself.[33] While, as Bruno Latour reminds us, the capacity to sense events should come with "sensitivity"—the ability to respond or, in the term offered by various feminist new materialist scholars, a "*response*-ability"—the lack of response despite the knowledge generated by surveillance became, in this case, proof of guilt.[34] In this way, we attempted to close the gap separating the possibility of sensing a certain event (of distress) and the obligation to intervene.

Fig 6: Analysis of March 29, 2011 Envisat satellite image showing the modeled position of the "left-to-die boat" (yellow diagonal hatch) and the nearby presence of several military vessels that did not intervene to rescue the migrants. Courtesy of Forensic Oceanography and SITU Research.

BORDER ENVIRONMENTALITY

Taking as starting point the United Kingdom's "hostile environment" policy but using it as a conceptual lens to explore the complex relations between migration, borders, and media across different terrains—the cities, oceans, deserts, and mountains that have been rendered inhospitable to migrants—what we see at work is a distinct form of border control, an immanent field of governmental intervention operating across different terrains, or, to use Foucault's language, a form of *environmentality*. While this notion has been taken up mostly in the context of environmental studies, Jennifer Gabrys usefully reconceptualizes it in more general terms as the multiple ways in which "environments, technologies, and ways of life [are] governed through… particular environmental distributions."[35]

This expanded notion of the environment as governance provides us with a number of fresh insights. To start with, it allows us to challenge essentialist conceptions of the environment. Indeed, while the latter is commonly understood as a "neutral or passive term describing the environs of humans," that which is around and clearly differentiated from the actions of humans, environments, as we have seen, are far more than "natural" backgrounds to human action.[36] They are "a sign for the dynamic relationships between entities, within and around us and across different scales, temporalities, and strata," that shape human (in)action in decisive ways.[37]

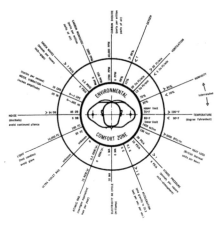

The first circle is the bearable zone limit. Outside this limit great discomfort or possible damage is encountered. It is also necessary to consider: infra-red radiation, ultra sonic vibration, noxious gases, dust, pollen, and heat exchange with liquids and solids.
Note: All data here are subject to qualification, refer to reference sources; for complete information see bibliography.

Fig 7: One of the most prominent diagrams in Henry Dreyfuss's renowned design standards guide *The Measure of Man* (New York: Whitney Library of Design, 1967). It encapsulates a well-engrained modernist vision that sees human beings as sharply separated from and constantly under threat from different environmental forces. This vision produces the understanding that architecture's role is to create a shelter to protect humans from that which threatens them: the environment. It presupposes a stark ontological distinction between human beings and their surroundings—one that has been cogently criticized by Adrian Lahoud, who reveals the colonial, Eurocentric roots of this clichéd vision. See, for instance, his lecture "Origins, Shelters, Traps," at Iowa State University College of Design, February 7, 2018, https://www.youtube.com/watch?v=ZKqcpoL4DY4.

Second, this reconceptualization of "hostile environment"(s) allows us to better perceive the connections that exist between the weaponization of the Mediterranean Sea and the strategies of UK border control. In both cases, environment should be understood not simply as a site of border control but rather as one of its modes of operation. This was effectively captured by the NGO Corporate Watch, which argued that the rationale of Theresa May's policies could be summarized as follows: "if the government can't actually seal tight the external borders, it can push unwanted 'illegals' to leave, or deter others from coming in the first place, by making it near impossible to live a normal life."[38] As this quote reveals, May's hostile environment policies have conjured up a diffused "atmosphere of surveillance," a form of racialized violence that has become, in terms proposed by Christina Sharpe, as pervasive as the weather.[39] In this sense, their aims and modes of operation are not dissimilar from the policies that, as we have seen, turn the terrains migrants are forced to cross on their way to Europe (oceans, deserts, mountains) into hazardous environments, producing death and suffering on a vast scale.

Finally, the notion of "hostile environment"(s) allows us to shed a different light on the becoming hostile of environments as a result of extractive practices, climate change, and armed conflict—some of the many intertwined factors that lead migrants to seek opportunities beyond borders in the first place. As Rob Nixon has suggested, displacement should be understood not simply as "the movement of people from their places of belonging" but also as "the loss of the land and resources beneath them, a loss that leaves communities stranded in a place stripped of the very characteristics that made it inhabitable."[40]

This perspective carries implications that are deep and that we can only start to fathom here. It demands, to start with, that resistance to border violence be rethought both as the possibility of escaping toxic milieus and as a struggle against what Malini Ranganathan calls "environmental unfreedoms," all those "threats to our water, air, food, land, schools, and homes" that "mark contemporary racialised environments" and "constrain our individual and collective potential."[41] What is at stake here is not only the freedom to move, which has been one of the main rallying cries for border struggles across and beyond

Europe, but also the freedom to settle and stay put. This approach also suggests that struggles around migration and borders might be further grounded in a posthuman ethics that connects the movement of people to the movement that is inherent in all vibrant matter and its infinite combinations.[42] For if, as Achille Mbembe suggests through his formulation of an "ethics of the passerby," we are all existentially only passersby on this earth and through life, if the flow of life unites us in a multispecies and multi-elemental belonging, and if we are contingently tied to but also inherently detached from (without being indifferent to) the multiple locations we come to cross through our life trajectories, then any claim to territorial possession is always tenuous.[43] After all, as Claire Colebrook reminds us, from an ecological perspective, "life *is* displacement in the face of one's milieu becoming hostile."[44] The claims to exclusive territoriality and belonging that nation-states have established and that are policed by borders thus begin to fracture and appear for what they are: illusions of control and fixity for the privileged few that scar the surface of a world in which different *strata*—including human bodies—are always on the move at different speeds and scales.[45] When looking at bordering practices from this perspective, we might begin to detect a secret, deep, and elemental solidarity between environments and migrants. At times, we might be able to catch a glimpse of it coming to the surface and materializing furtively—such as when, in the winter of 2014, high winds toppled part of a new metal fence erected in the French port of Calais to prevent migrants from slipping onto UK-bound ferries.[46] In this, as on many other occasions, "hostile environment" policies in all their guises come up against the unruly force of human movement and of the elements alike.

Fig 8: Migrant fence toppled by high winds in the French port city of Calais. The fence had been built to prevent migrants from boarding UK-bound ferries illegally. © Philippe Huguen/ AFP/Getty Images.

CHARLES HELLER is a researcher and filmmaker whose work has a long-standing focus on the politics of migration. In 2015 he completed a PhD in research architecture at Goldsmiths, University of London, where he continues to be affiliated as a research fellow. He is currently based in Geneva, conducting a postdoctoral research supported by the Swiss National Fund.

LORENZO PEZZANI is an architectural researcher. In 2015 he completed a PhD in research architecture at Goldsmiths, University of London, where he is currently lecturer and leads the MA studio in Forensic Architecture. His work deals with the spatial politics and visual cultures of migration, with a particular focus on the geography of the ocean.

1   James Kirkup and Robert Winnett, "Theresa May Interview: 'We're Going to Give Illegal Migrants a Really Hostile Reception,'" *Telegraph*, May 25, 2012, https://www.telegraph.co.uk/news/uknews/immigration/9291483/Theresa-May-interview-Were-going-to-give-illegal-migrants-a-really-hostile-reception.html.

2   Kirkup and Winnett, "Theresa May Interview."

3   For an overview of fatalities recorded along these different border zones, see the International Organization for Migration's "Missing Migrants Project," http://missingmigrants.iom.int.

4   See the list of migrant deaths at the European borders established by UNITED for Intercultural Action: http://unitedagainstrefugeedeaths.eu/about-the-campaign/about-the-united-list-of-deaths.

5   Joseph Nevins, *Operation Gatekeeper: The Rise of the "Illegal Alien" and the Making of the US–Mexico Boundary* (New York: Routledge, 2002), 144. As an example of the work we have produced in the context of the Forensic Oceanography project, see "The Left-to-Die Boat," https://www.forensic-architecture.org/case/left-die-boat.

6   Michel Foucault, *Security, Territory, Population: Lectures at the Collège de France*, 1977–78 (New York: Palgrave Macmillan, 2007), 20–23.

7   Foucault, *Security, Territory, Population*, 22–23. For an insightful discussion, see Federico Luisetti, "Geopower: On the States of Nature of Late Capitalism," *European Journal of Social Theory* 18, no. 3 (October 2018): 327–342.

8   Peter Sahlins, "Natural Frontiers Revisited: France's Boundaries since the Seventeenth Century," *American Historical Review* 95, no. 5 (December 1990): 1424.

9   Sahlins, "Natural Frontiers Revisited," 1423.

10   Bernard Debarbieux and Gilles Rudaz, *The Mountain: A Political History from the Enlightenment to the Present* (Chicago: University of Chicago Press, 2015), 57.

11   Ellen Churchill Semple, *Influences of Geographic Environment on the Basis of Ratzel's System of Anthropo-Geography* (New York: Henry Holt and Company, 1911), 214.

12   Semple, *Influences of Geographic Environment*, 292. A more recent example of this double function of the sea as barrier and bridge has been offered by Renaud Morieux in his historical account of the construction of the maritime frontier across the English Channel. Willy Maley, "'Is It a Barrier? Is It a Bridge?': The Channel: England, France, and the Construction of a Maritime Border in the Eighteenth Century, by Renaud Morieux," *Times Higher Education*, June 2016, https://www.timeshighereducation.com/books/review-the-channel-england-france-construction-maritime-border-eighteenth-century-renaud-morieux-cambridge-university-press.

13   Duncan Depledge, "Geopolitical Material: Assemblages of Geopower and the Constitution of the Geopolitical Stage," *Political Geography* 45, no. 2 (2015): 1. For more on Grosz's notion of "geopower," see Elizabeth Grosz, Kathryn Yusoff, and Nigel Clark, "An Interview with Elizabeth Grosz: Geopower, Inhumanism, and the Biopolitical," *Theory, Culture, & Society* 34, no. 2–3 (May 2017): 129–146, https://journals.sagepub.com/doi/pdf/10.1177/0263276417689899.

14   Juanita Sundberg, "Diabolic Caminos in the Desert and Cat Fights on the Río: A Posthumanist Political Ecology of Boundary Enforcement in the United States–Mexico Borderlands," *Annals of the Association of American Geographers* 101, no. 2 (March 2011): 318–336, https://doi.org/10.1080/00045608.2010.538323.

15   Vyjayanthi Rao, "Speculative Seas," in *The Sea-Image: Visual Manifestations of Port Cities and Global Waters*, ed. Güven Incirlioglu and Hakan Topal (New York: Newgray, 2011), 124.

16   See Maribel Casas-Cortés and Sebastian Cobarrubias, "A War on Mobility: The Border Empire Strikes Back?," in this volume.

17   Brett Neilson, "Between Governance and Sovereignty: Remaking the Borderscape to Australia's North," *Local-Global Journal* 8 (2010): 126, http://mams.rmit.edu.au/56k3qh2kfcx1.pdf.

18   Philip E. Steinberg, *The Social Construction of the Ocean* (Cambridge, UK: Cambridge University Press, 2001); Thomas Gammeltoft-Hansen and Tanja E. Alberts, "Sovereignty at Sea: The Law and Politics of Saving Lives in the Mare Liberum," DIIS Working Paper (2010): 1–31.

19   Ruben Andersson, "A Game of Risk: Boat Migration and the Business of Bordering Europe," *Anthropology Today* 28, no. 6 (December 2012): 7–11, https://doi.org/10.1111/j.1467-8322.2012.00910.x.

20   Keller Easterling, *Extrastatecraft: The Power of Infrastructure Space* (New York: Verso Books, 2014), 14.

21   See "Death by Rescue," https://www.forensic-architecture.org/case/death-by-rescue.

22   We expand on this notion in Charles Heller and Lorenzo Pezzani, "Liquid Violence: Migrant Deaths at Sea and the Responsibility of European States," in *Transit: Art, Mobility, and Migration in the Age of Globalisation*, ed. Sabine Dahl Nielsen (Aalborg: Aalborg University Press, 2019).

23   Stuart Elden, "Land, Terrain, Territory," *Progress in Human Geography* 34, no. 6 (2010): 804.

24   Karin Knorr Cetina, "The Synthetic Situation: Interactionism for a Global World," *Symbolic Interaction* 32, no. 1 (2009): 64.

25   Philip Steinberg and Kimberley Peters, "Wet Ontologies, Fluid Spaces: Giving Depth to Volume through Oceanic Thinking," *Environment and Planning D: Society and Space* 33, no. 2 (April 2015): 247–264, https://doi.org/10.1068/d14148p.

26   Jennifer Gabrys and Helen Pritchard, "Sensing Practices," in *Posthuman Glossary*, ed. Rosi Braidotti and Maria Hlavajova (New York: Bloomsbury Academic, 2018), 394.

27   CIVIPOL, "Feasibility Study on the Control of the European Union's Maritime Borders," European Commission, April 7, 2003, http://www.ifmcr.org/assets/documents/files/documents_ifm/st11490-re01en03.pdf.

28   CIVIPOL, "Feasibility Study."

29   CIVIPOL, "Feasibility Study."

30   Sundberg, "Diabolic Caminos"; Jason De Leon, *The Land of Open Graves: Living and Dying on the Migrant Trail* (Oakland: University of California Press, 2015).

31   See Forensic Oceanography, "Left-to-Die Boat."

32   Charles Heller and Lorenzo Pezzani, "Liquid Traces: Investigating the Deaths of Migrants at the EU's Maritime Frontier," in *Forensis: The Architecture of Public Truth*, ed. Anselm Franke and Eyal Weizman (Berlin: Sternberg Press, 2014), 656–684.

33   Lorenzo Pezzani and Charles Heller, "A Disobedient Gaze: Strategic Interventions in the Knowledge(s) of Maritime Borders," *Postcolonial Studies* 16, no. 3 (September 2013): 289–298, https://doi.org/10.1080/13688790.2013.850047.

34   Bruno Latour, "The Anthropocene and the Destruction of the Image of the Globe," Latour's Fourth Gifford Lecture, University of Edinburgh, March 1, 2013, https://www.giffordlectures.org/videos/anthropocene-and-destruction-image-globe. Karen Barad, *Meeting the Universe Halfway: Quantum Physics and the Entanglement of Matter and Meaning* (Durham, NC: Duke University Press, 2007).

35   Jennifer Gabrys, *Program Earth: Environmental Sensing Technology and the Making of a Computational Planet* (Minneapolis: University of Minnesota Press, 2016), 191.

36   Rafi Youatt, "Interspecies," in *The Oxford Handbook of Environmental Political Theory*, ed. Teena Gabrielson et al., vol. 1 (Oxford: Oxford University Press, 2016), 212, https://doi.org/10.1093/oxfordhb/9780199685271.013.4.

37   Carrie Hamilton and Yasmin Gunaratnam, "Environment," *Feminist Review* 118, no. 1 (April 2018): 1, https://doi.org/10.1057/s41305-018-0096-9.

38   See "The Hostile Environment: Turning the UK into a Nation of Border Cops," April 8, 2017, https://corporatewatch.org/the-hostile-environment-turning-the-uk-into-a-nation-of-border-cops-2.

39   Darren Ellis, Ian Tucker, and David Harper, "The Affective Atmospheres of Surveillance," *Theory and Psychology* 23, no. 6 (December 2013): 716–731, https://doi.org/10.1177/0959354313496604; Christina Elizabeth Sharpe, *In the Wake: On Blackness and Being* (Durham, NC: Duke University Press, 2016).

40   Rob Nixon, *Slow Violence and the Environmentalism of the Poor* (Cambridge, MA: Harvard University Press, 2011), 19. We are grateful to Nishat Awan for pointing us to this formulation.

41   Malini Ranganathan, "The Environment as Freedom: A Decolonial Reimagining," *Items: Insights from the Social Sciences*, June 13, 2017, https://items.ssrc.org/the-environment-as-freedom-a-decolonial-reimagining.

42   Jane Bennett, *Vibrant Matter: A Political Ecology of Things* (Durham, NC: Duke University Press, 2010).

43   Achille Mbembe, *Politiques de l'inimitié* (Paris: Édition la Découverte, 2016), 173–179.

44   Claire Colebrook, "Transcendental Migration: Taking Refuge from Climate Change," in *Life Adrift: Climate Change, Migration, Critique*, ed. Andrew Baldwin and Giovanni Bettini (London: Rowman & Littlefield International, 2017), 119.

45   Andrew Baldwin and Giovanni Bettini, *Life Adrift: Climate Change, Migration, Critique* (London: Rowman & Littlefield, 2017), 16–18.

46   "Calais Migrant Fence Blown Down by Wind in French Port," BBC, December 27, 2014, https://www.bbc.com/news/world-europe-30613475.

Urban Intermedia: City, Archive, Narrative

Eve Blau

Urban Intermedia: City, Archive, Narrative is a multimedia research project, methodological experiment, and exhibition that is part of an ongoing exploration of new collaborative practices and projects that bring together scholarship, design, and media around the study of cities.[1] As a capstone project of the Harvard Mellon Urban Initiative (2013–2018)—a multi-year, cross-university research and teaching program, supported by funding from the Andrew W. Mellon Foundation—*Urban Intermedia* engages the objectives of the initiative: to connect scholars and designers to develop new visual and digital methods and cross-disciplinary approaches to the study of urban environments, societies, and cultures.[2] Four city-based research projects, in Berlin, Boston, Istanbul, and Mumbai, directed by Harvard faculty, form the core of the project. Conceived as *portals* into different geographies and urban issues, these projects open a broad field of comparative urban study.[3]

Three foundational ideas have guided the Harvard Mellon Urban Initiative and the *Urban Intermedia* project. The first: no discipline "owns" the city, an idea that acknowledges that each discipline produces its own forms of knowledge but also has its own blind spots or "residues" (as Henri Lefebvre called them) that "evade its grasp" and can be approached only through other disciplinary frameworks.[4] The second: the fixed categories by which we have traditionally understood the urban no longer hold. They have been undermined by the multiplicity of disparate urban formations that are transforming cities across the planet. In order to understand the dynamics of emerging conditions and the proliferating differences they produce, urban research needs to be both specific and site-based, as well as comparative across geographies and cultures. The third: we must engage directly with the relationship between the tools and objects of urban research—with how the digitized information, communication, and media technologies we use to visualize and understand urban environments are changing both the ways we research and the kinds of knowledge we produce from it. These conditions call for direct critical engagement with the dynamic and synergistic relationship between the instruments and the objects of research.

As points of departure, these ideas inform a set of research questions around urban processes, conditions, and practices. Together they provide the comparative ground between the individual city-based research projects and the issues they raise: (1) What can we learn about urban processes if we look at the inter-relation of the *planned and the unplanned*; how do formal and informal practices work together to shape the city? (2) What does the urban imprint of patterns of migration and mobility tell us about the modalities of inclusion and exclusion, and the complex ways that claims on space are made by (or denied to) different groups? (3) How does the relationship between nature and technology create and sustain urban environments; how do technical

Fig 1: View of the *Urban Intermedia: City, Archive, Narrative* installation at the Aedes Architecture Forum, Berlin, January 2018. All images © Harvard Mellon Urban Initiative.

Fig 2: Still from the Berlin narrative, *City-Fabric: Between Systems and Sites*, Berlin: Experimental Ground, Urban Intermedia, 2018.

infrastructures shape natural landscapes in processes of urbanization; how do natural resource flows (material and energy) impact urban and larger territorial ecologies?

The overarching agenda of each research portal is to probe the blind spots of established narratives—focusing on topics and sites considered outside the dominant conceptual frameworks of urban research on those cities. Boston: Race and Space, for example, brings into focus the long-standing racialized policies and exclusionary practices that produced the enormous disparities (in terms of access to housing, jobs, public transportation, and social amenities) between predominantly white and nonwhite inner-city neighborhoods, which persist today. Mumbai: Claims on the City examines places in the megacity that acknowledge and commemorate the cultures and environments of those excluded from the space of global capital flow. Istanbul: Metropolitan Flux shows the collusion between government-sponsored large-scale planning and unregulated private development that enabled the massive expansion of the city into the European and Asian hinterlands on both sides of the Bosporus. Berlin: Experimental Ground reveals how the city's large-scale urban grid and block system was a structuring device that, rather than producing uniformity and dullness, engendered complexity and difference—supporting a productive urban mix of social uses, classes, and practices—and shows how this resilient urban form has been appropriated as a platform for a wide range of successive uses and constituencies.

The challenge for the *Urban Intermedia* project was how to present both the research findings and the methods developed in the course of investigating each city through its disciplinary blind spots, and to do so through the archival and analytical materials used and produced in the course of the research itself. This challenge became its own project—a collective project—developed collaboratively over the course of a year by the curators (Robert Pietrusko and I), the faculty directors of each city-based research portal, and an extensive team of doctoral and design students and recent Harvard Graduate School of Design graduates (see credits in footnote 1). In the pages that follow, I would like to focus on *this* project and the methods that were conceived to realize it—to represent conditions that resist representation and to construct arguments and stories that are more nuanced, multifaceted, and plurivalent than the disciplinary frameworks of any one field of inquiry.

Complexity is theoretical and empirical. Conceptually, as Manfredo Tafuri pointed out, a project that seeks to speak across disciplines, whether through a new kind of "intermedia" language or by some other means, must not only "ceaselessly question" its own methods and materials but also "continuously reconstruct itself" as a project.[5] This involves not only "incorporating uncertainty" into the methods and critical frameworks of research but also conceiving of the project itself as an experiment—the real task of which, according to Tafuri, is to expand or "widen" the scope of the project "by taking apart, putting together, contradicting, provoking languages and syntaxes" in order to push the project "outside of its own boundaries" while nevertheless remaining "solidly anchored to the ground."[6] To chart such a course is to venture into perilous interdisciplinary territory, especially if the object of study is the urban.

Henri Lefebvre had a great deal to say about the perils and pitfalls of interdisciplinary urban study. "The urban phenomenon, taken as a whole," he asserts in *The Urban Revolution*, "cannot be grasped by any specialized science [because] no science can claim to exhaust it. Or control it. Once we have acknowledged or established this, the difficulties begin. How many of us," he asks, "are unaware of the disappointments and setbacks that resulted from so-called inter- and multi-disciplinary efforts? The illusions of such studies, and the myths surrounding them have been abundantly criticized"—indeed, extensively by Lefebvre himself.[7] The main problem is one of terminology—of language—which Lefebvre calls the "academic Babel" that produces "scientific hermeticism" and results in interdisciplinary "confusion."[8] Yet the complexity of "the urban phenomenon," Lefebvre acknowledges, requires disciplinary cooperation, precisely because of the blind spots that emerge out of it: "the farther a given science pushes its analysis, the more it reveals the presence of a *residue*. It is this residue that evades its grasp. And, although essential, it can only be approached using different methods."[9] He goes on to propose that "if every discipline were to succeed in bringing into view some residue, they would all soon become irreducible."[10] And, although "the complexity of the urban phenomenon is not that of an 'object,'" it can perform useful theoretical work as a *virtual object*—a theoretically possible object that "envelops a whole range of problems" that are too complex to be grasped by any field alone.[11] In fact, Lefebvre suggests, a new field could emerge, "a differential field" of urban praxis that could engage the full complexity of the urban, including the disciplinary residues of urban research, in terms of "the urban problematic."[12]

Lefebvre's notion of the virtual object of urban research as a conceptual tool for bridging disciplinary boundaries and for advancing a differential field of urban praxis that would make visible the accumulated blind spots of urban research informs both the critical framework of *Urban Intermedia* and the operative concept of *media* on which it is based. That concept (of media) is envisaged as a convergence of *science-based* and *culture-based* conceptions of medium—that is, as a matrix constituted of both the *environment* and the *means by which we engage and understand it*.[13] This convergence is itself conceived in ecological terms, as an ecosystem that is never static but is in a permanent state of disequilibrium, continuously triggering new sets of interactions between the environments and the cultures they support.

More specific questions about the dynamic and synergistic relationship between the tools and objects of urban research follow from the continuously transforming project of urban research, questions that revolve around the interrelation of physical and digital media: How are the materials and methods of urban research—and by extension the stories we tell with them—being transformed by new media formats and technologies? In this context, what constitutes an archive, and how might physical archival materials be incorporated into digital forms of urban scholarship? Is it possible to tell stories and construct arguments that speak across disciplinary boundaries through a shared media language? And how would such a "shared media language" challenge the dominant conceptual frameworks of urban research?

These theoretical questions drive the empirical research and the discursive format of the *Urban Intermedia* project and exhibition, which consist of a series of visual narratives composed of the research material gathered over three years of archival research and fieldwork in Berlin, Boston, Istanbul, and Mumbai. Digitized and animated, to unfold in space and over time, the narratives are constructed using a range of digital design techniques, developed by Robert Pietrusko, that allow us to combine the technologies and working methods of animation, drawing, typography, photography, 3D graphics, video, and other (physical, digital, and electronic) media technologies (see figure 3).

Conceptually, we imagine a virtual plane—an infinite white media surface—on which the images, maps, and other assembled materials are layered and brought into registration with one another. Once placed on the media surface, an image or piece of media never disappears. It remains an independent (virtual) object that can always be accessed. The virtual plane allows us to create densely layered assemblages that can be manipulated and reassembled as we explore the different spatialities and temporalities of the sites, and the layered social, political, and cultural meanings of the conditions and processes to which they give access. It also allows us to examine those conditions at multiple scales, from different perspectives, and across space and time, and to generate animated visual narratives exploring their meanings.[14] While the starting point of each narrative is always the present moment—the issues, topics, questions, and debates that are of urgent contemporary concern—the present is engaged historically and spatially through dense intermedia matrices, challenging any unitary understanding of urban environments and processes and leaving viewers to construct their own meanings from the material presented.

Each narrative is structured to tell its story without written or verbal narration (except for the occasional intertitle, a technique borrowed from silent films). Research material and media are left to narrate stories and shape arguments through their own visual languages and through the spatial and temporal relationships generated by animating new juxtapositions and adjacencies.

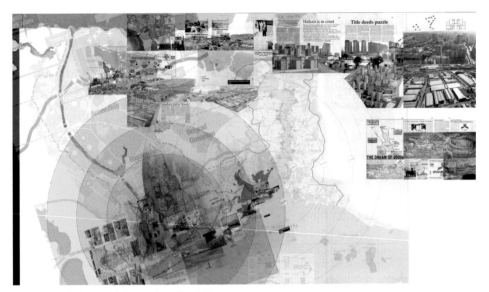

Fig 3: Virtual plane with layered media. Still
from the Istanbul narrative, *Making of an Edge*,
Istanbul: Metropolitan Flux, Urban Intermedia,
2018.

Iterative and incremental, the narratives capture a process of experimentation that involves a set of protocols, adopted in uncertainty, that transform the spatiotemporal unfolding of the narrative into a process of exploration and discovery. In the exhibition, the "final" narratives are presented in videos projected onto screens.

One of the three Berlin narratives, *City-Fabric: Between Systems and Sites*, for example, examines what makes the old inner-city district of Luisenstadt (today, part of Mitte and Kreuzberg and one of the principal sites of creative clustering in Berlin) such fertile, experimental ground (see figures 2 and 4). The narrative begins with the historical evolution of Berlin—through a sequential layering of historical maps, surveys, and plans that are brought into dialogue with one another. Luisenstadt emerges in relation to the region, its geology and its topography, and the growth of the city over centuries. As a low-lying, marshy swampland unsuitable for building, the site was one of the last inner-city districts of Berlin to be urbanized—beginning with a canal project by the landscape architect Peter Josef Lenné that was connected to a citywide system of waterways and parks. Zooming into the site, the layers thicken: new information and media create diverse entryways into a range of topics, questions, and lines of research. The canal (which made "nature suitable for culture") created the conditions for urban development: the expansion of infrastructure, the evolution of new institutions and legal codes, and the generation of new social practices and forms of cultural production.[15] These processes are examined through multiple lenses focusing on the intersection of technological innovation, political conflict, patterns of industrial development, migration, and settlement. Layering and animation make it possible to visualize processes of change and conditions of difference though narratives that are diachronic and synchronic—adding complexity and dimension to the multiple stories they bring together. Assemblages produce new knowledge. Through them, we begin to understand how planned and unplanned interventions, formal and informal practices, operate together to shape the organization and use of space in the city.

Other discoveries emerged out of the process of assembly. When we began materializing the narratives, we had detailed and carefully developed story lines and arguments that we wanted to build out of our research materials. But as the narratives began to take shape, so too did the images, documents, film footage, and other media but not in the way we anticipated. These materials would not stay within the confines of a single story line. Instead, they kept adding layers of information and introducing topics, critical perspectives, and new points of view that would break out of the original story line and send the narratives spinning off in new, unscripted directions. It became clear to us that the visual narratives we were constructing were uncontainable in terms of story line. Understanding that dynamic was critical to developing the project.

Fig 4: Sequence of stills (pages 214–217) from
Berlin narrative, *City-Fabric: Between Systems
and Sites.*

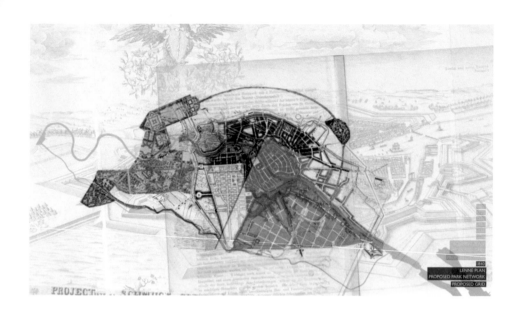

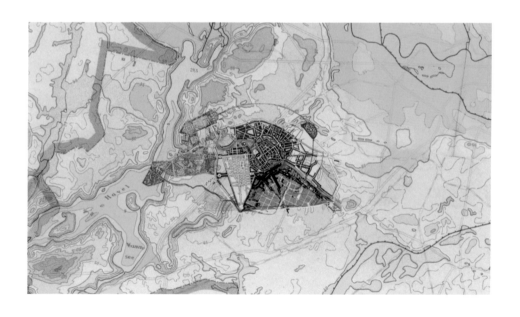

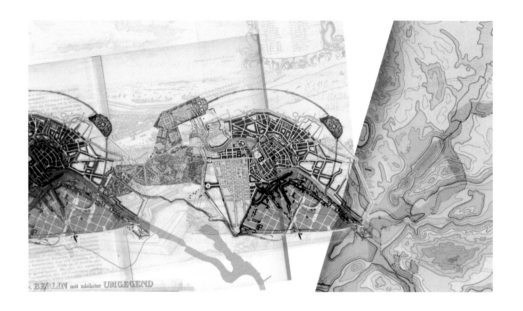

On one level, this uncontainability can be seen as a function of the "analog surplus value" of visual images—their potential and tendency to transmit information beyond the capacity of verbal language or to communicate more information about an object than verbal statements about the same object generally do.[16] As Otto Neurath, the Viennese philosopher of science and inventor of ISOTYPE (International System of Typographic Picture Education) argued, images invite multiple and conflicting readings and interpretations. Neurath called this ability—to shape and transfer (complex) information about the social and material world in a way that leaves the object itself open to shifting interpretations and meanings over time—the "either-or quality" of visual images or visual text: their capacity to embody a contradiction. He saw their most critical didactic value in "the teaching of how to argue."[17] The openness of the visual text, composed of images and other graphic forms of documentation, is a function of how (visual) texts themselves are constructed and the role of spatial design in their telling.

This is especially true in the context of the *Urban Intermedia* project. The narratives are constructed through a process of assembly, which is a method of composition that operates in terms of relationships—proximity, distance, juxtaposition, superimposition, transparency, opacity, and so on—that are spatial and visual. The process of assembly is very different from the process of explication as a way of telling stories and constructing arguments. The narratives that unfold are not only multiply layered and dense, they are also fundamentally open-ended, provisional, and mutable—continuously suggesting other stories that could be told with the same materials. They also tend to be nonlinear, to go backward and forward in time and to move freely in space. Assembly, in other words, leaves explication—the analytic process of explanation—to the viewers or users of the narratives. In doing so, it opens the narratives and the work as a whole to overwriting, to further imbrication, and to counternarration (see figure 5).

The concept of "intermedia" emerged over the course of our work and out of our practice. A hybrid word, *intermedia* references both the methods of digital compositing—by which the different media are brought together, hybridized, and animated in digital narratives—and the cultural significance of those capabilities for ways of knowing and producing knowledge about cities. As media theorist and designer Lev Manovich points out, these methods (of layering, remixing, and combining media of all kinds) were enabled by software programs developed in the early 1990s.[18] The software production environment of After Effects, for example, allows designers to "remix not only the content from different media [physical, digital, electronic] but also their fundamental techniques, working methods, and ways of representation and expression." The capabilities of After Effects and other digital design technologies make it possible to bring together the previously unique "languages of cinematography, animation, computer animation, special effects, graphic design, typography, drawing, and painting" to form a "new *metalanguage*."[19] But "when physical or electronic media are simulated in a computer, we do not simply end up with the same media as before," Manovich argues.[20] Instead, the techniques of digital compositing that make it possible to combine multiple levels of imagery with varying degrees of transparency, using interactive working methods that make the results immediately visible, fundamentally change both what the images look like and what they can say: "By adding new properties and working methods, computer simulation fundamentally changes the identity of given media."[21] Through these methods, the distinct languages of different media interact at the deepest structural levels. They hybridize, exchange properties and techniques, and, in the process, generate new hybrid "intermedia" languages that are both richer and more complex.[22] While this hybridized media language "inherits the traits" of other image media, it is a "true hybrid" with its own "distinct identity" that "is not reducible" to any of those media formats.[23]

"Deep remixability," as Manovich characterizes the "interactions between the working methods and techniques of different media" in the hybridized compositive media language of intermedia narratives, is also a critical component of research.[24] Deep remixability gives us access to new methods of experiencing and representing, and therefore also of navigating, understanding, interacting, and communicating with others about the conditions we seek to understand. At the same time, any one of the intermedia narratives can be disaggregated into the individual elements of which it is composed, and each one of those elements can be independently accessed, manipulated, and incorporated into any number of other compositive intermedia narratives (see figure 6).

In *Urban Intermedia*, we make this point, and the process it involves, explicit. Each narrative, therefore, generates its own archive, which comprises all the media used in the narrative and which scrolls across the bottom of the screen as the narrative unfolds above it. In the archival register, each piece of media is identified and documented along with its source when it first appears in the narrative, so that each document, photograph, map, film or video clip, or other object retains its historical and material integrity as an object. Synchronized with the narratives, the algorithmically generated archival register (which also includes an image of each object) functions both as visual documentation (footnotes/bibliography) for the visual text and a rolling repository from which any number of different narratives could be constructed (see figure 7).[25]

The open-ended dialogic format of *Urban Intermedia* is key to both the criticality and potential uses of the project. It is open-ended in two senses: First, the meaning of each particular story is purposefully not fixed. The overlapping of temporalities

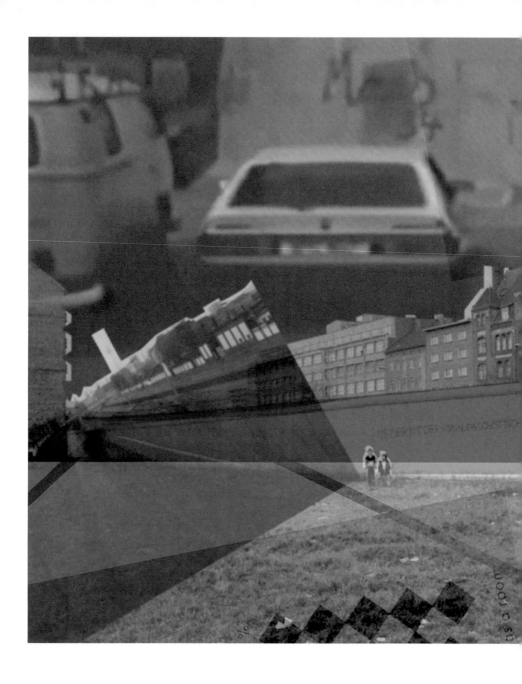

Fig 5: Sequence of stills (pages 220–223) from Berlin narrative, *City-Fabric: Between Systems and Sites*, showing methods by which temporalities and modes of representation are overlaid, allowing different media to tell stories about places and events simultaneously from different points of view and continuously suggesting other stories that could be told with the same materials.

Fig. 73—74.
Kanalprofile der Ber-
liner Kanalisation.

(Maasstab 1:50.)

Fig 6: Sequence of stills (pages 224–227) from
Berlin narrative, *City-Landscape: Rescaling
the Urban*, Berlin: Experimental Ground, Urban
Intermedia, 2018.

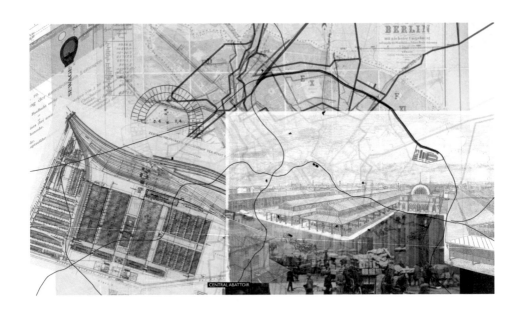

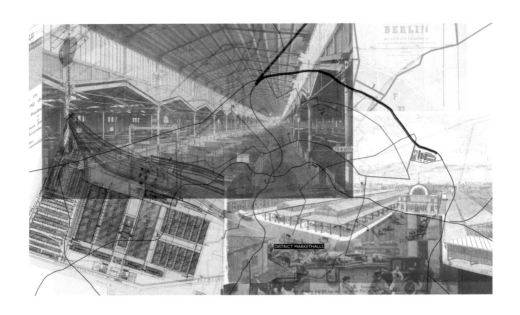

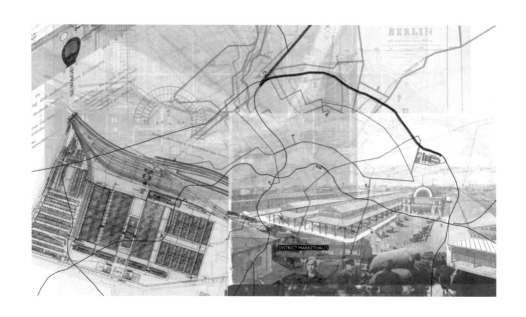

and spatialities and the composite modes of representation replicate the complexity of the urban environments and conditions they represent, and compel viewers and users of each narrative to actively construct the meaning of any particular episode and weave together the multiple story lines that comprise the narrative itself. Second, the project is part of an ongoing study of inherently dynamic conditions that make it necessary to go back and forth between city, archive, and narrative. Permanently unfinished, *Urban Intermedia* is what Umberto Eco called an "open work"—a work that is integral and complete in itself yet open to experience and interpretation—"because in every reception the work takes on a fresh perspective for itself."[26]

This brings me to the final, third point about the open-endedness of the *Urban Intermedia* project: It is not a tool, nor is it an app or a platform. It is an experimental research-driven project—an urban research project—that brings together the media and materials of multiple disciplines to tell stories and construct arguments that speak across disciplinary knowledge bases through a kind of shared media language. The possibility of a shared media language emerged (like so many other aspects of the project) over the course of the work and through collaborative practice. Just as it became clear that the visual narratives we were constructing could not be contained within a single story line, we also came to realize that the hybridized intermedia language through which we were telling the stories was itself creating this shared vocabulary and syntax—a common media language that gave us access to multiple modes of interpretation. Increasingly, as we collaborated, we found that we were not only narrating stories in more prismatic and nuanced ways but also reading them through more diverse lenses as well (see figure 8).

The open-ended format of the intermedia project is central to its critical purpose: to engage issues that are multifaceted, contradiction filled, politically charged, and highly contested—issues that are irreducibly complex and uncontainable—like the urban phenomenon itself. It is a format that is suited to speculation and experimentation, to opening up a field of study and exploring new kinds of collaborative practices and projects around the study of cities that combine scholarship, design, and media.

Fig 7: Still from Berlin narrative, *City-Fabric: Between Systems and Sites,* showing archival register at the bottom of the screen.

Current's

रस्त्यावरचे विक्रेते (रस्त्यावरच्या विक्रेत्यांच्या उपजिविकेचे संरक्षण आणि रस्त्यावरच्या विक्रेत्यांचे नियमन करणे) अधिनियम, २०१४

(२०१४ चा ७ वा अधिनियम)

THE STREET VENDORS (PROTECTION OF LIVELIHOOD AND REGULATION OF STREET VENDING) ACT, 2014

(ACT NO. 7 OF 2014)

CURRENT®

Fig 8: Sequence of stills (pages 230–233) from Mumbai narrative, *Space*, Mumbai: Claims on the City, Urban Intermedia, 2018, showing methods used to convey multiple ways of understanding any particular condition: how urban infrastructure in Mumbai is layered, and how it both connects and divides places and groups who inhabit and circulate through infrastructural layers.

EVE BLAU teaches the history and theory of urban form at the Harvard Graduate School of Design. She is the author of *Baku: Oil and Urbanism* (Park Books/University of Chicago Press, 2018), *Project Zagreb: Transition as Condition, Strategy, Practice* (Actar, 2007), *Shaping the Great City: Modern Architecture in Central Europe* (Prestel, 2000), *The Architecture of Red Vienna 1919–1934* (MIT Press, 1999), and *Architecture and Cubism* (MIT Press, 1997), among others. Blau is director of research at the GSD, co-director of the Harvard Mellon Urban Initiative, and co-curator of the research project and exhibition *Urban Intermedia: City, Archive, Narrative*.

1   *Urban Intermedia: City, Archive, Narrative* traveled to the following venues (and cities): the Aedes Architecture Forum (Berlin), January 27–February 21, 2018; SALT (Istanbul), March 6–April 1, 2018; CSMVS (Mumbai), April 15–May 9, 2018; and Harvard University Graduate School of Design (Boston), August 23–October 14, 2018. For more information, see Travis Dagenais, "At GSD, a Tale of Four Cities," Harvard Gazette, September 21, 2018, https://news.harvard.edu/gazette/story/2018/09/urban-intermedia-is-a-tale-of-four-cities. The exhibition was curated by Eve Blau and Robert Gerard Pietrusko; installation design by Eric Höweler, David Hamm, and Caleb Hawkins; exhibition coordinated by Gül Neşe Doğusan Alexander; art direction by Robert Gerard Pietrusko; production by Scott Smith; web design and development by Nil Tuzcu, Namik Mačkić, and Rob Meyerson; and brochure design by Claudia Tomateo. The Berlin team consisted of Eve Blau (research director), Igor Ekštajn (research associate), Max Hirsh (research associate), Pedro Aparicio, Silvia Danielak, Mikela De Tchaves, Emma Goode, Adam Himes, Eli Keller, Michael Keller, Aleksandra Kudryashova, Namik Mačkić, Scott Smith, and Claudia Tomateo; the Boston team consisted of Stephen Gray (research director), Alex Krieger (research director), Caroline Filice Smith (research associate), Hannah Gaegler, Emma Goode, Jeremey Hartley, Renia Kagkou, Annie Liang, and Erica Rothman; the Istabul team consisted of Sibel Bozdoğan (research director), Gül Neşe Doğusan Alexander (research director), Nil Tuzcu (research associate), Marysol Rivas Brito, Ece Cömert, Adam Himes, Hazal Seval, and Dana Shaikh Solaiman; and the Mumbai team consisted of Rahul Mehrotra (research director), Kate Cahill (research associate), Smita Babar, Enrique Aureng Silva Estrada, Emma Goode, Mark Jongman-Sereno, Gabriel Munoz Moreno, Aditya Sawant, Esa Shaikh, Apoorva Shenvi, Claudia Tomateo, Sonny Xu, and Jessy Yang.

2   The Harvard Mellon Urban Initiative is itself part of the Mellon Foundation's Architecture, Urbanism, and the Humanities initiative launched in 2012 to support and promote research and pedagogy on the history of cities as distinct forms of human cohabitation and social organization—forging connections in research universities between schools of architecture and programs in the humanities and experimenting with new models of teaching that incorporate studio methods into the investigation of large humanistic questions and broadly based research projects in major global cities. See "Architecture, Urbanism, and the Humanities," Mellon Foundation, https://mellon.org/initiatives/architecture-urbanism-and-humanities. For more information on phase one of the initiative, "Reconceptualizing the Urban: Interdisciplinary Study of Urban Environments, Societies, and Cultures" (2013–2018), visit http://mellonurbanism.harvard.edu.

3   The city-based research portals were directed by Rahul Mehrotra (Mumbai), Stephen Gray and Alex Krieger (Boston), Sibel Bozdogan and Gül Neşe Doğusan Alexander (Istanbul), and Eve Blau (Berlin).

4   Henri Lefebvre, *The Urban Revolution*, trans. Robert Bononno (Minneapolis: University of Minnesota Press, 2003), 55, 56.

5   Manfredo Tafuri, *The Sphere and the Labyrinth: Avant-Gardes and Architecture from Piranesi to the 1970s*, trans. Pellegrino d'Acierno and Robert Connolly (Cambridge, MA: MIT Press, 1978), 12.

6   Manfredo Tafuri, *Theories and History of Architecture*, trans. Giorgio Verecchia (New York: Harper & Row, 1976), 104; Tafuri, *The Sphere and the Labyrinth*, 13.

7   Lefebvre, *Urban Revolution*, 53.

8   Lefebvre, *Urban Revolution*, 54.

9   Lefebvre, *Urban Revolution*, 54, 55–56 (emphasis in the original).

10   Lefebvre, *Urban Revolution*, 56.

11   Lefebvre, *Urban Revolution*, 56, 58.

12   Lefebvre, *Urban Revolution*, 3–5, 58.

13   See, for example, John Naughton, "Net Benefit: How the Internet Is Transforming Our World," keynote address for the UK Marketing Society, February 28, 2006, https://memex.naughtons.org/wp-content/Keynotefinal.pdf; John Naughton, "Blogging and the Emerging Media Ecosystem," background paper for an invited seminar to Reuters Fellowship, University of Oxford, November 8, 2006, http://davidgauntlett.com/wp-content/uploads/2018/08/Naughton-Blogging-and-Media-Ecosystem-2006.pdf.

14   A range of Adobe Creative Suite programs were used to produce the narratives; however, the principal animation software was After Effects; other applications, including Photoshop, Illustrator, Media Encoder, and InDesign, were used to process and annotate the media. Additional software used in the exhibition included Max/MSP/Jitter, and Processing.

15   This phrase is from Frank Eberhardt, "Der Luisenstädtische Kanal Wird Eröfnet," *Berlinische Monatsschrift*, May 15, 1852.

16   Fred I. Dretske, *Knowledge and the Flow of Information* (Cambridge, MA: MIT Press, 1981), 137.

17   See Otto Neurath, *International Picture Language/Internationale Bildersprache*, trans. Marie Neurath (Reading, UK: University of Reading, 1980); see also Eve Blau, "Isotype and Architectural Knowledge," in *Emigré Cultures in Design and Architecture*, ed. Alison J. Clarke and Elana Shapira (London: Bloomsbury, 2017), 29–44.

18   Lev Manovich, *Software Takes Command* (New York: Bloomsbury, 2013), 44–46, 246–249.

19   Manovich, *Software Takes Command*, 268–269 (emphasis in the original). Manovich notes that After Effects continues to be the most popular, widely used, and best-known application. "After Effects' UI and tools bring together fundamental techniques, working methods, and assumptions of previously separate fields of filmmaking, animation, and graphic design. This hybrid production environment, encapsulated in a single software application, is directly reflected in the new visual language it enables—specifically, its focus on exploring aesthetic, narrative, and affective possibilities of hybridization." Manovich, *Software Takes Command*, 246, 247.

20   Manovich, *Software Takes Command*, 289.

21   Manovich, *Software Takes Command*, 278, 287, 289.

22   Manovich, *Software Takes Command*, 169.

23   Manovich, *Software Takes Command*, 260.

24   Manovich, *Software Takes Command*, 285, 305.

25   The algorithm and software for the archival register were developed expressly for the project by Robert Pietrusko.

26   Umberto Eco, *The Open Work*, trans. Anna Cancogni (Cambridge, MA: Harvard University Press, 1989), 4 (emphasis in the original).

Maps that
Move
Matthew W.
Wilson

236

In some recent writings, I suggested "maps that move" as a way to question the role of systemization and capture in geographic representation, particularly in our current moment, when geovisualizations of big data abound.[1] In doing so, I want to take up a particular kind of map that moves: animated maps. On the top in figure 1 is a still from an animated map of Lansing, Michigan, by Allan Schmidt, created in the late 1960s.[2] On the bottom is a still from an animated map of tweets related to Ferguson, Missouri, created in 2014 by Carto, a web-based mapping company, and published in the *Washington Post*.[3]

Both animations are born out of incredible leaps in computing and geographic representation, although they are separated by nearly fifty years. Both attempt to represent the spatiality of social phenomena across a map plane. Both are meant to inspire as well as instruct. And yet there was and is an uneasiness in these productions, as they rub against an establishment cartography as well as a persistent critique of the command and control of geographic representation. Far from attempting to resolve these tensions, I hope to get a little muddy in their mixing. In what follows, I present some map animations from the cartographic archives, reading them with and against the grain of cartographic scholarship and spatial theory. My conclusions are tentative: the techniques of cartographic animation and the techniques of cinema are sutured, and as such, they enable ways of thinking and acting through map animation beyond the purely effective. I want to explore some potential epistemological irreducibilities, not in order to reconcile their remainders but, as Donna Haraway insists, to "stay with the trouble."[4]

To illustrate this trouble, let us take up some writings by Doreen Massey and Ken Field. I begin with Doreen Massey, whose ruminations on space, time, and representation beg us to unsettle our most basic assumptions and consumptions regarding spatiality and liveliness. What bothers Massey is articulated at the beginning of *For Space*: "Equations of representation with spatialisation have troubled me; associations of space with synchrony exasperated me; persistent assumptions of space as the opposite of time have kept me thinking; analyses that remained within the discursive have just not been positive enough."[5] Massey continues: "Representation is seen to take on aspects of spatial*isation*... setting things down side by side; of laying them out as a discrete simultaneity. But representation is also... fixing things, taking the time out of them."[6] Here, Massey sorts out a series of formulations offered a century earlier in *Matter and Memory*, by Henri Bergson, on the opposition between duration and space. The trouble with the relationship between duration (as time) and spatialized representation (as space) is at the heart of Massey's argument of "space as the dimension of multiple trajectories, a simultaneity of stories-so-far... as the dimension of a multiplicity of durations. The problem has been that the old chain of meaning—space-representation-stasis—continues to wield its power. The legacy lingers on."[7]

This is perhaps where our slack-jawed viewing of animated maps begins to take a critical turn. Massey argues, "Space conquers time by being set up as the *representation* of history/life/the real world... The very life, and certainly the politics, are taken out of it."[8] Another reaction to the reduction of space to stasis, although less philosophically sublime, can be located in the writings of behavioral cartographers on the topic of animated maps. At its most abbreviated, fewer than 140 characters, is the tweet by Ken Field (of the GIS software company Esri): "I'm wondering when people will realize the animated ectoplasm twitter maps don't actually show anything."[9]

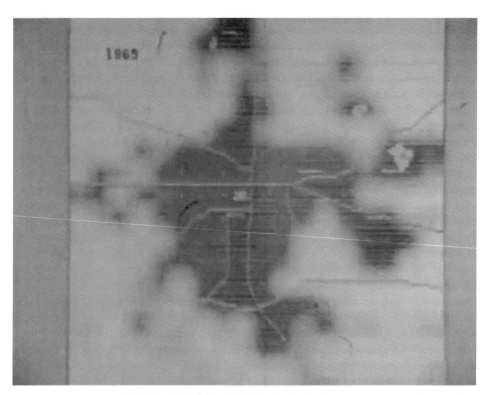

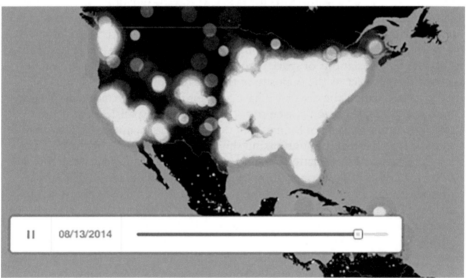

Fig 1: Top: still from Allan Schmidt's 1967 animated map of Lansing, Michigan. Courtesy of Allan Schmidt. Bottom: still from Carto's animated map of user-generated posts on Twitter related to the Ferguson, Missouri, protests, August 13–14, 2014. Map by Simon Rogers. Courtesy of Carto.

Undoubtedly a lob at Carto and at the proliferation of these kinds maps of Twitter data, Field's critique might be read alongside a persist iness in the development of animated cartography. While there is much critique, we might draw parallels to Danny Dorling's suggestion, twent years earlier, regarding animated cartography: "There is no reason why the map should remain fixed while the action is played out upon it."[10]

While Massey does not directly address animated maps, we can perhaps read into her critique of the stultifying effect of these geographic representations. Cartographer and spatial theorist alike are unsettled by the animated map, perhaps sharing in a recognition that in the worst case, these representations serve to stabilize and depoliticize space and spatial relations, and at best, they are just not effective devices for communicating information about space.

But let's "stay with the trouble" and introduce another theorist into the mix to think through the implications of animated maps *as cinema*. In *Cinema 1*, Gilles Deleuze begins by working through Bergson's thesis about memory, movement, and images on cinema. "In short, cinema does not give us an image to which movement is added, it immediately gives us a movement-image."[11] The operations of cinema to produce a movement-image, a concept from Bergson, requires some technical conditions, which include: "not merely the photo, but the snapshot... the equidistance of snapshots; the transfer of this equidistance on to a framework which constitutes the 'film'... It is in this sense that the cinema is the system which reproduces movement... as a function of equidistant instants, selected so as to create an impression of continuity."[12] Deleuze continues:

> But it is here that the difficulty arises. What is the interest of such a system? From the point of view of science, it is very slight... one of analysis... Did it at least have artistic interest? This did not seem likely either, since art seemed to uphold the claims of a higher synthesis of movement, and to remain linked to the poses and forms that science had rejected. We have reached the very heart of cinema's ambiguous position as "industrial art": it was neither an art nor a science.[13]

The development of animated maps mimics this ambiguity; it is neither an art nor a science. And while there have been significant attempts to claim that animated cartography is a science, it has been a slippery subject. Consider these key entries in the history of animated cartography: Norman Thrower, in a piece titled "Animated Cartography" in the *Professional Geographer* in 1959, establishes the key furniture in the development of the field. He writes: "Although in the past the animated drawing has been associated particularly with entertainment and advertising, it is being used increasingly for scientific illustration. Maps lend themselves particularly well to animation; by the use of this technique we can add another dimension to cartography—time."[14] This additional dimension would be nontrivial. Years later, Bruce Cornwell and Arthur Robinson would review the field. By 1966 a number of computing developments including the CRT display and drawing "light pen" had further evolved the process of successive frame animations with film, drawing directly from the film industry.[15] Jacques Bertin insists in 1967 that movement was an "overwhelming" variable. He writes that movement "so dominates perception that it severely limits the attention which can be given to the meaning of the other variables... real time

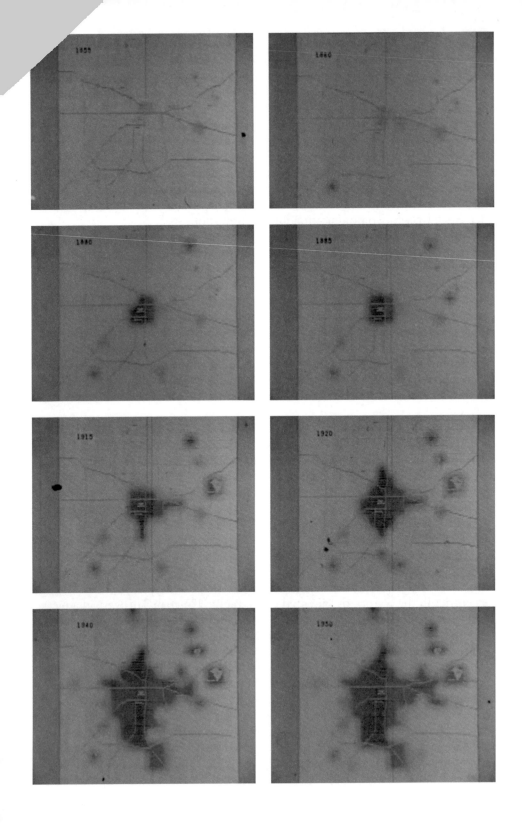

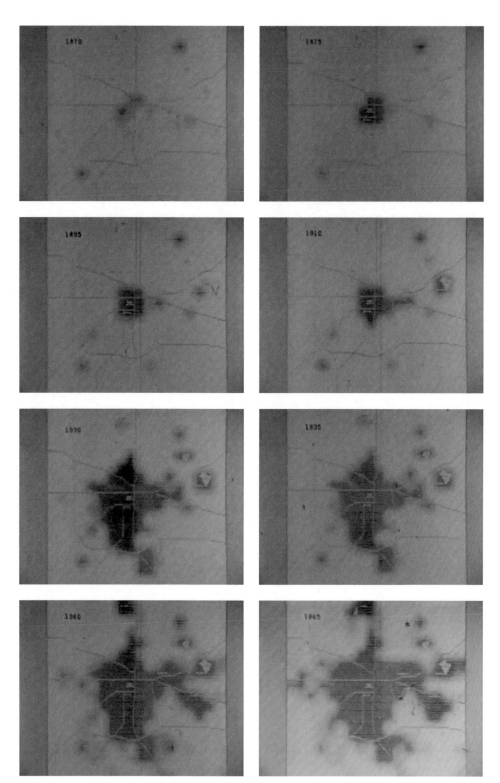

Fig 2: Stills from Allan Schmidt's 1967 animated map of Lansing, Michigan, https://www.youtube.com/watch?v=aySwJKK6i2s. Courtesy of Allan Schmidt.

Maps that Move

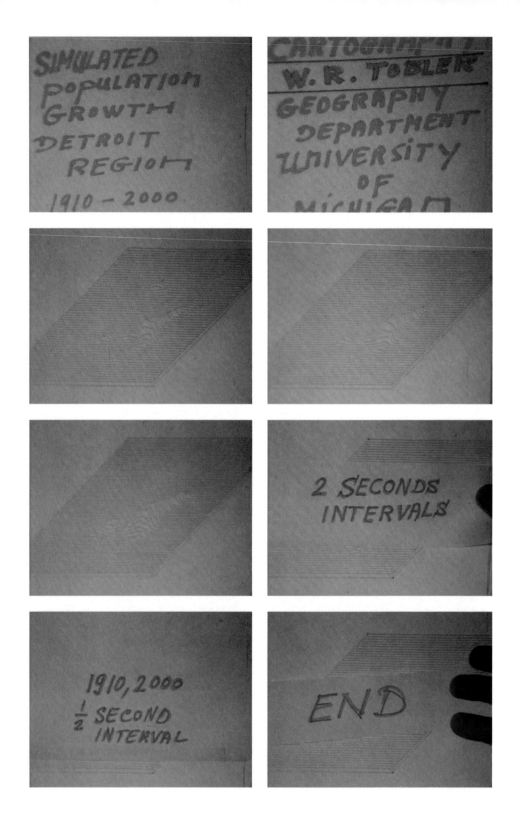

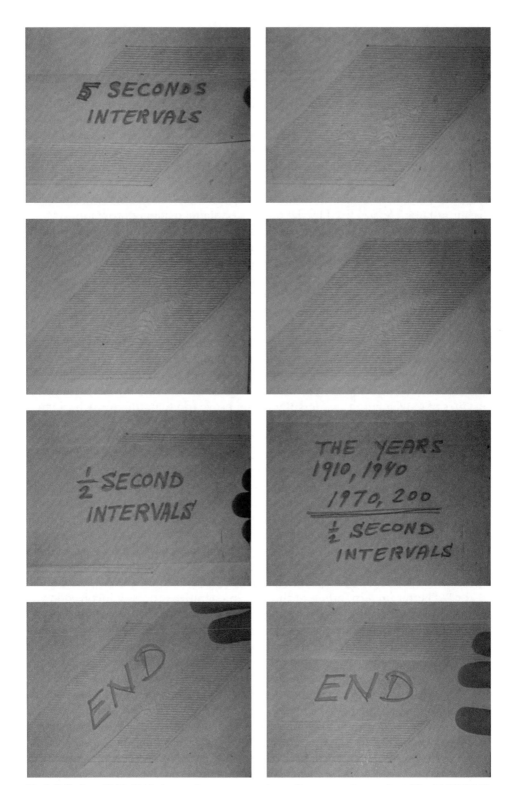

Fig 3: Stills from Waldo Tobler's experiment with animated map surfaces,

https://www.youtube.com/watch?v=kRsF9S8JqBl.

is not quantitative; it is 'elastic'… though we are not yet able to determine all the factors of this variation."[16]

Despite the development of these factors, animated cartography proceeded with wide-ranging experimentation. In 1967 Allan Schmidt created "A Pictorial History of the Expansion of the Metropolitan Area" of Lansing, Michigan, while at Michigan State University (see figure 2). Here, he used a new program called SYMAP, short for the synagraphic mapping method, developed in 1963. Waldo Tobler and his student Frank Rens at Michigan were similarly experimenting with these methods for drawing three-dimensional surfaces.[17] In these experiments (see figure 3), you can see how Tobler was adjusting the intervals of exposure to these successive map snapshots to tune the qualities produced by these "equidistant instants." Space, fixed by the outputs of digital mapping programs, was made to move through film. Hal Moellering, another student of Tobler and John Nystuen, experimented with these filmed instants to "develop a feel for a spatial and temporal dynamics associated with traffic crash production" (see figure 4).[18]

With their roots firmly in the quantitative traditions born out of the University of Washington and in the thematic cartographic traditions born out of the University of Wisconsin, experiments in animated maps attempted to tame and define the ineffability of spatiality. Staying with the trouble, created by their opposition of time and space, these experiments were both fascinating and vexing in their status as science and art. Moellering would go on to explore real-time animations with 3D maps, enabling the user to navigate and visualize spatial processes.[19] However, Bertin's 1967 warning about the "overwhelming" qualities of movement in cartography would prove too tempting for behavioral cartographers.

In 1995 Alan MacEachren would write in *How Maps Work* that movement was not just one additional variable in cartography but several—drawing on work produced with Dave DiBiase, among others.[20] He writes, "What is probably true, however, is that on a dynamic map, things that change attract more attention than things that do not and things that move probably attract more attention than things that change in place."[21] The ineffability of movement in cartography would require more variables. MacEachren would chart six: display date, duration, order, rate of change, frequency, and synchronization.[22] These variables of movement would enable a new generation of cartographic study of cognitive processes, which would tame the animated map. As Mark Harrower and Sara Fabrikant argued in 2008, "better understanding of the human cognitive processes involved in… highly interactive graphic displays is fundamental for facilitating sense-making… Better understanding will lead to greater efficiency in the complex decision-making required to solve pressing environmental problems and societal needs."[23]

Indeed, work around animated maps would become work investigating the potential for interactive maps. In the experiment published in 2011 by Carolyn Fish, among others, we can see the crystallization of these methods, born in the serendipitous experiments of the 1960s (see figure 5).[24] The questions, largely unchanged since the time of Robinson and Tobler, remain: How do we ensure that map readers receive the message encoded in the representation? What visual variables of movement can be better resolved to better enable new map users?

Interestingly, the *subject* of such animated maps recedes into the background. Maps become static surfaces for use in decision-making. Environmental crisis, social struggle, demographic shifts—this content matters less in the fine-tuning

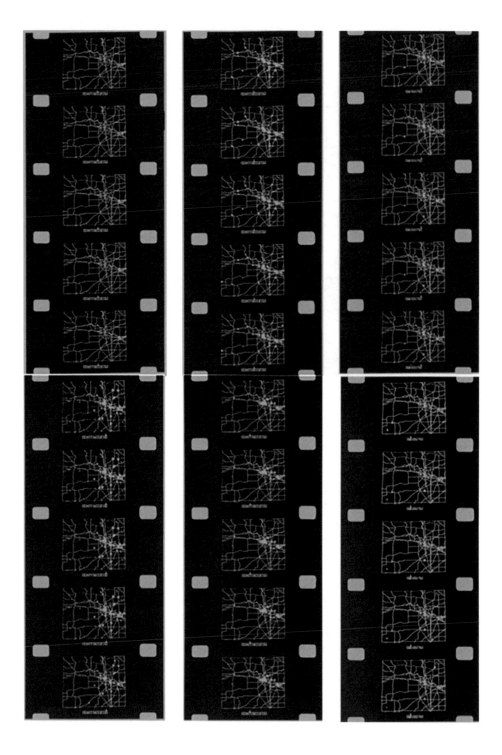

Fig 4: Stills from Hal Moellering's experiments with filmed instants. From Harold Moellering, "The Potential Uses of a Computer Animated Film in the Analysis of Geographical Patterns of Traffic Crashes," *Accident Analysis and* *Prevention* 8, no. 4 (December 1976): 215–227.

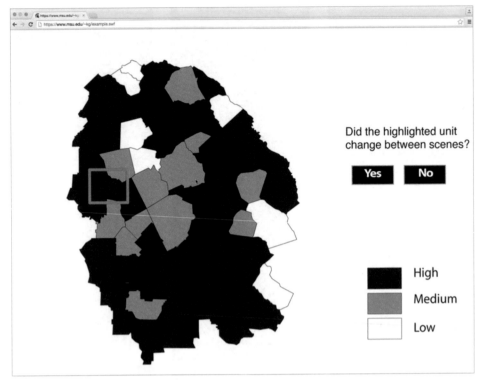

Fig 5: Still from Carolyn Fish et al., experiment with animated cartography, 2011. From Carolyn Fish, Kirk P. Goldsberry, and Sarah Battersby, "Change Blindness in Animated Choropleth Maps: An Empirical Study," *Cartography and* *Geographic Information Science* 38, no. 4 (October 2011): 350–362.

of the map instrument. The trouble of the ineffable, of occupying neither science nor art, is the problem to be resolved. However, what might it mean to stay with the trouble, to maintain the "mysterious interaction between computer display and human visual processing systems," as Danny Dorling and Stan Openshaw argued in 1992, in the midst of the GIS wars, as the role of GIS in geography came under scrutiny?[25]

This essay ends with Geoff Dutton, a student and researcher at the Harvard Lab in the late 1960s and 1970s. In a class project from 1969, Dutton created a piece of electronic cartographic art, testing out central place theory in a nest of three orders of lights representing interacting cities. The work attempts to adjust our vision to the regularity of human life amid chaos. In 1979 Dutton draws this work forward in "American Graph Fleeting," the first animated map hologram. In figure 6, we see two individuals watching a short film of the animation in the hologram, representing a rotating 3D drawing of population density in the United States. More than an artifact for precisely measuring the effectiveness of cartographic design, these animations invoke what Jacques Rancière describes as the "art of cinema," which "exists through the play of gaps and improprieties."[26] Or as Danny Dorling aptly states in 1992, "Cartographic animation is a strange concept."[27] Indeed, as Harrower and Fabrikant write, "there is the very real risk that mapping technology is outpacing cartographic theory."[28]

Fig 6: Dutton's "American Graph Fleeting,"
produced at the Harvard LCGSA in 1979, was
perhaps the world's first (and only) animated
map hologram viewable in the round. Courtesy
of Geoff Dutton.

The mystery of map animation may lie in its unresolvable tension, neither art nor science, of fixing space and opposing time, of equidistant instants and the movement-image of film. Perhaps the potential of "maps that move" is precisely in their uncanny appropriateness for our space-times. And this is where Massey might help direct such a critical cartography of animated maps. This is the problem, she writes: "Loose ends and ongoing stories are real challenges to cartography."[29] The static map tends toward closure, space as stasis. Perhaps "maps that move" might mobilize design to think about the intervention in cartography differently, as shifting the ways the world is experienced and represented, to be *for space* in all its liveliness, surprise, and disruption.

MATTHEW W. WILSON is associate professor of geography at the University of Kentucky and visiting scholar in the Center for Geographic Analysis at Harvard University. His most recent book is *New Lines: Critical GIS and the Trouble of the Map* (University of Minnesota Press, 2018).

1   This essay is based on "Movement: Strange Concepts and the Essentially Subjective" in Matthew W. Wilson, *New Lines: Critical GIS and the Trouble of the Map* (Minneapolis: University of Minnesota Press, 2017).

2   Allan Schmidt, *A Pictorial History of the Expansion of the Metropolitan Area* (Lansing: Michigan State University, 1967). Schmidt said, in personal communication with the author, that after completing the SYMAP correspondence course, he was hired by Richard Duke at Michigan State University as assistant director of the METRO project, funded by Ford. Schmidt wrote to Fisher to request a copy of the SYMAP software, and a programmer converted it from running on an IBM 7094 to the CDC 3600 at Michigan State. Here, he motivated a group of graduate students to record every subdivision at the state land registry, to map the coordinates of these subdivisions as individual snapshots for the eventual animated map.

3   Brian Fung, "Watch Twitter Explode along with Ferguson," *Washington Post*, August 14, 2014, www.washingtonpost.com/blogs/the-switch/wp/2014/08/14/watch-twitter-explode-along-with-ferguson; see also the larger version of the map hosted by Carto, http://srogers.cartodb.com/viz/4a5eb582-23ed-11e4-bd6b-0e230854a1cb/embed_map.

4   Donna J. Haraway, *Staying with the Trouble: Making Kin in the Chthulucene* (Durham, NC: Duke University Press, 2016).

5   Doreen Massey, *For Space* (London: Sage, 2005), 13.

6   Massey, *For Space*, 23.

7   Massey, *For Space*, 24.

8   Massey, *For Space*, 30.

9   Kenneth Field, Twitter, June 17, 2014, http://twitter.com/kennethfield/status/478775510386741248.

10   Daniel Dorling, "Stretching Space and Splicing Time: From Cartographic Animation to Interactive Visualization," *Cartography and Geographic Information Systems* 19, no. 4 (1992): 215.

11   Gilles Deleuze, *Cinema 1: The Movement-Image*, trans. Hugh Tomlinson and Barbara Habberjam (New York: Bloomsbury Academic, 2013), 2.

12   Deleuze, *Cinema 1*, 5.

13   Deleuze, *Cinema 1*, 6.

14   Norman J. W. Thrower, "Animated Cartography," *Professional Geographer* 11, no. 6 (1959): 10.

15   Bruce Cornwell and Arthur Howard Robinson, "Possibilities for Computer Animated Films in Cartography," *Cartographic Journal* 3, no. 2 (1966): 79–82.

16   Jacques Bertin, *Semiology of Graphics* (Madison: University of Wisconsin Press, 1983), 42.

17   Waldo R. Tobler, "A Computer Movie Simulating Urban Growth in the Detroit Region," *Economic Geography* 46 (June 1970): 234–240.

18   Harold Moellering, "The Potential Uses of a Computer Animated Film in the Analysis of Geographical Patterns of Traffic Crashes," *Accident Analysis and Prevention* 8, no. 4 (December 1976): 217.

19   I share in this academic genealogy. My adviser at the University of Washington, Tim Nyerges, read for his PhD with Moellering at Ohio State University (graduating in 1980). While Nyerges's work does not emphasize the movement of the map, per se, his interest in the ways in which map and map interactions can impact decision-making and planning is approached from a similar perspective: that the perception of a map is something that can be controlled for in behavioral experiments with maps. See Timothy L. Nyerges, "Geographic Information Abstractions: Conceptual Clarity for Geographic Modeling," *Environment and Planning A* 23 (1991): 1483–1499; Timothy L. Nyerges, "Analytical Map Use," *Cartography and Geographic Information Systems* 18, no. 1 (January 1991): 11–22; Timothy L. Nyerges, "How Do People Use Geographical Information Systems?," in *Human Factors in Geographical Information Systems*, ed. David Medyckyj-Scott and Hilary Hearnshaw (London: Belhaven Press, 1993), 37–50.

20   MacEachren articulates a response to the deconstructive trend in postmodern scholarship as it targets cartography: "What is needed, I believe, is a more balanced perspective on cartographic research that attempts to merge the perceptual, cognitive, and semiotic issues of maps as functional devices for portraying space and the sociocultural issues of how these portrayals might facilitate, guide, control, or stifle social interaction." And while he states that he is no longer an adherent of the map communication model, the move toward map design research has its most significant roots in a functional map design moment. See Alan M. MacEachren, *How Maps Work: Representation, Visualization, and Design* (New York: Guilford Press, 2004), 11.

21   MacEachren, *How Maps Work*, 280.

22   MacEachren, *How Maps Work*, 281–287. Note that duration, rate of change, and order were three initial variables of dynamic maps as developed from MacEachren's team at Penn State; see David DiBiase, Alan M. MacEachren, John B. Krygier, and Catherine Reeves, "Animation and the Role of Map Design in Scientific Visualization," *Cartography and Geographic Information Systems* 19, no. 4 (1992): 201–214.

23   Mark Harrower and Sara Irina Fabrikant, "The Role of Map Animation for Geographic Visualization," in *Geographic Visualization: Concepts, Tools and Applications*, ed. Martin Dodge, Mary McDerby, and Martin Turner (New York: Wiley, 2008), 62.

24   Carolyn Fish, Kirk P. Goldsberry, and Sarah Battersby, "Change Blindness in Animated Choropleth Maps: An Empirical Study," *Cartography and Geographic Information Science* 38, no. 4 (October 2011): 350–362, 357.

25   Daniel Dorling and Stan Openshaw, "Using Computer Animation to Visualize Space-Time Patterns," *Environment and Planning B: Planning and Design* 19 (1992): 644.

26   Jacques Rancière, *The Intervals of Cinema* (New York: Verso, 2014), 11.

27   Dorling, "Stretching Space and Splicing Time," 215.

28   Harrower and Fabrikant, "Role of Map Animation," 49.

29   Massey, *For Space*, 106–111.

Cartographies of Distance
Leah Meisterlin

UPFRONT POSTSCRIPT

Eleven days after an earlier version of this text was presented at the Center for Spatial Research's Ways of Knowing Cities conference at Columbia University, Waldo Tobler passed away at the age of eighty-eight. The talk featured work in progress and new opportunities for constructing urban knowledge by clarifying the premises of spatial research, by returning to and reestablishing some first principles of cartographic analysis. What had started with thorny but straightforward research questions about inequities in everyday urban experience had come to present far thornier and circuitous epistemological and methodological questions. In trying to map known differences between individuals and groups, I found myself up against fundamental questions about how we know cities through mapping at all. More appropriately, I was up against the limits of common cartographic thinking—questioning the ways knowledge is produced through relationships drawn on a map.

Tobler was not explicitly referenced in the talk, but these questions are impossible without his contributions. Implicit throughout the project, and throughout this text, is the impact of his First Law of Geography.[1] What follows is an attempt at taking that law seriously—by not taking it for granted—perhaps more seriously than it was intended. Everything is indeed related to everything else. And near things are more related than distant things. I remained convinced: somewhere in the many meanings of *related* and the changing definitions of *near* and *distant* lie the questions of how we construct and navigate the human environment. From the local causes and effects of globalization to remarkable shifts in worldwide demographics to the appropriation of virtual space as public space, the qualitative and quantitative relationships between near (and less near) things speak to both how we make the world in which we live and how we live in it together.[2]

MAP AS SITE

It is true that new opportunities for urban representation (both graphically and politically) have extended broadly with the recent ubiquity of and advances in digital mapping. From Google and Socrata to Esri, Leaflet, Mapbox, and Carto, we have seen the creation and development of several platforms, portals, and tools that offer ever-growing access to geospatial data and wider-reaching mapping capability.[3] Now more than ever, individuals and communities can find and represent spatial information in ways that are situated, meaningful, and compelling. We can locate ourselves and our advocacy within a statistical landscape of greater possibility (if not certainty): several voices might be heard, and multiple perspectives may be offered. It is also true that this expansion has happened within a particular cartographic space held almost axiomatically as the scalable and neutral container for the representation of those voices and perspectives. Such an infinite Cartesian container constitutes the standardized framework that enables the promise of widespread (and often called democratic) data collection, digitization, and visualization—and through which wildly complex sociogeographic phenomena are modeled and reconstituted, bubbling up to the surface of the map. The consistency, clarity, and commonality of the (x, y) form the basis for a declared universality—a shared reference against which differences are measured, across which narratives are traced and made comparable, and in which the spatial advantages of some at the expense of others are sometimes seen.

And yet the collected and collective leveling of the mapped proverbial playing field is also understood to level and flatten the contours of diversity and difference in our cities. The popularization of digital mapping and GIS (geographic information systems) must not be confused for the democratization of the map or of cartographic practice. Despite the proliferation of data and the accessibility of geovisualization tools, countermapping persists because—in the rational, and sometimes hopeful, claim to neutrality—that standardized framework belies something else we already know is true: space is not neutral.[4] Mapping what happens in cities is both an investigative tool and an epistemological position; it is both implicit and complicit in the social reproduction of urbanism.[5] Nonneutral and nonscalable, community-based, participatory, and radical countermapping persists precisely because cartographic reasoning—more explicitly than other modes of knowledge production and more overtly than other interpretative devices—quite literally entails drawing (upon) and enforcing a worldview.

This persistence of countermapping—this unrelenting insistence on developing alternative maps alongside the breakneck growth of quasi-scientific and positivist data mapping approaches—may be better described as a resistance.[6] Narrative digital maps establish personally relevant landmarks from geotagged POIS (points of interest) while resisting the Cartesian substitution of the space of experience with a coordinate plane. Psychogeographic and social tracings derived from mobile phones and GPS receivers resist the imposition of that plane as a means of normalizing disparate perspectives. Participatory GIS and grassroots advocacy mappings resist authoritative data visualizations as representative of the issues, questions, concerns, and priorities of the communities they represent.[7] And nearly all critical cartographies and countermapping practices resist standardized, quantitative, algorithmic logics as the prima facie generative principle for the creation or the communication of spatial knowledge claims.

To be clear, the recent shared history of digital mapping technologies and the multiple forms of mapping practices they enable—quantitative or qualitative, normative or alternative, positivist or interpretivist—raises difficulties for mapping as a mode of urban research and as a basis for urban intervention.

While popular-populist digital tools augment opportunities for information-cartography for more communities, the spaces they describe and the claims they produce remain delimited by an unquestioned frame. If the aims, analyses, and agendas of mapping align with the map's space, then this cartographic container must be understood as integrally cooperating in the construction of those claims. Moreover, any form of sociospatial resistance reliant upon these tools and thus subject to their frame—whether mapping as intervention or map-based research informing advocacy, design, or policy—also reifies the very structures, technologies, politics, and systems of representation against which their resistance is organized.

That resistance risks reification carries a crucial but sometimes paralyzing suspicion and critique of commonly deployed digital mapping technologies. (For example, and with notable exceptions, geographers and critical cartography theorists notoriously do not map.) But neither criticism nor abstinence have diminished the acceleration of normative mapping technologies or mitigated the scope of their impact on evolving urbanisms. As thoroughly researched, contextually responsive, and vividly descriptive as they may be, uniquely framed and tightly individualized countermaps do not scale toward influencing urban policy and decision-making with the same persuasive efficiency of authoritative, data-driven, quantitative, GIS-based results. For that reason and despite the risk, shying away from the exploratory, explanatory, and communicative potentials of digital mapping technologies—for me, as for many interested in the map as an instrument of intervention—is simply not an option. Instead, it is precisely where sociopolitical resistance risks structural reification that the map, with its imbricated technologies, data sources, analytical underpinnings, and representational standards, becomes (once again) a site of necessary interrogation, engagement, reflection, and operation. Swerving past paralysis while holding onto critical suspicion, I propose a defiant and willful cartographic action: a more pointed persistence aimed at the logics inherent in the already almost-pervasive norms of spatial analysis and exercised upon this site through its native technologies and on their declared terms.

This is to say, I propose wielding the capital-P power of data-driven, GIS-based mapping upon the data map itself—using the methods of digital spatial analysis to better understand the representations of space they produce. Redirecting this sort of persistence keeps the GIS analyst-cartographer locked within the tools, registers, datasets, and products of most urban GIS analysis, as a site of research intervention. It allows urban researchers to ask how the analytical assumptions and geometric preconceptions of popular data-driven mapping have established and reinforced a totalizing map logic that (literally, figuratively, and representationally) bounds the types of knowledge produced via cartographic reasoning, the descriptions of space drawn with data, the evidence they provide for urban policy-making, and even the questions asked through GIS.[8] Positioning the map as the site of urban research (and conducting that research through mapping) is an insurgent act of persistent resistance concerning pluralistic knowledge of and within cities while seeking to reconfigure, retool, and redeploy the data map as a device for the production of that knowledge. For design and planning, it reorients urban drawing toward research questions that ask what it could pragmatically mean to map multiple, coincident, and collocated environments from information culled from the processes that produce their difference. Insofar as representation is an instrument for understanding, it asks which (and how many) frameworks for understanding the city control the instrument of the map.

THE CARTOGRAPHIC FATES

But, first, how to map? Asking *how* to map the uneven and multiple patterns we understand as comprising pluralistic spaces—and, again, how to do this via GIS-based, systematic, and data-driven means—reveals fundamental assumptions in and opportunities for the ways we map digitally. The resistance inherent in critical and countermapping practices calls attention to the limits of geometric cartography, to its deployment as a rationalized abstraction of lived experience, and to the implications of that process. Together, the digital map's representational claim of comprehensiveness and rigid locational precision combine to foster a bidirectional misdirection—from information to map and back again. As digital information is plotted, the map implies that the perceptual and lived proximity to located points is fixed and universal. As information is derived from the map, the process of measurement implies that new findings are agnostic and generalizable. While neither implication is logically justified, this back-and-forth between map and information also implies that finding an alternative approach is not simply a matter of finding an alternative to the Cartesian structure of the GIS-derived drawing. The institutions of the (x, y) grid and the Euclidean derivation of spatial relationships, despite their flattening and normalizing effects, are not solely culpable for hindering the data-based visualization of difference.[9] Rather, the cartographic framework under consideration here is more than the organizational geometry of the map; it is that which governs the process of translation between geometry and spatiality, between placing information on a map and taking information from it.[10] It is a process now largely overlooked or simply unseen by most mapmakers and map users, including architects and urban planners. The newfound ease and ubiquity of GIS software and digital cartography have produced and popularized a collection of techniques as standard forms of spatial analysis in urban research, given methodological protocols so fundamental that they begin with the core geometric-geographic elements of the map: the point, the line, and the polygon—abstracted representations for Location, Distance, and Area.

The growth of the Internet followed almost immediately by the ubiquity of geolocated services it enables has facilitated a strange resurrection of geography and mapping. After distance was declared dead during the 1990s—as many predicted its oncoming obsolescence given the connective capacity of the World Wide Web—a set of primarily quantitative and promisingly nonacademic mapping practices emerged.[11] Several factors contributed to this shift including, but certainly not limited to, the opening of the United States' global positioning system (GPS) to commercial uses and the development of new GIS technologies for nonexpert applications. Geographical insights were quickly heralded as key to strategic and entrepreneurial success, whether in tech start-ups or real estate or politics. But as we map more than ever before, the elements of the map have not revived equally.

Distance may not be dead anymore—at least not as an empirical measure of the geometrically traversable ground between known, finite locations—but she isn't quite a phoenix yet either. Distance is still struggling to rise—overshadowed by her sisters Location and Area, obscured by their digital, ready-made traces and mapped manifestations including the dropped pin, the assemblage of dots into densities, and their aggregation into the choropleth and "heat" map. Whether for policy-making or market analysis, whether identifying food deserts or strategizing health care or planning emergency response, the bigness of our data and the hunt for user-friendly, human- and machine-readable patterns have conspired in favor of mapping by default settings.[12] The dominance of Area and Location and the dominance of their representations speak to the dominance of one back-and-forth process of analytical mapping; one way of understanding space through points, lines, and polygons; one cartographic container into which we continue to compress and contort what we know about cities.

A full discussion of the recent and longer histories of these cartographic fates is beyond the immediate scope of this essay and requires its own future treatment, as does their relationship to Western spatial knowledge production through enumeration, incrementalization, and quantification.[13] That said, I introduce the mythological metaphor to underscore the power of their inscription on the cities and regions we draw and the control they wield over how we think about and make the city through these drawings. Location enumerates and plots; Area incrementalizes and bounds. Together they unitize, collect, and summarize by sociospatial quantum. They aggregate. They reveal comparative densities of human interest and activity—of people, of crimes, of exploitable resources, of property values, of electoral votes, and so on—as static snapshots and as moments in time. Area and Location have dominated digital mapping. Distance, however, as an epistemological instrument, as a force greater than the Euclidean length of a line, has remained underexamined and underutilized.

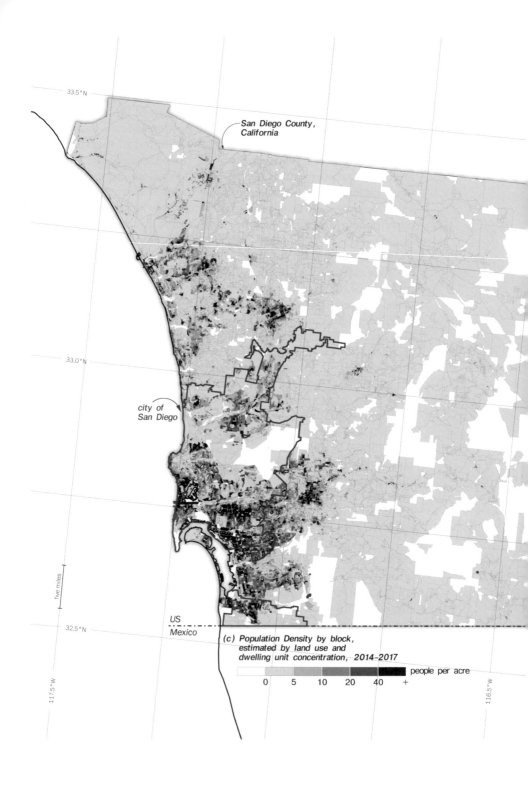

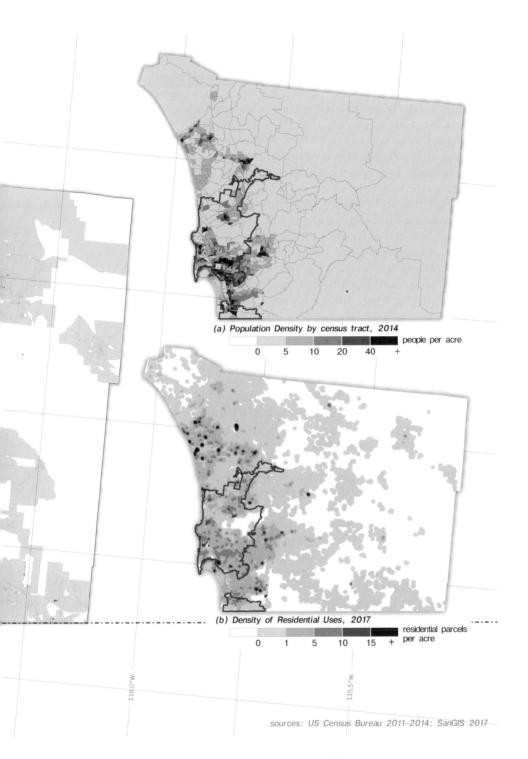

Fig 1: "Density in San Diego County, CA."
(a) Choropleth, population per acre by
census tract; (b) Kernel density "heat" map,
residential units per acre; (c) Dasymetric
estimation by housing distribution, population
per acre by block. All maps courtesy of
the author.

The influence of Area and Location over environmental and urban decisions is not unquestioned, of course. Both the conceptual and the practical nuts and bolts of spatiotemporal aggregation continue to receive attention, particularly where they engender false knowledge claims through misuse or misapplication, including the ecological fallacies described by the Boundary Problem and its growing list of cousins.[14] Each of these problems cautions about the interpretative effects of spatial summary, asks which areal units bound the specific spatial phenomena being mapped, or describes the variability of included (and excluded) limits and factors. Still, this act of unitized collection presupposes conceptual equivalencies between locations and between areas—between points and between polygons—equivalencies that may carry little meaning on the ground or for different individuals and that have become prerequisites for deriving actionable information from mapped information. But when we aggregate beyond meaning, we create patterns where there were none. And yet the bigger our data grow, the more tautological our cartographic models become in order to fit it all in and still keep that container from cracking. In other words, the simultaneous growth of digital information and digital mapping has created a codependent, positive feedback loop between Location and Area: with ever-greater amounts of geotagged information come farther-reaching collections of incrementalized boundaries to help make sense of that information. Whether the result of intention or negligence, it works to preserve the integrity of a hegemonic framework and all in support of that framework's claim to epistemological efficacy.

For the record, though, Area and Location are not to blame for their sister's struggle, and their maps are only red herrings. Their maps remind us that the proliferation of spatial data and tools has not truly democratized map*ping* as practice and process. The metaphor reminds us that the map is as prescriptive as it is descriptive, that as long as we draw from one unified worldview coded for us by others, we will continue to build the world in its image. When asking how to map as an iterative, interpretative, analytical process between digital information and digital drawing, the question serves to remind us that there are other options and that one such option might be to empower Distance as we have empowered Area and Location.

EARLY EXPERIMENTS IN MAPPING
DISTANCE AND DIFFERENCE

So, now, what to map? If the site of analysis is the map centered on a diversity of experience, and specifically where the appearance of difference is obscured by the standardized prioritization of area and location, then the *what* and *where* of that map might be anything and anywhere. As an opportunistic example, this investigation begins with gender and notions of everyday access, drawing from feminist geography and feminist GIS for the groundwork and methodological advantages they offer. Gendered differences in individual urban experience have been consistently demonstrated through a generation's worth of research, but these differences result from processes that common digital mapping techniques are not equipped to render at citywide scales. They constitute an ideal test site for methodological inquiry and innovation largely because men and women are spread more evenly than other demographic categorical groupings, and thus comparing their geographic distributions cannot describe their relatively uneven experiences.[15] Simply put, plotting points, measuring densities, and aggregating within shared boundaries fails to confirm the systemic differences between genders with respect to the availability and reachability of urban opportunities as well as the myriad spatial practices that emerge from those differences.[16] Reorienting the conclusions of prior research as new premises effectively holds location (where individuals live) and area (city blocks, neighborhoods, and so on) constant and, as a result, requires operationalizing alternative variables. It demands mapping distance in search of difference. Such an approach would also offer intersectional advantages if applied across areas and between identity groups to reveal finer-grain distinctions within neighborhoods that are commonly depicted as experientially homogenous and broader commonalities between individuals living in different corners of the city.

Our standard frameworks for interrogating distance-based access to the city are geometrically straightforward and rather computationally attainable. We measure either from one location to another or outward in unchallenged, incremental units of feet, miles, or minutes. Though we might not always use these resultant areas as aggregation units, we deploy these distances to create areal descriptors of accessibility, of neighborhoods, of catchment, and of association and similarity. We deploy both approaches in the planning of transit systems, zoning regulations and incentives, real estate investment, and customer bases or market analyses. We rarely, if ever, question whether movement through these areas or the time available for such movement is uniform, finding it much harder to render the constraints on distance resulting from who we are and the lives we live there.

This difficulty is because distances that reflect the spatial experience of the city cannot be dependent upon geometries mapped irrespective of those experiences. Both conventional approaches invoke or compare distances as proxies for access or actionable proximity, but neither raises these measures to the analytical value given to location and area. Mapping the separation between locations privileges origins and destination (points), assuming a void between those points. Mapping the dimensions of a neighborhood or the area described by a radius privileges the boundary, assuming a homogeneity of experience within its edges. Thus, mapping access might call for new experiments in analytical cartography that

Distances:

*from one location
in San Diego, CA*

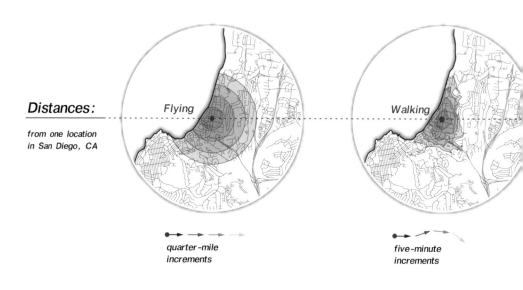

Flying

Walking

quarter-mile
increments

five-minute
increments

sources: SanGIS 2017

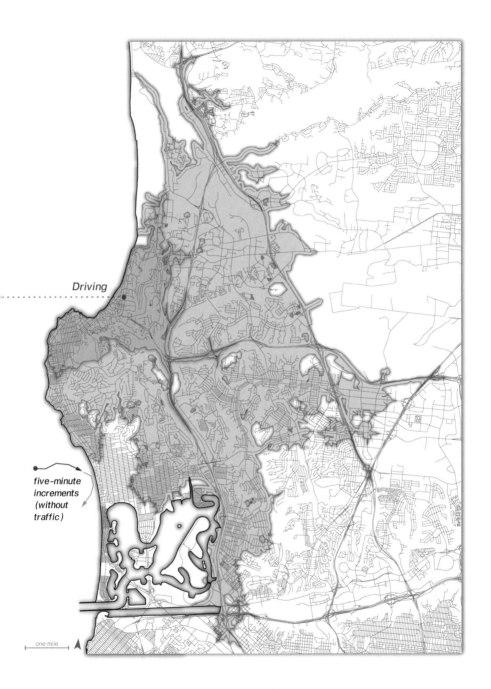

Driving

five-minute
increments
(without
traffic)

one mile

Fig 2: "Distance as Blast Radius."

do not rest on distances as measured or distances as mapped, but rather on distances as lived.

Further, despite the growth of new digital tools and available datasets, this distance as lived—as the product of perception and agency, constraint and opportunity, access and intent, directionality and morphology—is yet to rise from the ashes, yet to appear out of the ether of ubiquitous digital mapping, a revelation of promised pluralism and democratized, open data.[17] Distance as a vector of volition operates within and against the uneven geography of the city—this is the distance that carves territory for some while creating new margins and corralling others therein. This is the line that works alongside points and polygons to describe and prescribe the nonneutral terrain of urban space.

The recent history of feminist GIS and spatial analysis also provides an advantageous starting point for developing techniques to visualize such difference. Almost all GIS-based mapping of comparative urban experience as access to the city—and, by extension, any meaningful right to that city—depends on two precedent methods.[18] The first includes mapping the relative location of quotidian errands as an indication and fuzzy description of the concurrent distances that comprise our perceived and lived spaces. Examples of these range from hub-and-spoke diagrams illustrating connections between individuals' homes and their various destinations to newer animated densities of GPS tracings across streetscapes. Underpinning these drawings is an equivalent association between access and action, between proximity and motion. Accessible destinations are defined as those that are accessed. The second precedent makes this association explicit by mapping time. Specifically, Torsten Hägerstrand's work on time-geography, and the resulting space-time aquarium, has been employed to considerable effect in feminist and humanities GIS.[19] The analytical strength of Hägerstrand's invention is that it uses a third, vertical axis to situate the two-dimensional map with respect to time, reconciling the seemingly radical notions that it takes time to move from one point to another, that one moves between locations to spend time at each, and that none of us can make more hours in the day. Despite its conceptual elegance, the aquarium as a cartographic container begins to break down as it fills up: the more narratives it includes, the less legible their distinctions.

What these approaches share is an individually scaled, sampled, and volunteered data collection methodology predicated on travel diaries and surveys. They describe individuals' paths as reported by these individuals and generally require time-stamped information. Gathering or deriving such information is certainly possible for very large proportions of a city's population using, for example, mobile phone data, but the drawbacks are significant if not prohibitive. Compiling narratives sufficient for generalizability is resource intensive, (digitally) marginalized populations often remain uncounted, and the ethical compromises required to collect and analyze them at urban-level scales are rightfully unresolved.

The experiments and test maps included here take seriously the empirical findings of feminist geography, the conceptual construct of Hägerstrand's premises, and the inherent political potentials of each by radicalizing large, authoritative datasets available across jurisdictions throughout the United States. As part of continuing research focused on midsized US cities, these maps depict San Diego County, California, or portions thereof, using information summarized and averaged by census tract from the American Community Survey to isolate neighborhoods with significant differences between the commute times of men and women.[20] Zooming into these neighborhoods with employment data, the aim is not to find causal conclusions regarding the source of commute disparities but to map an image of the city through which individuals move and to which they have everyday access.[21]

The first attempt at such a mapping (figure 3, read as a single map), in a neighborhood where most people drive to work, depicts the five-minute drivable area for four commuters living on one block if they were to deviate from the quickest driving route to their places of primary employment. The nonresidential buildings within those areas are represented as a summary of possible destinations to which these commuters have quick access, while solely residential uses (planned and zoned as improbable destination locations) recede. The map quickly hints at how meaningful access to the city is more than measurable distance. It includes both the constraints and the necessities of daily life. Access has directionality: what might be only a few minutes away may not be accessible if it is in the wrong direction, especially if one is pressed for time or if there is another option "on the way."

The familiarity of this observation masks its potentially profound implications for describing access. This is one illustrative first attempt at a simple mapping of a daily constraint (getting to work) and a common decision (a five-minute detour). That said, this attempt takes advantage of now standard computational and cartographic capacity to empower and problematize distance as vector, as experienced both in space and through space. In so doing, it implies new possibilities for redescribing and redefining areal concepts of catchment, reach, or neighborhood and suggests an approach to mapping information wherein area is subject to distance and time—wherein boundary follows the line. Further, because it maps individuals that live together, it decouples notions of access from the (x, y) of a single location—instead delineating the distance to urban resources as dependent upon not one, or even two, but a complex matrix of locations with interrelated possibilities at each.

By all accounts, any definitional understanding of distance as simultaneously dependent upon all locations should worry most map users. In an era of GPS-enabled and personalized wayfinding,

Four Neighbors: Five Minutes

four neighbors' 5-minute
deviation from their quickest commute routes

home

sources: SanGIS 2017, LODES 2017

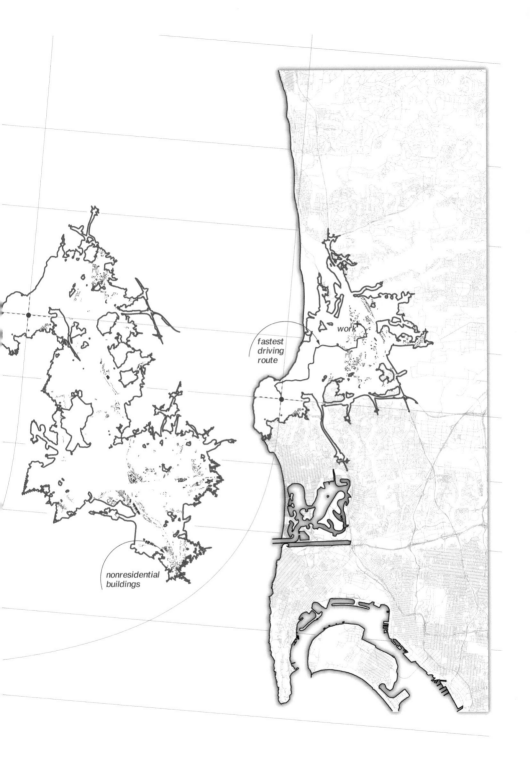

Fig 3: "Four Neighbors: Five Minutes."

the map already knows its distances as a function of its locations: embedded information that we must trust if the map is to serve as a tool for finding anything. But deriving geometry is not the same as reading spatiality. Mapping to find lived distance presupposes that the map—its frame, its scale, its perspective, its contents, and its authority—is unstable. Mapping to empower distance means mapping in search of a cartographic framework that can accommodate difference without flattening or normalizing it, that demands the rigor of systematic analysis without claiming comprehensiveness, and that leverages the quantity of our collected geographic information without the seduction of Haraway's "god trick."[22] The map is drawn with an appreciation for collocation and with attention to cardinal relationships and geographic scale, but these are not held as privileged properties. Rather, what is forefront is the shared scale of urban space-time and one common daily practice.

The daily practice of commuting, however, is not standardized. That is, none of us experience the city as a blast radius from a single location or even as standard distances emanating from a vector. Rather, we make choices and seek opportunities as we move through space, knowing each moment spent on movement constrains our available options. The twenty-four-hour day is a zero-sum game. Drawing more explicitly from the intersection of time-geography and theories of structuration, the distances from one person moving through time and space must be recalibrated and comparatively rescaled when related to the distribution and accessibility of urban resources.[23] Another attempt (figure 4, again read as one map) compares the reachable area for two commuters living on the same block, holding all variables constant aside from the location of each job. Translating from information to map, the drawing assumes an eight-hour workday and a standard set of at-home commitments, calculates the commute time along the quickest driving route, and summarizes the distance each could travel to accomplish a one-hour errand or excursion to a variety of possible destination types. (One might imagine the warping, shrinkage, and rescaling if time constraints were greater for either commuter.) All else equal, the difference between a ten-minute commute and a thirty-minute commute yields predictable consequences for the time left available to access what the city offers. One commuter passes through much more of the city, but having forty additional minutes in the day creates meaningful spatial flexibility and more choice. As a result, these two commuters appear to have comparable opportunities.

Within the constraints of time is where mapping empowered distances begins to reveal new differences, where experiential limits shift while locations stay in place. The comparability of those two commutes fails to hold when each commuter loses an hour. Working longer, a sick child, or even unanticipated traffic—anything that might take more time—does not affect daily possibilities evenly, and the flexibility inherent in the shorter commute cannot account fully for the difference. Here, the morphology of the city (the organization of highways and streets, as well as variable land use concentrations across the region) paired with the distance and direction of each commute compound the effects of lost time, and one person loses more of her city than the other.

What began as an experiment in mapping distances in the context of difference has become an exercise in describing the structural spatial processes that engender those differences. This is a map of two cities centered on one block, where access, variability, and vulnerability are unequal. Perhaps more importantly, it describes planned and designed effects of everyday marginalization and resilience that are not dependent on location, that cannot be rendered by plotting points or creating density maps, and that we will miss if we take distance for granted in the back-and-forth of cartographic analysis.

Empowering distance distinguishes forms of access that are dependent upon location from those only related to it. In so doing, it challenges the normalizing frameworks that delimit map-based knowledge production by producing dynamic boundaries that are subject to the variations and constraints of the catchments they aim to describe—that can be individualized and multiple while collocated, and that may ultimately reflect pluralism. A more equally tripartite employment of the map's geometric components further challenges the primacy of today's popular-populist GIS approaches, thereby creating an opening for time and difference to operate within two-dimensional GIS mapping and suggesting new visualizations of citywide patterns by activating area (via aggregation) only after activating distance. Such a cartography of distance also challenges a map's flattened and neutral, snapshot claims by implicating the many maps that produced its information and their limitations, whether transit planning or zoning codes, suggested-routing algorithms, or housing and jobs spatial policy. By reinterpreting and remapping GIS-based data derived through processes of governance and planning, these drawings act within bidirectional cartographic reasoning while self-consciously maintaining the map's position as a site of investigation and ongoing intervention. As a result, the maps begin to reveal where movement, choice, and necessity meet the social inequities and structural conditions manifest in the city's prior enumerations, spatial parsings, mapped designs, and urban plans—each colluding and incrementally contributing to its built environment. And while these drawings cannot accomplish an image of how individuals, in turn, act upon those conditions, tracing their own cartographies of distance between locations and across these derived boundaries, they do begin to render how the geometries of point and area function, for some, as geographies of tether and barrier.

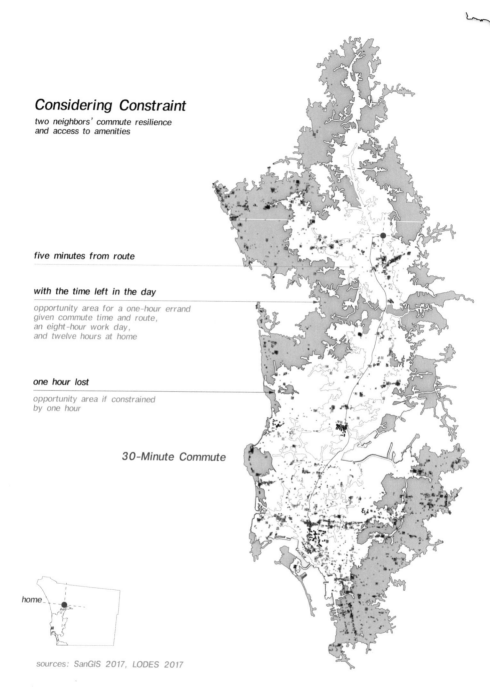

Considering Constraint

two neighbors' commute resilience
and access to amenities

five minutes from route

with the time left in the day

opportunity area for a one-hour errand
given commute time and route,
an eight-hour work day,
and twelve hours at home

one hour lost

opportunity area if constrained
by one hour

30-Minute Commute

home

sources: SanGIS 2017, LODES 2017

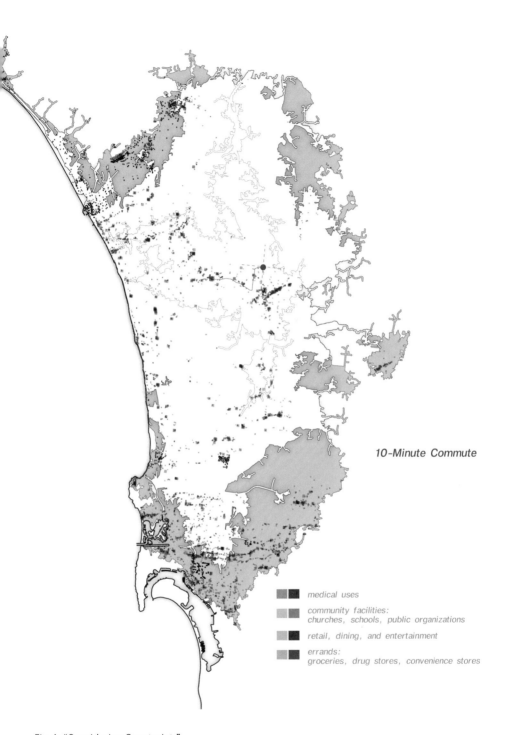

10-Minute Commute

medical uses

community facilities:
churches, schools, public organizations

retail, dining, and entertainment

errands:
groceries, drug stores, convenience stores

Fig 4: "Considering Constraint."

LEAH MEISTERLIN is an urbanist, GIS methodologist, cartographer, and assistant professor at Columbia University's Graduate School of Architecture, Planning, and Preservation. Broadly, her research engages concurrent issues of spatial justice, informational ethics, and the effects of digital technologies on the representation of social and political space. Her current research explores the ways in which urban processes are defined, described, and disrupted by map-based models of distance within GIS frameworks.

1   Waldo Tobler, "A Computer Movie Simulating Urban Growth in the Detroit Region," *Economic Geography* 46, no. 2 (1970): 234–240. See also Harvey J. Miller, "Tobler's First Law and Spatial Analysis," *Annals of the Association of American Geographers* 94, no. 2 (June 2004): 284–289.

2   Originally published in 2008, these two sentences appeared on the landing page of my personal website for the better part of the last decade.

3   Versions of this development and expansion of digital mapping capability go by many names, each with slightly different connotations than the next. "Neogeography" works well to describe the cartographic explorations of nonspecialists, citizen scientists, and interested individuals and communities.

4   Throughout this text, "countermapping" describes the collection of mapping and GIS practices aimed at asserting and visualizing minority or underrepresented perspectives, particularly to counter positivist and authoritative maps and/or geographic exertions of power as experienced by those groups. For reference and examples, see Dianne Rocheleau, "Maps as Power Tools: Locating Communities in Space or Situating People and Ecologies in Place?," in *Communities and Conservation: Histories and Politics of Community-Based Natural Resource Management*, ed. Peter J. Brosius, Anna Lowenhaupt Tsing, and Charles Zerner (Walnut Creek, CA: AltaMira Press, 2005), 327–362; Renee Pualani Louis et al., "Introduction: Indigenous Cartographies and Counter-Mapping," *Cartographica: The International Journal for Geographic Information and Geovisualization* 47, no. 2 (January 2012): 77–79; John Schofield, ed., *Who Needs Experts?: Counter-Mapping Cultural Heritage* (Burlington, VT: Ashgate, 2014); Craig Dalton and Liz Mason-Deese, "Counter (Mapping) Actions: Mapping as Militant Research," *ACME: An International E-Journal for Critical Geographies* 11, no. 3 (2012): 439–466.

5   Theorizing the role of the map in society has a long and broad history. Scholarship on GIS and society is admittedly more recent and is receiving renewed attention with the growth of social media, open data movements, mobile smart phones, "smart" city proposals, and the GIS software and platforms discussed here. In short, (digital) mapping and its effects are pervasive, influencing decisions across scales including those made by individuals through the course of their Internet-connected days. For reference and examples, see Jeremy W. Crampton, "Maps as Social Constructions: Power, Communication, and Visualization," *Progress in Human Geography* 25, no. 2 (June 2001): 235–252; J. B. Harley, "Deconstructing the Map," *Cartographica* 26, no. 2 (Summer 1989): 1–20; Reuben Rose-Redwood, "Introduction: The Limits to Deconstructing the Map," *Cartographica: The International Journal for Geographic Information and Geovisualization* 50, no. 1 (March 2015): 1–8; Matthew W. Wilson, *New Lines: Critical GIS and the Trouble of the Map* (Minneapolis: University of Minnesota Press, 2017).

6   Annette M. Kim's two-part operational definition of maps as "visual representations of spatial relationships" that also assert "knowledge claims that are inherently political" is extremely valuable here. Annette M. Kim, *Sidewalk City: Remapping Public Space in Ho Chi Minh City* (Chicago: University of Chicago Press, 2015), 75.

7   Annette M. Kim, "Critical Cartography 2.0: From 'Participatory Mapping' to Authored Visualizations of Power and People," *Landscape and Urban Planning* 142 (October 2015): 215–225. See also several examples collected in Meghan Cope and Sarah Elwood, eds., *Qualitative GIS: A Mixed Methods Approach* (London: Sage Publications, 2009).

8   As digital mapping increases within architecture, urban design, and planning, such a persistence concerns foundational representational questions within those fields. They are not, however, unexamined questions elsewhere and are deeply tied to those within closely related fields of critical cartography and critical GIS that ask who maps, what form those maps take, and how the map operates in society. See, for example, Jeremy W. Crampton and John Krygier, "An Introduction to Critical Cartography," ACME: An International E-Journal for Critical Geographies 4, no. 1 (2006): 11–33; Sarah Elwood, "Thinking outside the Box: Engaging Critical Geographic Information Systems Theory, Practice and Politics in Human Geography," Geography Compass 4, no. 1 (January 2010): 45–60.

9   Indeed, given the need for a shared referent to measure any difference, the grid's malleability via map projection offers a variety of perspectival manipulations and prioritizations. Even the online dominance of the Mercator— while certainly problematic for its areal distortions and its apparent assumption that nautical wayfinding is among the highest global mapping priorities—is more of a symptomatic criticism of widespread mapping practices than a causal critique.

10   See, for example, Taylor Shelton, "Spatialities of Data: Mapping Social Media 'beyond the Geotag,'" GeoJournal 82, no. 4 (August 2017): 721–734.

11   See, for example, Frances Cairncross, The Death of Distance: How the Communications Revolution Will Change Our Lives (Boston: Harvard Business School Press, 1997).

12   For example, see Jeremy Crampton, "GIS and Geographic Governance: Reconstructing the Choropleth Map," Cartographica: The International Journal for Geographic Information and Geovisualization 39, no. 1 (March 2004): 41–53.

13   For reference, see Alfred W. Crosby, Measure of Reality: Quantification and Western Society, 1250–1600 (Cambridge, UK: Cambridge University Press, 1997); Jeremy W. Crampton and Stuart Elden, "Space, Politics, Calculation: An Introduction," Social & Cultural Geography 7, no. 5 (October 2006): 681–685; Jeremy W. Crampton, "How Mapping Became Scientific," in Mapping: A Critical Introduction to Cartography and GIS (Malden, MA: Wiley-Blackwell, 2010), 49–61.

14   Together, these problems (including the Modifiable Areal Unit Problem and the Uncertain Geographic Context Problem) describe the myriad ways that aggregating spatial information to areal units can lead to conclusions that might be quantitatively valid but fail to reflect conditions on the ground. These logical fallacies stem from the ecological fallacy, manifesting geographically depending on different factors such as the internal homogeneity assumed within an areal boundary, scalar mismatch, and inappropriateness of boundary types. S. Openshaw, "Ecological Fallacies and the Analysis of Areal Census Data," Environment and Planning A 16, no. 1 (January 1984): 17–31; Mei-Po Kwan, "The Uncertain Geographic Context Problem," Annals of the Association of American Geographers 102, no. 5 (September 2012): 958–968.

15   Spatial patterns between demographic groupings are more readily perceivable by aggregation when the locations of included individuals and communities cluster or segregate by area (as in, for example, mapping income groups).

16   See, for example, Mei-Po Kwan, "Gender and Individual Access to Urban Opportunities: A Study Using Space–Time Measures," Professional Geographer 51, no. 2 (May 1999): 211–227; Risa Palm and Allan Pred, "A Time-Geographic Perspective on Problems of Inequality for Women" (working paper, University of California, Berkeley, 1974).

17   Mapping "lived experience" is not without its problems. Some of these, including the distinction between mapping narrative accounts versus structural constraints on daily possibilities, are addressed later. Additionally, mapping is implicated in lived experience in ways that cannot be decoupled for analytical or conceptual clarity. We navigate with Google Maps and Waze, often geotagging ourselves along the way on social media platforms; we move through the city aided by complex cultural-historical and perceptual mappings of our space(s), which have also been organized and planned through layers of prior mappings. Any attempt at drawing lived spatial experience must concede that the resulting drawing is not a sterile instrument for recording and research but a confounding intervention and just one of many mappings at play. (Cf. note 5.)

18   It is worth noting that leveraging "access" as a proxy to compare urban experience follows a slightly different methodological history than analyzing the "geographic distribution of access" as such. Certainly, the two intersect (as is demonstrated above and below via cumulative opportunity areas). That said, the former has historically required individually recorded and reported data in the form of surveys, travel diaries, or tracking, whereas the latter rests on the descriptive analysis of geographic relationships between land uses and amenities.

19   Torsten Hägerstrand, "Diorama, Path, and Project," *Tijdschrift Voor Economische En Sociale Geografie* 73, no. 6 (December 1982): 323–339; Allan Pred, "The Choreography of Existence: Comments on Hägerstrand's Time-Geography and Its Usefulness," *Economic Geography* 53, no. 2 (April 1977): 207; Mei-Po Kwan, "GIS Methods in Time-Geographic Research: Geocomputation and Geovisualization of Human Activity Patterns," *Geografiska Annaler: Series B, Human Geography* 86, no. 4 (December 2004): 267–280; Mei-Po Kwan, "Is GIS for Women? Reflections on the Critical Discourse in the 1990s," *Gender, Place & Culture* 9, no. 3 (September 2002): 271–279; Harvey J. Miller, "A Measurement Theory for Time Geography," *Geographical Analysis* 37, no. 1 (January 2005): 17–45; Fang Ren, Daoqin Tong, and Mei-Po Kwan, "Space-Time Measures of Demand for Service: Bridging Location Modelling and Accessibility Studies through a Time-Geographic Framework," *Geografiska Annaler: Series B, Human Geography* 96, no. 4 (December 2014): 329–344; Charles Travis, "Transcending the Cube: Translating GIScience Time and Space Perspectives in a Humanities GIS," *International Journal of Geographical Information Science* 28, no. 5 (May 2014): 1149–1164.

20   Neighborhoods were chosen based on the results of a Getis-Ord Gi* cluster analysis of the difference in mean commute times for men and for women by census tract. The home locations (blocks) presented in these examples belong to tracts within significant clusters, where women have longer commutes than their male counterparts on average. United States Census Bureau, 2015 American Community Survey 5-Year Estimates.

21   United States Census Bureau, LEHD Origin-Destination Employment Statistics 2015 (Washington, DC: US Census Bureau, Longitudinal-Employer Household Dynamics Program).

22   The "god trick" is a "view of infinite vision," of "seeing everything from nowhere." Donna Haraway, "Situated Knowledge: The Science Questions in Feminism and the Privilege of Partial Perspective," *Feminism Studies* 14, no. 3 (1988): 581–582.

23   Briefly, this intersection shows that social processes are constrained by structural conditions and that such structures are geographically manifest and operative within GIS. See, for example, Roger P. Miller, "Beyond Method, beyond Ethics: Integrating Social Theory into GIS and GIS into Social Theory," *Cartography and Geographic Information Systems* 22, no. 1 (January 1995): 98–103; Jakub Novák and Luděk Sýkora, "A City in Motion: Time-Space Activity and Mobility Patterns of Suburban Inhabitants and the Structuration of the Spatial Organization of the Prague Metropolitan Area," *Geografiska Annaler: Series B, Human Geography* 89, no. 2 (June 2007): 147–168; Allan Pred, "Place as Historically Contingent Process: Structuration and the Time-Geography of Becoming Places," *Annals of the Association of American Geographers* 74, no. 2 (March 1984): 279–297.